THE
SELF-HEALING
MIND

THE SELF-HEALING MIND

MIND

AN ESSENTIAL FIVE-STEP
PRACTICE FOR OVERCOMING
ANXIETY AND DEPRESSION,
AND REVITALIZING YOUR LIFE

GREGORY SCOTT BROWN, MD

HARPER WAVE

An Imprint of HarperCollins*Publishers*

This book contains advice and information relating to health care. It should be used to supplement rather than replace the advice of your doctor or another trained health professional. If you know or suspect you have a health problem, it is recommended that you seek your physician's advice before embarking on any medical program or treatment. All efforts have been made to assure the accuracy of the information contained in this book as of the date of publication. This publisher and the author disclaim liability for any medical outcomes that may occur as a result of applying the methods suggested in this book.

THE SELF-HEALING MIND. Copyright © 2022 by Gregory Scott Brown, MD. All rights reserved. Printed in the United States of America. No part of this book may be used or reproduced in any manner whatsoever without written permission except in the case of brief quotations embodied in critical articles and reviews. For information, address HarperCollins Publishers, 195 Broadway, New York, NY 10007.

HarperCollins books may be purchased for educational, business, or sales promotional use. For information, please email the Special Markets Department at SPsales@harpercollins.com.

FIRST EDITION

Designed by Nancy Singer

Library of Congress Cataloging-in-Publication Data has been applied for.

ISBN 978-0-06-309447-5

22 23 24 25 26 LSC 10 9 8 7 6 5 4 3 2 1

For Patsy, Trevor, and Tram-Anh

CONTENTS

THE
SELF-HEALING
MIND

INTRODUCTION

In early spring of 2020, a longtime patient reached out to shake my hand as our therapy session came to a close. Almost immediately, he realized his blunder.

"How long do you think we'll be doing this?" he laughed, as he bumped his elbow against mine.

I could only shrug in reply. At the time, the United States was just beginning to see the rise of COVID-19 cases, but I had no idea the coronavirus pandemic was about to ripple across the world like an earthquake, changing the entire health-care landscape, including mental health delivery as we once knew it. I also could not have predicted that, because of infection control mandates, I'd have to close my office to in-person visits a few weeks later. Life was changing— and quickly. I began to see my patients virtually, doing what I could to connect with them through tablets and screens. I also had to put many of my favorite wellness practices on hold, including my regular visits to the yoga studio, and more carefully consider how to encourage my patients to continue their own self-care regimens.

As the novel coronavirus continued to spread across the country, I, like many other mental health professionals, noticed an uptick in requests for new appointments. There were many reasons for that. Some people felt increasingly isolated by stay-at-home orders and social distancing guidelines. Others were having trouble adjusting to working from home or struggling to manage their kids as they attended online school. Some were just worried about the virus and its potential long-term impact on their families or businesses. People were coping as they could; yet, for far too many, the situation lent itself to increased anxiety and negative thinking. In some cases, I also saw substance misuse relapses as people turned to alcohol or drugs to help manage their stress.

COVID-19 was far from the only problem haunting the country. In the wake of George Floyd's and Breonna Taylor's murders by police, xenophobia against Asian Americans, and a chaotic news cycle, images of brutality and overt civil unrest were delivered into our homes each day. Not only were we getting a daily dose of the thousands of people dying from this new and insidious virus, but we were also watching the cumulative physical and emotional trauma of millions of Americans of color being played out on our smartphones and television sets. The combination took a heavy toll on all of us, and soon mental health was on everyone's mind. We thought about it more, even if we weren't always talking about it. Although this book was years in the making, the turbulent events of 2020 led me to reassess the state of my own mental health, while simultaneously treating patients in my outpatient practice. It became even more vital that I record my thoughts about the importance of self-care and mental health maintenance on paper.

My work offers me the opportunity to hear so many stories—treating patients in my office, as well as hosting conversations about mental health with athletes, musicians, actors, and journalists in an effort to help reduce mental health stigma. Many of these discussions involve people who have grappled with depression or sleep difficulties, or have experienced a rocky relationship at home. Some people just need someone to talk to—a neutral sounding board, someone with whom they can safely blow off steam as they work through their thoughts and feelings.

Practicing psychiatry is humbling, even in the best of circumstances. No psychiatrist is omniscient, and as the mind is such a perplexing entity, we need to be open to different ways of thinking as well as different ways of addressing common issues. I learn quite a bit from my patients as well as from people outside my clinic that I have conversations with about mental health. I'd even go so far as to say, some days, these conversations are almost a form of therapy for me, the person who is supposed to be giving the advice. Sometimes one of my patients will share a personal insight and I'll think: *That's an interesting idea, I haven't thought about things quite that way before.* Or: *That's a great approach to better managing that thought. It sounds like something I should try.* I found myself listening for those nuggets of wisdom more than ever during the summer of 2020, as the Black Lives Matter movement and widespread protests against racial injustice seemed at their height. As one of the few Black psychiatrists in the United States—we make up less than 5 percent of the field, all told—it felt like everyone wanted to know my take on things. My patients, my friends, and even some reporters in the media wanted my insights about the effect race has on mental health, as well as how we might learn to better understand and communicate with one another in order to more effectively address racial injustice. Almost every day, when I was alone, I'd ask myself those same questions again and again—and struggle to come up with concrete answers. I tell you this because, in order to be in a better position to both give and receive advice, it's important to admit that we don't have all of the answers.

I don't have all of the answers.

That said, my role is to help my patients find their own purpose, balance, contentment, and hope by sharing what I know about medicine, science, and faith. In doing so, I hope they will understand why living with mental health can bring them closer to fully experiencing the moments of happiness that come along with it. While professional mental health care can be a vital part of this journey, it is not the only factor at play. The bulk of patients don't see their psychiatrist that often, for a number of factors including demand and health insurance restrictions.

Sometimes it's once a week, but more often it's once a month or even less. If you're meeting with a therapist who isn't authorized to prescribe medications, typically visits are more frequent, but they can also be expensive unless you have expendable income or exceptional health insurance. That's why it's so important to understand that the life you live off your therapist's couch, in those days and hours between sessions, is really where the most important work takes place. That's the place where acts of self-care can—and will—make a big difference to your overall mental and physical well-being.

Taking the Objective Approach

Mental health care is a nuanced field—to the point where some have argued it's as much an art as it is a science. I remember, early in my training, I asked my favorite mentor which antidepressant I should prescribe for a particular patient. I was surprised when she replied with a confident grin and her warm, Southern drawl, "Six of one, half a dozen of the other. Doctor, you pick."

I don't share this story to suggest that practicing psychiatry is rolling the dice—or that all antidepressant medications are interchangeable. Rather, I share it because the brain is complex. People are complex. The different treatment options available are—you guessed it—also complex. So, as you work to help someone struggling with mental illness, there are a wide variety of options for determining how to best proceed. You quickly see that our thoughts, feelings, and behaviors are not solely the result of neurochemical shifts in the brain. It's not that simple. The context matters a great deal, and it must be considered as we look for ways to help ourselves and the people around us feel better.

In medical school, I learned about the scientific method, how to read and interpret clinical data, and the importance of supporting my opinions with facts. Physicians are trained to think objectively. In fact, while I was rotating at a community hospital in Houston as a third-year medical student, the senior faculty members loved to quiz us about complex medical cases. As we presented to them—and tried to explain what we thought the issue might be—we could count on being asked, "What is your evidence for that assertion?" Trying to answer with a feeling, an inclination, a medical story, or even clinical experience was not the way to satisfy the gray beards in the long white coats. In fact, such a strategy would likely lead to quick and public embarrassment. It didn't take long for me to learn that, in order to avoid humiliation, your best bet was to stock up on studies. Citing a credible source, say a clinical report from the *New England Journal of Medicine*, was the best way to support your theory and keep the critics at bay.

This objective approach to medicine is partly responsible for the Western health-care system's status as one of the most advanced and trusted in the world. In the United States, medications are approved by the Food and Drug Administration, thoroughly tested, and then retested for safety and efficacy. Doctors do not heal based on intuition but prescribe evidence-based treatments based on what has been proven to work. If a particular regimen does not have verifiable proof to back up its use, it is almost immediately classified as wishful thinking or pseudoscience.

That's why, historically, the idea of self-care as a credible medical intervention has been so difficult for so many people—both doctors and patients—to adopt. It's ironic: Even though the practice of taking an active role in protecting one's own well-being, especially during times of heightened stress, dates back to the earliest medical writings, people still look down on it as a form of quackery. Yet, day by day, the body of evidence supporting the efficacy of self-care grows. Scientific studies are demonstrating that activities like physical exercise, yoga, meditation, and spiritual practices have a place in promoting resiliency and mental health—and even alleviating the symptoms of common mental illnesses like depression and anxiety. When you start to look at the bigger scientific picture, the research clearly shows us that *this stuff works*. So why aren't we talking about it more?

A New Kind of Self-Help

If you have ever met with a psychiatrist—or even just thought about meeting with one—you understand that taking the steps necessary to make your first appointment isn't easy. You likely were experiencing powerful feelings of hopelessness, or perhaps an unrelenting need for guidance, to dismantle the stigma or pride that previously kept you from such an encounter.

Each patient I have worked with, and the thousands of conversations those sessions have produced, has shown me that the mind is complicated. Much more so than I was led to understand when I was in medical school. The mind's ability to dream, to love, to imagine, and to hope is a powerful force for good. Unfortunately, the mind is equally gifted at producing anxiety, self-doubt, and shame. Trying to balance these forces is not a simple task.

Psychiatric diagnoses for conditions like depression, anxiety, and post-traumatic stress disorder (PTSD)—just to name a few—come with guidelines for treatment. While there is no one-size-fits-all approach to helping people living with these issues, there's at least a game plan. Many of us will never meet the diagnostic criteria for these diseases, but some of us still live with unhappiness, loneliness, disconnection, and a lack of purpose. These conditions can influence the quality of our lives just as much as a diagnosed mental illness. They all but ensure we are not living our best lives. Simply put, we can't—until we find a way to live a life that embraces mental health.

Unfortunately, it's often easier said than done. As we try to bolster our mental health, we tend to look for simple answers. We desperately attempt to identify three easy steps to happiness. We search for the keys to success. We want to believe there is one thing—one simple thing—that can turn our life around and make it all better. Unfortunately, such quests usually result in a dead end.

That said, I can relate. I, too, am a student of books about improvement. As someone who wants the answers to life's quintessential questions—*Who am I? Why am I here?*—I find such books are almost irresistible. Certainly, self-help books played an important role in my upbringing. And, while reading them, they often did make me feel better in the moment. I thought they offered me an explanation for why I'm built the way I am, what makes me tick, what career would suit me best, and what kind of romantic partner I needed. I learned the habits of highly effective people. I grew to appreciate that there is courage in the ability to be vulnerable. I adopted the tools to win friends and influence people. I recognized the power of purpose.

Eventually, I found I had hit a self-help book wall. At a certain point, I found I could predict what was coming next, from the stories to the recommendations. I also found that I could follow the books' advice without much effort on my part. Initially, I was a self-help sponge, soaking up all the advice I could. I thought that, when life got challenging or downright ugly, these books had given me the tools I needed to fix whatever mess might be in front of me. That may be why I was caught so off guard when, in my early twenties, I slid into an overwhelming depression that was uniquely my own.

Although I am a psychiatrist, I am not immune to mental illness. And because of this, I can tell you with conviction that it is possible to have a strong understanding of your higher purpose and still feel incapable. You can fully accept the challenge to be vulnerable and still struggle to connect with others or to find the motivation required to carry you forward. I can also say, with certainty, that even the most resilient people can and do fall—sometimes, in response to what may seem like a small or inconsequential issue. I can tell you this because I sit across from patients, each and every day, who have endured such challenges. I have listened to their stories. I am one of them.

I can also tell you that you have more power when it comes to your mental health and well-being than you think. This isn't about trying to oversimplify the mind so you can feel good in the moment. There is no "happiness" pill a doctor can prescribe to you. These sorts of beliefs, too often, can lead to even more hopelessness down the line. We need to acknowledge that there are limitations to what science can explain about the brain, mental illness, and mental health. With that in mind, my aim is to provide you with the knowledge and tools that can help you make more informed decisions about how to best support your own resilience and overall wellness as you are out there in the world each day, living your life.

I was inspired to call this book *The Self-Healing Mind* to highlight ways evidence-based self-care improves mental health. Over time, I have learned that it's what you do in between sessions that, ultimately, has the most impact on how you feel. That's where you need to apply the different ideas or strategies we discussed in session to make positive changes. That said, this book is not intended to encourage anyone to replace professional mental health care, or to take medical treatment into your own hands. Rather, the aim is to show you how tools for sustainable wellness start and end with essential acts of self-care.

In the following pages, I will discuss a different way of thinking about mental health and the mind. It may diverge quite a bit from what you may have learned before. I openly challenge pervasive ideas about mental health, including that mental illness is a sign of weakness, that depression and anxiety are the result of a defective or injured brain, that knowing your purpose will automatically make your life easier, and that psychiatric drugs offer a quick cure. These ideas extend from my experience treating patients in my psychiatry practice, as well as my own personal life story. This composes Part I of the book—where I help the reader to look at these issues in a new way. That new foundational understanding sets up Part II, where I introduce practical techniques about how to use self-care to improve your mental health. Those topics will include how to give up on (let go of) the right things (like giving up on death), using breath work as medicine, moving your body to boost your mood, making the best food choices for your mind, and tapping into your inner spirituality that connects you with the world around you. My time as a psychiatrist—and a patient—has shown me what works and what does not. These are the lessons patients have taught me through hours of vital conversations, as well as those I've learned firsthand as I've pursued my own self-care journey for mental health.

My intention with this book is to provide you with the insights and skill set that can help you live with purpose, balance, contentment, and hope, regardless of what the world may throw your way. While I do not wish to suggest that all mental illnesses can be resolved outside the psychiatrist's office—or that there aren't situations where antidepressants or other drugs are both helpful and necessary—the truth is there are many things you can do outside of a clinical setting to help support strong mental health. That starts by reconsidering your definition of, as well as any preconceived notions you may hold about, what mental health actually is.

PART I

A CHANGE
IN PERSPECTIVE

Think about why you picked up this book. Some of you may have already seen a therapist or a psychiatrist in the past. Maybe you have even been diagnosed with depression or anxiety at some point, and you have been prescribed a medication or another form of therapy to help manage it. Perhaps the idea of potentially being labeled "mentally ill" has kept you from getting help altogether. Or maybe you don't fit neatly into any of these categories. You're just not fully satisfied with your life and are looking for ways to make some improvements. No matter who you are or what your experience has been, this book is for you.

Before you can start to adopt practices to help elevate you in between sessions, it's important to redefine the concept of mental health. The world is changing—and changing fast. We are long past the days of patients lying on a leather couch as a stoic shrink scribbles notes on a legal pad. Therapy has changed to keep up with the times and, on an even more positive note, mental health is less stigmatized than it once was. We also understand, more and more, that the most important work occurs in between and outside of the psychiatrist's office.

That means that there are many things each one of us can do outside of a clinical setting to bolster our mental health. Before we can begin, it is vital that we learn to move past outdated notions of "broken" brains and chemical imbalances. After all, you can't work toward mental health without first knowing what it is, exactly, that you are trying to achieve.

CHAPTER 1

REDEFINING MENTAL HEALTH

Start where you are. Use what you
have. Do what you can.
—*Arthur Ashe*

Most of us avoid talking about mental health—that is, unless we're sitting on a therapist's couch looking for advice. Even if you've never been there personally, I'll bet you know someone who has. Maybe it's your son or daughter—or your husband, girlfriend, or dad—and you're wondering how you can best show love and support. It's also possible that you're asking yourself: *How does a playbook about mental health and self-care relate to me?* Years before I became a psychiatrist, and spent time studying the mind, I would've asked that same question.

Now, I have come to realize that mental health is the driving force behind every decision we make; how we live, work, and love. But most important, achieving mental health begins with actionable self-care. Let's start by moving beyond the idea that self-care only translates to ritzy spa dates or expensive organic foods.

In fact, self-care, approached the right way, is a powerful evidence-based medicine for the mind. You just have to learn how to tap into it. There have been times when I've spent years working with patients, exploring different types of therapies, and looking for the perfect prescription, when ultimately the cure is in simple techniques that we so often take for granted—self-care practices like sleep, breath work, nutrition, movement, and spirituality. The challenge is learning how to fully utilize these skills in a way that feels doable. It's a process I've seen unfold in my own life, as well as with patients like John.

The first time I met him, he was in his mid-fifties, and sitting anxiously in the waiting area of my office. John was wearing a heavily starched button-down shirt and designer jeans. I could see him clutching a can of sparkling water in his hand, and he exuded a cool dad kind of vibe. Frankly, he looked like he'd rather be anywhere else than in that chair. From my office door, I could see John relentlessly scanning the perimeter, as if he were afraid that he might run into someone from work.

John drove a sports car, ran marathons, and was a total technology geek. By the time I called his name, he was a nervous wreck. To be honest, that's not uncommon. I get it. Many people don't know what to expect the first time they meet with a psychiatrist, and that uncertainty can lead to a lot of fear. For some people, an hour a week conversing on the therapy couch is just part of what you do as a responsible adult: Eat three meals a day, go to the gym, show up to work on time, and have a reliable shrink on call just in case. Most of us, however, don't fall into that category.

John was afraid that an appointment with any mental health professional, which included meeting with me, would mean he had officially "lost his mind," and from that point forward, there'd be no turning back. Because of this fear, he completely avoided the couch where my patients usually sit, and he was also careful not to make eye contact with me as he passed it—a gesture that brought a subtle but empathetic smile to my face. Instead, he took a seat at a small round table in the corner of my office. So I pulled up a chair and sat across from him.

Before I could introduce myself, John shifted back in his seat and said, in a calculating tone, "Okay, Mr. Brown. Fine. Maybe I'm drinking too much." He was intentional about not calling me "doctor," probably to create even more distance from becoming an official "psych patient." It didn't bother me, so I just went along.

"Well, nice to see you," I said.

"Sorry," he said, with a sweeping gesture of his hands, belying his discomfort. "I'm John. Hi," he continued and extended a firm handshake.

"So how much drinking are we talking about?" I asked.

"I don't know," he replied. "A couple of beers every day. Maybe more."

"Did you come here on your own?"

"Yeah, I did," he said. "Well, I mean, I brought my wife with me. But she didn't make me come," he replied motioning toward the door.

After spending the hour speaking with John, it became clear he came to see me that day only to appease his wife, because as he put it, "I love her, but she's the boss."

However, her concerns aside, he didn't really think he had a drinking problem. He did acknowledge work was increasingly stressful;

he was spending more time alone, and he enjoyed winding down at the end of the day with a few beers. What was wrong with that? Eventually, John's wife, with his permission, joined the conversation. She mostly agreed with his assessment, but she said his feelings of stress were negatively affecting their marriage, as well as John's relationship with extended family and friends. He hadn't told me that.

So, here was my dilemma: Was John mentally ill?

John would be the first to tell you he absolutely was not; he made good money, he had a beautiful family and loyal friends, and he was self-sufficient. The idea that he might have a mental illness was simply out of the question for him; in fact, he interpreted it as being on the verge of insulting. As for professional opinions, if you put five psychiatrists in a room, you would likely hear five different opinions about whether or not he met criteria for a particular psychiatric diagnosis, and if he did, there would surely be some colorful debates about which one. Regardless, it was obvious to me that John wasn't *well*. He freely acknowledged he was not living his fullest life, because he was drained, was stressed out, and wanted to feel better than he did. He was coping with the stress of a demanding career with alcohol, and his wife was concerned by the toll it was taking on their family. It was important to them both that things changed for the better.

Over the next few months, our discussions revealed that John was not only drinking too much, but he was also struggling with some mild symptoms of depression, like having a hard time falling asleep at night, feeling tired during the day, and often losing his train of thought at the office. He was sleeping downstairs on the couch most nights with a Netflix series on auto play in the background, and sex with his wife was essentially nonexistent; he just wasn't "in the mood" anymore.

Drinking provided quick relief by slowing down his thoughts and allowing him to feel detached. It was an easy escape from reality that in the moment made him feel better, but the effect wore off quickly and he found himself wanting to "go there" more often, even throughout the day. Despite his admissions, he still didn't exactly fit into the defined criteria for major depressive disorder. That didn't mean I couldn't help him, because definitions and semantics, especially when we are talking about heavily stigmatized topics like mental illness, too often pose a barrier to treatment. Even if John didn't fit neatly into a diagnostic box, there were still ways to improve his mental health.

Understanding the Difference Between Mental Health and Mental Illness

Have you ever thought about the difference between mental health and mental illness? Most people haven't. Understanding the distinction between the two is an important step for activating your self-care playbook.

Mental health isn't just another term for mental illness; instead, I'd like you to think about mental health as the state of living with purpose, balance, contentment, and hope. This way, you can also see why your lifestyle choices play a vital part in supporting your own mental health.

The American Psychiatric Association (APA) defines mental illness as "health conditions involving changes in emotion, thinking, or behavior (or a combination of these) . . . associated with distress and/or problems functioning in social, work or family activities." While the *Diagnostic and Statistical Manual of Mental Disorders* (*DSM*), the psychiatrist's diagnostic guidebook, lists symptoms linked to specific mental illnesses, it quickly becomes apparent that it's missing some situations that would cause many of us serious emotional distress. For example, there is no diagnosis for loneliness, or neglect—and no diagnosis for feeling like you don't have a purpose. Although these are not mental illnesses, per se, they can have a profound impact on your mood and your life. That's why it is so important to think beyond common perceptions of mental illnesses when considering whether or not paying attention to your mental health is worth your while. It's something all of us need to pay attention to. Your ultimate intention, and mine, should always be pursing mental health.

If I asked you about "mental health" on the fly, you might start reciting a list of diagnoses that fit into the APA's definition of mental illness without even knowing it: depression, anxiety, bipolar disorder, substance abuse, or schizophrenia. You might also refer to a popular movie or book that features someone struggling with mental illness, like *Silver Linings Playbook* or *Girl, Interrupted*—or even bring up a completely fictional character like Sherlock Holmes or Batman's nemesis, the Joker. Some people may even start talking about a friend or loved one who has been diagnosed with a mental illness. There's good reason for this. Someone starts talking about mental health and our mind immediately goes to everything that could go wrong with it—instead of what can go right.

After spending hours in conversation with my patients, as well as learning from my own battle overcoming depression, I personally understand that mental health means that your mind is firing on all cylinders, giving you both the confidence and the ability to achieve your intentions, whatever they may be. It's about overcoming challenges and embracing joy. Simply put, mental health is the mode of being that each and every one of us should be working to pursue, not only to prevent the potential onset of mental illness but to live richer and more fulfilling lives.

It's not any different from the distinctions we make between physical illness and health. Most of us now understand that there's no sense in waiting to get sick to take care of our bodies. We work toward physical health, whether by improving our diet, cutting back on alcohol, or regularly going to the gym. There's more to our efforts than just wanting chiseled abs or toned arms—though both are definitely nice to have. It's about doing the things we need to do to feel our best.

One glass of green juice or a couple of rides on a spin bike isn't going to get you to that optimal state. Acquiring physical health does not happen overnight. It's something that requires ongoing work and maintenance. No matter how in shape you may be today, if you don't continue to pay attention to what you eat and find time for movement, you may find yourself at risk for chronic health conditions like high blood pressure, heart disease, or diabetes tomorrow. The pursuit of physical health is a lifetime journey. As you may have guessed, mental health is no different. It is also a process that requires active and continuous engagement with your mind, regardless of how fit you may believe it to be.

As you steer away from the idea that mental health is a set of diagnosable illnesses—or reduce the concept to the chemical reactions taking place in your brain—you learn that you have the ability and agency to implement the kind of positive changes to make yourself, and your life, *better*.

Despite the pervasive notion that it's the doctor who can cure what ails you, unfortunately, there is still much that doctors don't understand about the inner workings of the mind. While scientific studies are published every day offering remarkable new observations about the different molecules and processes that give rise to thoughts, feelings, and actions, such findings are not easily translated into specific mental health disorders or, by extension, effective treatments. Even without those actionable insights, there is hope. In the end, when it comes to your mind, you will soon find that there is no better expert than you—and you hold the tools you need to address and maintain your mental health.

As a psychiatrist, the work I do with my patients in session is important, but it's just the tip of the iceberg. Because the truth is, real therapy begins the moment my patients walk out the door and back into their own lives. That's where they can put the strategies we may have discussed into action, as well as develop new strategies on their own. That's where they can apply what they've learned to break the mental or emotional habits that may have been holding them back. And that's where they can learn to become a truly active participant in their wellness journey as they work toward mental health.

Diagnosing Mental Illness

Years after finishing medical school, there were some cases where I still had trouble distinguishing between what was likely a normal emotional response to a stressful life event and a psychiatric condition that warranted medical intervention. Most of my colleagues would admit to similar feelings. It is not always easy to determine whether someone has a mental illness. Most of the patients who walk through my office doors exhibit symptoms of depression or anxiety—or a combination of the two. That's not necessarily a surprise; they are the two most commonly diagnosed mental illnesses, affecting millions of people in the United States and around the world. The diagnostic challenge I face is whether or not a patient's melancholic mood after the loss of a spouse, for example, is a temporary and expected response or something that might require more aggressive treatment. How can you, or I, know for certain?

Unfortunately, there are no objective measures, like a blood test or X-ray, for mental illnesses or emotional distress. To determine whether someone may be suffering from a mental illness, psychiatrists rely on the *DSM*, what some in the field refer to as our "Diagnostic Bible." The *DSM* is just shy of one thousand pages and includes an incredible amount of useful information about mental illnesses, including both epidemiological and diagnostic data. Page over to the section on generalized anxiety disorder and you'll find its common symptoms as well as checklist criteria that help mental health professionals give a proper diagnosis.

Despite advances in neuroscience technology, including brain imaging studies that determine which brain regions are active in response to changes in mood, the diagnostic process really boils down to a doctor asking—and the patient honestly answering—a list of basic questions. *Over the past month, have you felt depressed, isolated, or hopeless? Have you lost interest in doing the things you usually like to do? Are you feeling a lack of energy? Are you having any problems sleeping? Any changes in appetite? What about feelings of guilt or worthlessness?* If the patient answers yes to any of those questions, it is important to follow up to understand the details. *How long have you felt this way? Have you experienced this kind of situation before? Do you have a family history of depression or mental illness? How are these feelings affecting your day-to-day life?*

The specific symptoms that a patient may be experiencing are important, of course, but so is the duration of those symptoms and the context in which they present themselves. *In the case of the patient who just lost a spouse, how long has he or she felt sad and hopeless? Has it been for a month or an entire year? Is it affecting their work? What about their relationships with friends and loved ones? Is the situation leading to suicidal thoughts?* The story matters—and it matters a great deal—as the psychiatrist determines a diagnosis and the appropriate course of treatment.

Let's face it, if you are feeling worthless, unmotivated, spending most of your time alone, and have lost interest in the things you once enjoyed, you may be suffering from depression. You may also just be going through a slump. With some careful listening, a doctor should be able to determine the difference as they learn more about the severity and duration of your symptoms. But it is not always that cut-and-dried. The *DSM* provides a diagnostic blueprint—as well as many useful checklists—yet it's the patient's story that adds the real richness and value to the process. It's the nuances that matter most when you consider how to best help someone feel better.

I'd also be remiss if I didn't tell you that the *DSM* has some limitations. The book is an evolving body of work that has gone through several revisions since it was first published back in 1952. It's not without its biases. For example, until 1973, homosexuality was considered a mental illness. Despite its eventual removal, you could still find mentions of it as a qualifier or direct cause for other mental illnesses for almost another fifteen years. Luckily, those days are long gone. The *DSM* continues to include some diagnoses that remain controversial, including conditions like dissociative identity disorder (better known as multiple personalities) and disruptive mood dysregulation disorder.

Psychiatrists often debate the validity of these entries at institutional grand rounds and academic conferences; however, debates aside, professionals in the field require an accessible tool to help standardize the diagnostic process. That's why, in the mental health realm, perhaps more than any other area of medicine, professional opinion is equally as important as the *DSM*'s suggested criteria. Moreover, the *DSM*, despite its length, simply cannot account for every detail of a patient's story.

It could not, for example, explain John's relentless drive to succeed at everything he did. How, as the oldest son, he was forced to grow up before he was ready. And after losing his mother in high school, he was the one who had to hold it together for the sake of his father and his younger brother. John had given up running during the week because he thought it was taking too much time away from his family, but as an adult it had also been his way to unwind. It soon became clear that John's time on the trail was more than an escape, because for him it was as vital as the air he breathed. It was also his best medicine for quelling alcohol cravings when he was feeling stressed out—making it more likely he'd be refreshed and ready to connect with his family and friends once he did make it home. That's how self-care works.

Why Mental Health Matters

According to the World Health Organization, depression is one of the leading causes of disability worldwide. More than 260 million people struggle with it—and, believe it or not, anxiety disorders affect more people than that. While the numbers, at first glance, are staggering, they likely are not fully representative of the prevalence of these two common mental illnesses. Not everyone who is struggling with a mental illness knows that they are, and even those who do may not seek help for a number of reasons. The patients who fall into those two categories often just decide to keep muddling through, not realizing the long-term toll it can take on their lives.

Americans tend to talk a lot about resilience. We put a high premium on grit and pushing on through the uncomfortable things we may encounter in life. Yet emphasizing resilience in that way is a bit of a double-edged sword. Think about a physical injury. If you were to hurt your knee playing tennis and just try to tough it out, you might be okay for a little while. You could likely finish the match and maybe even keep playing the next day for a couple of hours, but eventually that injury is going to catch up to you. When you put too much wear and tear on the body, and don't give yourself proper time to rest and heal, you make it more likely that you'll end up with a more severe problem later.

Basketball fans are well versed in the tragic story of All-Star forward Kevin Durant from his days playing for the Golden State Warriors. The California-based basketball team, which had won three championships over the past five years, were just a few games away from a possible fourth title. In the middle of the 2019 NBA Western Conference semifinal game against the Houston Rockets, Durant jumped to shoot at the baseline and landed awkwardly on his right foot. He hobbled off the court, grimacing in pain, and was soon diagnosed with a strained right calf muscle.

The usual treatment for such an injury is rest, but with so much pressure on the team to win the championship, Durant, who was still nursing his injured calf, found himself back on the court to play the Toronto Raptors in game five. The Warriors hoped that Durant, well known as a juggernaut sharpshooter, could bring home the W and save the series. Unfortunately, after only twelve minutes on the court, Durant pushed too hard, this time rupturing his Achilles tendon. This more severe injury not only required surgery to fix but ended Durant's season as well as his team's championship aspirations.

Why am I telling this story? It's not just because I'm a basketball fan. My point is that taking care of your mental health is a lot like taking care of your physical health. The mind, much like the body, can only handle so much. While injuries to the mind may be much less obvious than a dramatic tendon break during a jump shot, pushing your mind beyond its limits is dangerous. If you ignore your mind when it's telling you to rest, if you continue to let it marinate in negative thoughts, or if you allow it to spin with overwhelming what-ifs, you are exposing it to further and, often, more severe problems.

Over the course of my career, I have worked with countless patients who had to acknowledge that if only they had talked sooner or opened up about what they were going through a little bit earlier to a family member, friend, or mental health professional, it would have saved them a lot of pain down the line. But, since we don't put the same premium on our mind-based illnesses as we do on physical ones, many people needlessly suffer and even exacerbate the thoughts and feelings that are causing them so much distress. Because we are so focused on mental illness, instead of mental health, we ignore all those little things that can add up to big problems down the line. That needs to change. We need to change the way we think about mental health, so that we can work each day to do the things we know will improve our mind in order to better embrace joy, connection, and personal growth.

The Role of Self-Care in Your Mental Health Journey

These days, you'll find a lot of people talking about "wellness," or the act of practicing healthy habits on a daily basis to improve your overall well-being. This emphasis on maintenance and prevention is changing the conversation about health, including mental health—and, today, wellness is a trillion-dollar industry that promotes physical activity, mind-body interventions like meditation, and brain-boosting food choices.

While not all wellness claims are backed by science, this blossoming movement has become a force that has expanded the mental health umbrella in ways that the psychiatric field could not have anticipated. While traditional medicine, in many cases, focused primarily on the brain and ignored the mind (we'll talk more about the difference later), those who work in the wellness field acknowledge that the mind is an integral part of a person's overall health. Some of the most candid conversations I've heard about anxiety or trauma outside my practice have taken place in yoga studios, in gyms, or even at the juice bar. There's something about these spaces, and their focus on growth and potential, that really encourages people to open up. At the end of a sixty-minute vinyasa practice at my local yoga studio, it's not uncommon for the teacher to end class with a story about something she struggled with during the week—as well as how she worked to overcome that challenge. These kinds of testimonies are not only contributing to the destigmatization of mental health overall, but also paving the way for people to understand that you can't have overall health and well-being without a commitment to its mental and emotional components.

While some psychiatrists may be quick to dismiss anything that is not an FDA-approved medication as fake science, it's really a complicated dance. As more peer-reviewed studies are published, medical doctors and researchers are continuing to learn that prescription medications are not the be-all and end-all for dealing with mental illnesses. Interventions like breath work, meditation, and mind-body practices like yoga have been shown to reduce anxiety, boost mood, improve sleep, and temper emotional distress. Similarly, the foods we eat can contribute to our mental well-being. There is an increasing body of evidence suggesting that nutrients like omega-3 fatty acids and B vitamins influence not only how the brain works but also how we feel. Moreover, learning to train the way we think, like training a muscle group during a workout, can help offset the type of thinking that can spiral into depression or anxiety. There are likely more options to help support mental health than you think out there. Also, there are many tools you can use to build more resilience, compassion, and contentment in your own life. We'll talk about all of these things, and more, in the following chapters of this playbook.

Your life brings the gifts of personality, discernment, choice, and purpose. Despite this, you may find yourself lost, at a crossroads, or trying to figure out who you are. Maybe you often feel misunderstood. Or like you are just coasting along without purpose, struggling to see how your time adds value to the billions who walked before you. Though I have never walked in your shoes, my personal and professional experience has taught me one thing above all else: You know a lot more about yourself than you think. While we are all unique combinations of circumstances and genes, one thing holds true: You want a mind that works for you and not against you. That is what mental health is about.

In the following pages, I'll discuss what I've learned about the art and the science of self-care—and why it is truly one of the most powerful things you can do to support your mental health. As you learn more about these different practices, take what you need and leave what you don't. There is no one-size-fits-all approach to mental health. There's only what works for you. My intention is for you to learn more about these different tools so you can look into your own mind to see what you require to live with purpose, balance, contentment, and hope. There are many things you can do outside the psychiatrist's office to support strong mental health. It's time to learn which ones are right for you.

CHAPTER 2

YOUR BEAUTIFUL MIND

Biology gives you a brain. Life turns it into a mind.
—*Jeffrey Eugenides*

Early in my training, a man I'll call Zeke was referred to me. During our first session, as I tried to get more details about his life, Zeke quickly interrupted me to ask, after only a few minutes, for a new antidepressant medication to fix, as he put it, "the chemical imbalance" in his brain.

I was still fairly new to seeing patients in the outpatient clinic, but Zeke was a seasoned pro when it came to mental health care. In fact, he was a psychotherapist himself. I soon learned that long before he'd met me, year after year, he'd go from one doctor to the next in the small clinic where I worked looking for the pill, or combination of pills, that would finally cure his depression and anxiety.

"The meds work for a little while and then they stop," he said. "I just need something that's going to work this time—and keep working."

"Which medications have you taken?" I asked, trying to get a feel for what had gone wrong. It's no secret that many patients don't find relief during their first experience taking an antidepressant. In fact, the Sequenced Treatment Alternatives to Relieve Depression (STAR*D) study, a large-scale project that looked at the effectiveness of medications in patients with mild to moderate depression, demonstrated that only about one-third of patients will see their depressive symptoms abate after being prescribed their first antidepressant medication. It's not uncommon for patients to have to try several different drugs, at different dosages, before they feel better. In some cases, prescription drugs don't work at all. Despite that knowledge, I didn't expect Zeke to start naming a veritable laundry list of different medications after I asked the question.

"Let's see . . . Prozac, Zoloft, Wellbutrin, Trazodone, Ambien," he said, with a stern look. "Celexa . . . Effexor. There were a bunch of others. Those should be listed there in the records."

Sure enough, as I perused his chart on my laptop, I saw the notes from his previous doctors. He wasn't joking—and I found myself somewhat dizzied by the list that extended down the screen. I'm not sure there is an antidepressant on the market that he hadn't tried at one point or another. And as I considered just what might help Zeke, I found myself flummoxed. Zeke was a mental health professional. He was already well versed in all the skills I usually introduce to patients. Yet, here he was, pleading for a new prescription to better manage what he believed, deep down, to be a brain that wasn't working the way it was supposed to work. He wanted me to fix him—and do it quickly.

Part of me understands the desire for a quick mood-boosting fix. Unfortunately, by the time patients reach the doors of my office—thanks to the stigma surrounding mental illnesses, health insurance limitations, and their desire just to push through—they are in desperate need of help. It's no wonder that they want to feel better, and to feel better as soon as possible.

In some ways, my experience with Zeke is a common story. Many of my colleagues have also met their own Zekes—patients who walk into the psychiatrist's office looking for a doctor to quickly diagnose the problem and set them up with a fast-acting treatment that will restore them to a more normal, balanced state. After all, an internist can reduce a patient's high blood pressure by prescribing an ACE inhibitor. A primary care provider can make fast work of a bacterial infection with some basic antibiotic treatment. And endocrinologists can dictate a personalized insulin regimen to allow diabetics to lead longer, healthier, and more independent lives. That's what medical doctors are taught to do, and it's also what patients expect of us. Pull out the prescription pad and make things better.

However, much of psychiatry doesn't lend itself well to this particular model of "fix me" health care. Treating disorders of the brain is a challenge, not only because the brain is so mysterious but because the brain gives rise to the mind. Understanding the difference between the brain and the mind is of vital importance—and something I will discuss in more detail later. Even as every psychiatrist has likely seen a patient like Zeke, there are a million little details about that particular patient's life, experiences, and perspective that make him or her distinct and unique. Those little variations add up and can lead to big differences in the way a mental health professional considers the challenges you face and the best way to address them.

As a psychiatrist, I hear people's stories every day, stories of loneliness, guilt, exuberance, and heartache. Like the recently divorced father who fills the hole in his soul with whatever drink will numb his sorrow. Or the woman who is living a good life, with a good job, and a good husband, but still feels unhappy. Or even the young gay man who is humorously self-deprecating in public but hates himself when left alone, living with an unspoken fear that he will not find footing in a world he believes does not accept him. While there may be some overlaps when it comes to what my patients may expect from me, the stories are as varied as the individuals who come seeking help. Although there is usually no perfect or quick solution to any of our struggles—no perfect therapy or magical pill—much of learning how to heal starts with an understanding about what mental health is and, more important, what it isn't.

Understanding Brain-Based Explanations for Mental Illness

Over the past few decades, advances in the field of neuroscience have changed the way we think about mental illness. Innovative technologies now allow us glimpses into a mysterious organ—and we have learned quite a bit about the brain's role in different illnesses. Because of these exciting research studies, you have likely heard prominent psychiatrists, therapists, and researchers frame their discussions about mental illness in terms of brain regions, neurons, and neurotransmitters. One prevalent view is that the bulk of mental illnesses arises from poor connectivity and communication within specific areas of the brain like the prefrontal cortex, the amygdala, and the limbic system. This view is not entirely wrong, as there are some notable instances where we can link changes in mood, personality, and behavior with damage to specific areas of the brain.

Take Phineas Gage. In the mid-1800s, this young hardworking

construction foreman had long been considered a kind and well-mannered gentleman by his colleagues at the railroad company, as well as his family and closest friends. After a series of misfortunes, the twenty-five-year-old shifted his attention at precisely the wrong moment, leading to an ill-timed explosion that sent a tamping iron—a three-foot steel bar—through Gage's left eye, through the front part of his brain, and out the top of his skull.

Miraculously, Gage survived the ordeal. He lost his eye, but otherwise recovered and returned to work. But he wasn't the same. Accounts from his friends, as well as his doctors, suggested that while Gage maintained some of his intellectual capacity, his personality was quite altered. He became disrespectful, callous, and difficult to work with. He was quick to anger—and he even started cussing like a sailor. Because of the noticeable changes in his demeanor, many prominent physicians and scientists at the time, who already had reason to suspect that frontal lobe damage could cause dramatic personality shifts, had even more evidence to support their claims. After all, the tamping iron had gone straight through Gage's left frontal lobe, causing notable physical damage to the area. Such hypotheses were not without merit. Brain imaging studies now suggest that damage in the frontal lobe is in fact associated with distinct behavioral changes. You also see this phenomenon in frontotemporal dementia, a type of neurodegenerative disease that targets the frontal lobes, where doctors will see changes to temperament and demeanor long before memory loss occurs.

Cases like Gage's raised questions about whether a brain aberration, specifically to the prefrontal cortex, might also account for mental illnesses like major depression or bipolar disorder. In 1966, a man by the name of Charles Whitman made headlines after climbing the iconic clock tower at the University of Texas at Austin with a rifle in hand. The former marine opened fire on the busy campus below, killing fourteen people and wounding more than thirty others before ultimately being shot and killed by police. Prior to this grisly event, Whitman had visited a campus psychiatrist, where he admitted to not feeling himself and grappling with fits of anger. Could there be clues in Whitman's brain as well? Perhaps, that might explain such heinous and inexplicable behavior.

When doctors completed an autopsy on Whitman, they discovered that he suffered from a glioblastoma multiforme, a type of aggressive brain tumor. The tumor had significantly compressed a part of the brain called the amygdala, known for its role in emotional regulation and fear processing. This finding raised some important questions: Would Whitman have committed such a terrible and violent act without having had a brain tumor? Could his actions have been avoided if the tumor had been successfully diagnosed and treated earlier? Unfortunately, we'll never know for sure whether it was the cause of his breakdown, or simply a mitigating factor that helped to further deteriorate an already vulnerable psychological state. However, the questions are still worth asking.

The bigger philosophical question that cases like Gage's and Whitman's inspire is how much of human behavior is dictated by a properly functioning brain. What kind of insults can it withstand—and which injuries might lead to mental illness? Unfortunately, despite the advances in research, it's hard to answer either question with any kind of specificity.

A Hundred Little Chemicals

While a brain-based explanation for common mental illnesses is compelling, there's one small problem: There's no definitive "depression" or "anxiety" region of the brain, per se. Studies show that several different brain areas are associated with a depressed mood, for example—including the amygdala, hippocampus, nucleus accumbens, and parts of the prefrontal cortex. But it's not like you can knock one of those sections out and a major depressive episode will immediately follow. It's not that straightforward.

With so many different regions involved with these most common conditions, scientists looked to the connections, or the neural circuits, between them. Each one of these circuits, made up of hundreds of thousands of neurons, sends important signals to different locations across the brain, and, in doing so, helps facilitate our every thought, feeling, and behavior. Each one of the brain cells making up a circuit contributes to this complex communication process by releasing unique chemical messengers called neurotransmitters.

There are over one hundred different types of neurotransmitters in the brain, providing the specific "messages" that govern the brain's functions. Science has identified only a handful that appear to play a specific psychoactive role (that impacts the way we think, behave, and feel). You've likely heard about serotonin before; it's sometimes referred to as a "mood" or "calming" chemical. You may have even heard about some of its cousins in the monoamine family—norepinephrine and dopamine. Other big players in the mood game include histamine, glutamate, gamma-aminobutyric acid (GABA), and acetylcholine.

Scientists have demonstrated that neurotransmitters communicate along different brain circuits to activate the specific brain regions involved with mood. That includes the limbic system, or the network of brain regions that are responsible for our emotional states, including the amygdala. Other parts of the brain, like the prefrontal cortex, have been shown to control executive function, or the higher-level cognitive functions like judgment and decision making—they appear to be involved with regulating our moods, too. And while scientists can't pinpoint one specific part of the brain and say that particular region is responsible for making you happy or sad, they have noted that too much or too little of a particular neurotransmitter—or activity of the receptors that pick up those neurotransmitters once neurons pass them to neighboring cells—is associated with mood disruptions.

Some of the earliest studies examining neurotransmitters and the brain noted that elevated levels of dopamine led to increased feelings of reward. Around the same time, in 1967, British psychiatrist Alec Coppen's work suggested that a lack of utilizable serotonin in the brain led to a depressed state, the so-called serotonin hypothesis of depression. It's easy to see why, with these breakthroughs, many hoped such studies could be translated into medications that could quickly, effectively improve mood in the patients who needed it the most by simply raising or lowering the levels of these chemicals circulating in our brain.

Researchers have spent almost a century trying to explain mental illness by the chemical reactions involving neurotransmitters, with good reason. If doctors could identify a particular chemical or process that had gone awry in the brain, there was the potential that they could directly treat the problem with medication. Such ideas led to increased intellectual curiosity about psychiatric medications in the early 1900s. By the 1950s, pharmacologic treatments for illnesses like schizophrenia and major depression were starting to take off. In 1957, the first academic paper was published that told the story of the drug imipramine, which increases levels of different neurotransmitters in the brain and was discovered to have antidepressant effects. By the 1970s, Coppen's serotonin hypothesis became the bedrock for the eventual development and utilization of selective serotonin reuptake inhibitors (SSRIs), drugs that block reuptake of serotonin by cells, leaving more of this neurotransmitter available to pass messages between brain cells. In 1987, the FDA approved Prozac, a new SSRI that boasted impressive rates of remission as well as an improved safety profile—and, within a year, it became one of the most widely prescribed drugs in the United States.

Throughout the 1990s, antidepressants grew in popularity and offered hope to millions of people who were looking for a pathway to a better life. Prozac was the first SSRI, but others, like Paxil, Zoloft, and Lexapro, soon came on the scene. According to data collected by the Centers for Disease Control and Prevention (CDC), there was a 400 percent increase in antidepressant prescriptions in adults and children over the age of twelve between 1988 and 1994. The so-called Prozac Revolution had begun—and people soon started to believe that fixing our chemical imbalances was the key to happiness.

Consider the marketing for these drugs. I remember one of the first Zoloft commercials to air on television. It depicted a sullen blobby face, suffering beneath a storm cloud, as a pensive bluebird watched from the sidelines. *While the cause is unknown,* the voiceover read, underscored by a jazzy clarinet, *depression may be related to an imbalance in natural chemicals found between nerve cells in the brain.* The message was simple, concise, and memorable. I was in my first semester of college when that ad first hit the airwaves. It wasn't uncommon for my friends and me to whistle the drug's catchy theme song when we went out for late-night food runs.

"Do I have a chemical imbalance or do you?" we would ask one another when we were stressed or anxious. The immediate reply was always "Maybe we need some Zoloft!"

For many of us, our earliest education about neurotransmitters and mental illness came from these types of advertisements. It would be a decade before I'd attend medical school and learn more about the brain—but those early commercials led to a strong belief that mental health was simply a matter of choice or bad genetics. It also supported the idea that SSRIs were the best and perhaps the only way to turn any frown upside down. Those beliefs undoubtedly changed the way both patients and psychiatrists thought about and treated mental illness.

How Antidepressants Work, and How They Don't

According to the CDC, tens of millions of Americans are prescribed antidepressants each year. In medical school and in residency, I was taught that SSRIs were the gold standard treatment for depression. Offering such drugs to patients was considered to provide their best opportunity for feeling better. My training all but ensured that my patients' path toward recovery would involve a prescription for Prozac or a similar drug.

As I had these conversations with patients, I was often asked what different antidepressant or psychotropic drugs did, and I'd do my best to explain why they could help. Prozac, Zoloft, and Lexapro are among the most famous antidepressants. They're SSRIs that work by blocking the reuptake of serotonin between neurons in the brain. In doing so, they increase the availability of serotonin, a neurochemical that has long been thought to contribute to mood.

SSRIs, however, are not the only class of antidepressants. SNRIs (serotonin norepinephrine reuptake inhibitors) like Effexor or Cymbalta increase serotonin levels—but they also up another brain chemical called norepinephrine that has been linked with improving mood and reducing anxiety as well. Other antidepressants, like Wellbutrin, target norepinephrine and dopamine, which can help improve energy and motivation.

Psychiatrists may also prescribe drugs called mood stabilizers for people in more extreme cases of emotional distress. You have likely heard of medications like lithium and Depakote. These drugs help control the swings between high and low moods, as often seen in conditions like bipolar disorder or schizoaffective disorder. These are pretty powerful drugs—and should only be used in specific circumstances. Although that didn't stop one of my patients, I'll call him Mike, from asking me to write him a prescription for lithium after he broke up with his girlfriend to help him "level out" his mood so he could better weather the transition.

"I'm not liking how I'm reacting to the stress," he told me. "I don't want to *feel* as much as I do."

I didn't write the prescription because that's not what these drugs are supposed to do. We have emotions for a reason. Our feelings help us not only to survive but to thrive in our environments—they give us additional information that help us make decisions, avoid dangers, and interact with other people. While our expected emotional swings can be inconvenient, they are a big part of what makes us human. We are supposed to experience emotion—and, because of that, our mood will not remain constant across all of life's trials and tribulations.

There are also FDA-approved drugs like ketamine, which block a special kind of glutamate receptor called N-methyl-D-aspartate (NMDA) and have been found to be effective for treatment-resistant depression. Ketamine promises a rapid reversal of depressive symptoms, and there is some evidence to show that the use of ketamine can potentially reverse suicidal thoughts as well. The problem is that the evidence isn't as clear when you consider its long-term impact on mood. Can ketamine alone cure depression and lead to a life of happiness? Like the other drugs used to treat depression, the answer is probably not.

There are, however, many potential medications that a doctor may give you if you are experiencing a mental illness. Each one of these drugs works on the brain in a slightly different manner. For the most part, their use is all based on the hypothesis that mental illness, whether it's depression, post-traumatic stress disorder (PTSD), or bipolar disorder, is the result of some sort of chemical imbalance in the brain. While these medications may make slight alterations to the neurobiology of your brain, they do not necessarily have the power to influence your mind. To truly recover from depression—or any other mental illness—you have to find the motivation to keep moving forward, to dream, to hope, and to embrace not only what is practical but what is possible. Those feelings are the ones that will carry you through the darkest nights into a brighter tomorrow, with the knowledge and faith that life is beautiful and good. Unfortunately, no pill can give you that.

It's also important to note that antidepressant medications can take weeks to work; most people don't feel a noticeable difference in their symptoms until two to three weeks after they start taking them. It's also possible that the medications may not take full effect for months. That's a long time to wait when depression or anxiety is hindering your ability to work, interact with your family or friends, or find joy in your everyday life. I should also reiterate that the first drug that a doctor prescribes may not be the right one. It is not uncommon for psychiatrists to have to prescribe a handful of different medications at different dosages to find a place where patients experience relief. Then, there's the problem of antidepressant tachyphylaxis. It's a mouthful, I know. That's the scientific term for when antidepressants just stop working. Sometimes, months, years, or even decades after you've found an antidepressant that works for you, it will just poop out. Scientists still aren't exactly sure how this happens, but it's why you see some patients constantly hopping from one drug to the next, hoping the latest one will hold them just a little longer than the last.

Some patients, like Zeke, immediately walk in my office door hoping that I will prescribe something that will instantaneously cure their mental illness. Prescribing medications, certainly, can be a vital part of a treatment regimen. But it's important that we clear up some important misconceptions. First, psychotropic drugs are not a quick fix. As mentioned, they don't always work right away—or, unfortunately, for some patients, at all. Equally important, when it comes to depression and anxiety (the two most prevalent mental illnesses in the world), the prescription drugs recommended to treat them will not make you happy, and they don't "cure" depression *or* anxiety. This statement may throw you off guard. It does for a lot of people. However, the value in these drugs is their ability to tame many of depression's most debilitating symptoms, including fatigue, insomnia, poor appetite, and low motivation. If you take an antidepressant and just wait for it to work—without doing anything else to help support your mental health—you may find yourself feeling even worse. It's not uncommon for these drugs to offer a false sense of hope as a result of unrealistic expectations—and, when they don't immediately kick into action, an even deeper sense of foreboding.

Every time I write a prescription for an antidepressant, I wonder what role it may have played in my own recovery some decades ago.

In hindsight, I likely would have benefited from one of these drugs. I wasn't sleeping well, I was tired all the time, I was losing weight, and I was suffering from a severe lack of motivation. An antidepressant could have helped me better manage those symptoms, at least temporarily. But I also know that any prescription wouldn't have helped me recover all on its own.

As I listen to the stories my patients tell me, I frequently see my own feelings and experiences reflected in them. Often, the people who come to see me are struggling through life's transitions or trying to find some kind of footing. They take the medications I prescribe, and I see them get better. I believe that is because I make sure they have reasonable expectations for what these drugs can and cannot do. An analogy I often share with my patients is that mental illness is like being stuck in a ditch. Medications can help get you out of the ditch, but it's your lifestyle that will keep you out of it.

Thinking beyond the Brain

Over the past few decades, the gold standard for psychiatric care shifted from doctors conducting hours of in-depth conversations on the therapy couch to pulling out the prescription pad to provide patients with mood-elevating medications. Better living through chemistry—the use of psychotropic drugs seemed quick, easy, and, for the most part, effective. But, as I mentioned earlier, up to a third of patients won't respond to antidepressant drugs, only show a partial response to treatment, or are plagued by unpleasant side effects that overshadow any relief they may find. Some patients may see their symptoms subside at first, but then find that the drugs are less effective over time.

I don't mean to suggest that psychiatric medications are not beneficial. The two-thirds of patients who find relief with that prescription are proof enough of that, and their use, as part of a comprehensive treatment program, has saved countless lives. Really, it's indisputable. Research studies have consistently shown us that medications like lithium, clozapine, and ketamine can reduce suicidal ideation in people at serious risk of harming themselves. Psychostimulants like Ritalin and Adderall have helped those struggling with attention deficit hyperactivity disorder (ADHD) better adapt at school, at work, or in life in general. And, of course, antidepressants like Wellbutrin, Zoloft, Remeron, and Prozac can reduce the severity and duration of debilitating depressive episodes, as well as help people better manage troubling symptoms like fatigue, poor appetite, and insomnia.

Yet, if mental illness can be explained solely by brain regions and neurotransmitters gone awry, these drugs should work for *everyone* who is struggling with a mental illness. There shouldn't be such large gaps in efficacy. As it turns out, when you try to distill mood, as well as other mental health problems, down to simple biological mechanics, there are still a lot of questions that require answers, especially if you want to help someone feel better.

This is just one of many reasons that trying to make scientific sense of your mood is such challenging stuff. While antidepressant and other psychoactive drugs have, no doubt, helped millions of patients across the globe, their widespread use has come at some cost to psychiatry as a whole. It has limited physicians' face-to-face time with patients, as short medication management appointments offer a quick alternative for those precious hours diving deeply into understanding the nuances of a particular depressive episode. It also helped to promote the idea that mental illness can be cured provided you find the right prescription drug. As a result, many people look no further than their biology for clues on how to feel better. This is to the detriment of both the doctor and the patient.

While it is easy to see the appeal of a brain-based explanation for mental illness, it leaves out what is most important in promoting mental health and preventing mental illness: the mind.

You may remember the name René Descartes from Philosophy 101 thanks to his famous one-liner, "I think therefore I am." This seventeenth-century mathematician was the first great philosopher on record to try to differentiate the mental and the physical parts of human beings. He defined the mind as the "thinking thing" and held it in stark contrast to the physical manifestation of our selves. Not to go too deep, Descartes believed that the mind was an immaterial substance that contained the essence of a person as an individual—the wonderful stuff that allowed man not only to think but to dream, doubt, imagine, believe, and hope. Many other enlightened thinkers have come to the same conclusion: that intangible human stuff, those things that makes each person unique and individual and, well, simply, *them*, is the mind.

In the centuries since, scientists and philosophers have hotly debated the so-called mind-body problem, with many leading neuroscientists hoping to find biological evidence of Descartes's "immaterial substance" within the contents of brain cells and neural circuitry. I sometimes wonder how Descartes, if he were alive today, might redefine his concept of the mind given the latest and greatest scientific findings. From my perspective as a mental health practitioner, the mind and the brain, despite the latest research studies, remain two distinct things. I cannot hope to come up with a definition to beat Descartes's but, for me, the mind is the mystery—it's the nuances, the experiences, the stories, and, more to the point, everything we don't know or understand about how the brain works to give rise to our thoughts and emotions.

If the brain is a Jackson Pollock canvas, I see the mind as the space between all those abstract splashes of paint. It's the music playing in the background, the canvas on the floor instead of an easel, the force required to get the splash of paint just so, the decision to use one color over another, and the reason why that cigarette butt was preserved in the gesso. The mind is not something you can see or feel or touch. It's the context surrounding your existence and experience. And it is that context, as much as the physical materials, that creates an individual human being—just as they provide the scaffolding for a unique work of art.

The entire framing of the mind-body problem makes it seem as if you have to choose one or the other to prescribe an effective treatment. I don't believe that's true, especially when thinking about how to support optimal mental health outside the psychiatrist's office. It's no mystery that the brain is an exceptional machine, comprised of a mélange of chemicals, cells, and circuits. The mind is equally compelling and should be treated with the same respect. Those spaces in the canvas hold truths and insights that cannot be re-created by amplifying a single neurotransmitter. They are the places where we can often go for relief when we find ourselves limited by the current state of medicine as it pertains to mental health treatment.

Let's go back to Zeke. While I did end up prescribing him a different antidepressant medication that first day he came to my office, he came back in a few weeks to tell me it wasn't working. In fact, he felt even worse than he had when he first came to see me. As we continued to work together, it became clear that Zeke didn't suffer from a "broken" brain. Rather, he was struggling with a long-standing but troubled marriage and frustrating dissatisfaction with a job he thought he was supposed to love—things that a drug, no matter how highly rated, cannot fix.

Eventually, Zeke gave up on searching for the perfect prescription and his misguided belief that the right medication could ease his troubled mind. In fact, he made the decision to move away from an antidepressant-driven approach to treatment long before I did, perhaps as a result of his own frustration or a realization that years down that path wasn't offering the solution he was looking for. Over time, at his request, I helped him reduce his medications from four pills a day, to three, to two, and, eventually, to one. At the same time, he also started exercising more, prioritized making his marriage work, and began exploring spirituality through the Buddhist faith.

This was a powerful lesson for me as his doctor and as someone who had to work hard to surface from my own depression. It was only when Zeke moved his focus away from finding a pill to "fix" the way he felt, as well as expecting me, as his physician, to provide the full cure, that he really started to get better. Implementing the right strategies outside the psychiatrist's office not only helped him better manage the parts of his life that were troubling him, but strengthened his overall mental health and wellness. That's what made the most meaningful difference.

Mental illness isn't a choice, but mental health can be. The work you put into learning about your mind, and figuring out what makes you tick, can not only reduce your risk for developing mental illnesses in the future but also lead to a more positive mindset and an improved quality of life today.

CHAPTER 3

HEALING BEYOND MEDICINE

Medicine is a science of uncertainty
and an art of probability.
—*Sir William Osler*

No one plans depression. I certainly did not.

As with most people who have never faced it before, my first major depressive episode caught me completely off guard. Yet, looking back, I can see hints of what was to come. Like many of my patients who share their stories with me, in my case, depression was always there, lurking in the background.

For as long as I can remember, I've been a dreamer. I spend a lot of time in my own head, being thoughtful and deeply intuitive. Even as a young child, I *felt* everything—and even the slightest impression of disappointment or displeasure from my family or friends would send my mind reeling. I was constantly questioning how I might have contributed to those feelings, even if I wasn't directly involved with the situation at hand. That's what depression can do. It can make you feel guilty about things you haven't done. It can test the limits of your perceptions, blurring the lines between what is rational and irrational. It can exhaust you in both body and spirit, making you feel like you are dragging yourself from one day and into the next. And it can lie to you, telling you if only you worked harder, did better, or tried more that life would not feel so hopeless.

Depression wasn't passed on to me by way of genetics or bestowed as a product of traumatic life events. I had one of those picturesque and upbeat childhoods, where I was surrounded by a family who loved and supported me. I had good friends and did well in school. By all accounts, I had everything going for me. If you listened to common wisdom, I'm not the type of person who should have ever struggled with a mental illness. In fact, when I was younger, I didn't even know anyone who had been depressed. Nor did I understand that this condition could have the power to ravage my own mind—especially since I felt like my thoughts, including the negative ones, were just a part of who I was, one of many components involved in my unique biological construction.

When I was twelve, I picked up an oboe for the first time. How I came to choose this unlikely instrument—while my friends tended to go for the clarinet, the trumpet, or the drums—seemed somewhat serendipitous. Just prior to my starting in the junior high school band, my dad, overhearing a soprano saxophone solo in a melodic jazz piece, remarked to me, "Son, that's beautiful. Is it an oboe?" It wasn't, of course, but somehow the name of the instrument stayed with me, and when it came time to select what I wanted to play, I gravitated toward this forceful, though sometimes melancholic, instrument. Within a few months of lessons, it seemed meant to be. I excelled, playing to accolades and awards across the state of Texas. By the time I graduated from high school, I had been accepted at the Juilliard School in New York City, the dream of any would-be classical musician. Everyone I knew was convinced I was on my way to performing in a prestigious symphony orchestra. I hoped they were right.

My high school graduating class was large—over eight hundred students. Of that group, only two of us were going to college in Manhattan: me and my high school sweetheart, an aspiring artist. The future looked bright for these two creative kids from suburban Texas. We were excited to get out into the big, bad city and make our respective dreams come true together. I was certain that the same discipline, work ethic, and determination that had contributed to my acceptance at Juilliard would see me through graduation and on to the orchestra of my choice.

Music opened so many doors for me. By the time I was twenty, I had given solo performances in the United States and abroad. My relationship, I believed, was also going strong. I should have been on top of the world; however, by my second year at Juilliard, I just didn't feel *right*. I was becoming more and more overwhelmed while the tide of those feelings slowly pulled me under.

At first, I thought the answer was just to work harder. That's the strategy that had sustained me in the past. The mantra of my youth was to work as hard as I could and then find time for self-care later, because I viewed self-care only as a reward for hard work. Despite the myriad of experiences that New York had to offer, you'd find me, night after night, playing for hours in one of the conservatory's closet-like practice rooms. Every once in a while, I'd venture out to listen to poetry slams at the Nuyorican Poets Cafe or to check out Egon Schiele paintings at the Neue Galerie with my girlfriend. But these occasions were rarities, and I'd spend as much time feeling guilty that I wasn't working on my music as I would enjoying the richness of the experiences and the company.

Looking back, I can clearly see that I was living under the misguided illusion that physical and emotional well-being were disposable commodities. Soon, the same traits that had allowed me to perform at such a high level throughout high school began to turn on me. After two years of pushing myself relentlessly, I lost all motivation to study, to work, to practice, to perform, or even to love. I didn't identify those feelings as depression, because I didn't know what it meant to be depressed, though now I understand how that's what was emerging. What I did know was that the situation had devolved to the point where I *had* to leave Juilliard and go back home. In doing so, I was also making the decision to leave behind music as well as my first love. I strongly believed it was the right thing to do, but I couldn't have anticipated how difficult it would be.

The Ebbs and Flows of Depression

Leaving music remains among the most difficult personal decisions I have ever made. The opportunities music brought me—including the validation that came with it—made it particularly challenging. Because of this, I regularly second-guessed my decision. Once I returned to Texas, those previously well-hidden undercurrents of despair started to crash, more and more, through the surface. Depression can wax and wane, which makes it difficult, at times, to identify. There are periods where it can feel like you're holding your head above water, and others when you are drowning.

From a distance, I probably looked okay to most people. I did what I needed to, and I was *functioning*, but every night, I lay in bed struggling to sleep. I had trouble connecting with my new class-mates, and it was almost impossible to make eye contact with them, especially when unfounded guilt made it difficult for me to even look at my own reflection in the mirror. My family was nearby, and remained supportive, but I had difficulty feeling their love for me, too. Depression took me to a place where I had lost all semblance of hope. I needed help, though, like many of my patients, I didn't realize it. I thought I could figure things out on my own because I was *getting by*.

After graduating from college, I started working as a research technician for an up-and-coming neuroscientist at the Texas Medical Center. It was at this time when I started to feel the full weight of depression. Every morning, as the sun would rise, I felt like I was being thrust in the deep end without knowing how to swim. Despite the fact that depression was slowly wearing me down, I was still trying to contribute to interesting research, publish papers, build my résumé, and find a place in medical school. I was going to fake it until I made it. I believed that was the only option. Perhaps, this mentality was a product of my unfounded belief that happiness was embedded in success, and that an educated African American man showing the slightest hint of weakness automatically equated to failure. Even as I was still doing my best to get by, several times a day I'd find it was all too much. I would make my way to the bath-room, lock the door, and sit on the floor with my face in my hands and just cry, only to leave, embarrassed by what I had just done.

I knew that what I was feeling was not normal. In fact, I was well aware that the negative thoughts and feelings I was experienc-ing were irrational and unwarranted. But I was too proud to admit that something might be wrong and that I couldn't handle my life on my own. So, I did what I'd always done. I soldiered on, doing my best to hide what was happening to me.

One morning, after another long and sleepless night, I finally hit bottom. As I started to ready myself for work, depression told me there was no point—there was no future for me. I couldn't even find the will to cry, which, in the moment, felt like just another in a long line of failures. That day, neither my body nor my mind would allow me to push through. Instead of going to work, as I was supposed to do, I lay down on the floor of my darkened closet and allowed an onslaught of regrets and recriminations to consume me. When my family found me there, hours later, I was too exhausted to meaningfully respond to their questions. They immediately called 9-1-1 to have me evaluated at the local emergency room.

Depression consumed me, and then spilled out like a collapsing dam, over all the barricades I had so carefully constructed to hide my pain and suffering. Why did it happen that day? I cannot tell you. Was there some meaningful event or conversation that preceded that desire to lie down and not get back up again that morning? Not really. Despite what you see in the movies, there isn't always some major crucible that leads to a crack in your psychological armor. More often than not, I've learned over countless conversations with colleagues and patients, seemingly small events are often the trigger for a major depressive episode. Those little things can, and quite often do, mean a lot.

There is no litmus test for emotionally traumatic events. What may seem inconsequential to you could end up being life or death for another person. One, because of all the lies depression tells us when we are in its sights. And, two, because often that one small thing is just the straw that breaks the camel's back. It is the culmination of a hundred, a thousand, a million little pains we carry—

the only difference being that, in that moment, your mind can no longer find a way to endure the burden.

Losing your will to go on, your motivation to succeed, or the hope that you will find happiness again—those are the decisions that depression makes for us. Unfortunately, for far too many people, it ends up being a life-or-death choice. As I sat on the bed in the ER that morning, answering questions from a safety checklist about whether I meant to harm myself, I realized I wanted to live. Over the next few months, by a little luck or by the grace of God, I found a path toward healing without ever being prescribed an antidepressant medication or getting the professional mental health care that would have helped ease my pain. Despite a seemingly impenetrable depression and emotional fragility that had me in its gridlock, mental illness eventually spared me. Hitting rock bottom led to a period of growth and maturity that allowed me to slowly feel better over time, and also to realize that mental health care works best when self-care is also part of the plan.

My experience with depression resulted in quite a bit of soul-searching during my medical training, because as I was learning about how neurotransmitters and pathways in the brain contributed to mental illness, I thought that all paths toward healing had to involve a medication to correct it. But how did I manage to get better without one? Throughout my training, I had seen how the advancements of modern medicine (including psychiatric medications) helped patients sleep better, manage anxiety, stabilize episodes of mania or psychosis, and emerge from periods of depression like mine. Medications were often part of a comprehensive treatment plan that undoubtedly improved and even saved lives. In my case, however—whether or not a chemical imbalance was the sole cause of my depression—I understood from personal experience that alternative treatments that didn't require a prescription—or could work in concert with one—did exist.

It meant there was the potential for healing *beyond* medicine.

Barriers to Entry

Often, when I talk about my own experience with depression, people will immediately ask why I didn't seek the help of a therapist. After all, that's what we're supposed to tell people who are struggling, right? If you need help, go get it. Make an appointment and talk to a mental health professional.

This is a totally appropriate thing to say if someone you care about is experiencing depression, or another mental illness is getting in the way of living their life the way they want to. Frankly, I'd love to see more people pursuing therapy. Unfortunately, securing an appointment with a psychiatrist or a therapist can be difficult.

This isn't just a matter of the stigma surrounding mental illness—even though that is still more prevalent than I'd like. With so many mental health advocacy organizations funding popular anti-stigma campaigns, as well as revered figures in sports and entertainment now going public with their own experiences in therapy, I might even go so far as to argue that stigma isn't the primary barrier anymore. Rather, it's a host of other, more practical factors that keep the average person out of the therapist's office.

First, therapy is expensive. If you look online, you can find prices ranging from $20 per hour to $275 per hour. But that $20 figure? It's a rarity. That's what therapists-in-training, with little to no experience, charge patients, and those appointments fill up fast. It's not unusual for patients looking for these more affordable sessions to wait months, or even longer, to see a doctor. Once they are in the door, there's no guarantee that there will be room on the schedule for recurring appointments if and when they are needed. If your insurance plan includes mental health benefits, you may be able to find a provider where you'll pay $20 to $50 out of pocket per session. Unfortunately, many private insurance plans don't cover therapy, except in very specific circumstances. Even *my* own health insurance plan doesn't cover mental health benefits.

It's also important to consider the associated costs of therapy. Therapy is a serious time commitment. That kind of commitment may require you to take time off work or find some extra hours away from your family, and making that happen comes with costs, both direct and indirect, too. Your job may not have the flexibility for you to go to regular appointments, and too often, workplaces will balk at your taking recurring sick time to cover those hours. If you can find an appointment outside your normal workday, you still may pay for transportation or a babysitter. When you put all those extras together, the end result is that many people who need psychotherapy just can't afford it.

There are issues surrounding supply and demand, too. The demand for therapy is high, especially in turbulent times. It's often a challenge to find a therapist who is accepting new patients, let alone a psychiatrist that you like and will want to work with. Rural areas, in particular, suffer from a lack of trained mental health practitioners. It's also important to note that not all psychiatrists offer psychotherapy, either. Many may work solely in a hospital setting or only see people briefly to manage medication regimens. And if you have specific preferences about the kind of practitioner you'd like to see? Maybe a female therapist or a psychiatrist of color—or someone who has experience with LGBTQ+ issues? This limits the pool of potential therapists even further.

It's important to find someone who "fits." Numerous research studies have demonstrated that factors like empathy, warmth, and a positive therapeutic alliance are just as important, if not more important, than any specific treatment interventions—important enough that the American Psychiatric Association has a specific task force that offers guidelines and recommendations about how psychiatrists and other mental health professionals (including licensed professional counselors, psychologists, and social workers) can better connect with patients so they will be more likely to benefit from treatment. Simply stated, if you don't have a good professional relationship with your therapist, you are less likely to benefit from the work you do in session.

I'm not trying to scare people away from therapy. I have seen firsthand the difference that these conversations can make in a person's life, and I will continue to beat the therapy drum in hopes of inspiring people to seek out the help they need. But it's important to acknowledge these barriers, because they highlight another reason why it's so important for people who are in pursuit of optimal mental health to think beyond the psychiatrist's couch.

Hints of Healing in Unexpected Places

Some people may be experiencing emotional distress to the point that they require hospitalization, usually after expressing suicidal thoughts. That's what happened to Orin, a patient I encountered when I was working in an inpatient facility some years ago.

You probably know someone like Orin. He had always taken great pride in providing for his family. He was the person people could count on to make things happen, whether it was to manage a complex project at work or help his daughter with her geometry homework. Unexpectedly, this army veteran in his mid-forties was abruptly laid off from his engineering job. It sent him reeling.

His wife picked up extra shifts to help pay the bills while Orin searched for a new position. No leads seemed to pan out. He felt like a failure, like he was letting down the people who mattered the most to him. Because of this, he started falling into a deep depression, and his daily battles with insomnia and diminished appetite soon transformed this burly, dark-skinned man into a pale, gaunt shadow of himself. Eventually, he couldn't find the motivation to do much of anything.

Over time, Orin and his wife started arguing more about trivial matters, while his teenaged daughter interpreted his growing desolation as indifference. He felt like, no matter where he turned, he just couldn't catch a break. He was exhausted, irritable, and wanted to be left alone. No matter how hard his family tried to connect with him, he pushed them away. He knew, deep down, that he was out of line, but from his perspective, what else could he do?

Within the year, Orin separated from his wife and took up residence in a small, sparsely furnished apartment. He had thought he wanted to be left alone, but now that he was passing time in this place, he was paralyzed by his feelings of isolation. In the middle of the night, he would call his brother, the only person he felt like he could still trust, just to talk. When he admitted to his brother that he was becoming more and more mesmerized by the loaded gun sitting on a table in front of him, wondering if everyone would be better off if he wasn't around, his brother immediately called for help. He was admitted to an inpatient facility for evaluation.

In the United States, the average psychiatric hospitalization lasts about ten days. Typically, patients like Orin are started on SSRI medications like Prozac or Zoloft for depression. Even though the best evidence suggests that these drugs can take several weeks to effect any noticeable improvement in mood, why, then, do most patients—including Orin—report feeling better much more quickly—usually within a couple of days?

The truth is, despite the amount of time psychiatrists spend discussing neurotransmitters and chemical imbalances, and the role antidepressants, mood stabilizers, and antipsychotics have in correcting them, healing comes in different forms. For example, they offer patients a much-needed reset on basic human needs like sleep, as we'll discuss further in Chapter 7.

While no one wants to spend a week in a psychiatric hospital, it works, in part, for patients like Orin because it removes them from an environment of isolation and despair and places them into one that offers three meals a day, a safe place to rest, supportive therapy groups, and empathetic doctors and nurses. It also offers patients hope—the belief that you can and will get better.

That belief matters more than you might think.

The Power of Placebo

During my final year of medical school, I traveled to Boston for a monthlong rotation at Harvard's McLean Hospital. There I worked on the adolescent residential treatment unit. Patients were admitted from across the United States, some for several weeks at a time. Throughout their stay, they received therapy groups, educational programming, family meetings, and regular sessions with a psychiatrist. The environment itself was cozy, supportive, and healing—a home away from home.

As part of my training there, I routinely met with a friendly attending physician to review studies or talk about interesting patient cases. Most of the conversations were bread-and-butter topics for a medical student: Freud's psychoanalytic theory, Erikson's stages of development, or the implications of the STAR*D trials on how we prescribe medication. But one day, she slid a ruffled, yet delicately stapled manuscript across the table to me.

"I'd like you to take a look at this," she said with a soft smile.

The paper was a landmark 2014 review, "Antidepressants and the Placebo Effect," authored by Irving Kirsch, PhD, a lecturer at Harvard Medical School. In this article, Kirsch made a bold claim: Most, if not all, of the therapeutic benefits of antidepressant medications are due to the placebo effect.

A placebo is nothing more than an inactive treatment—usually a sugar pill. They are generally used in clinical studies to compare with a real drug to see if that treatment is actually effective. But, sometimes, for reasons we are only beginning to understand, the mind believes that placebo works, and taking that "fake" treatment results in marked improvement from conditions including irritable bowel syndrome to chronic pain disorder. In the paper my attending asked me to read, Kirsch claimed that the placebo response could be responsible for up to 82 percent of the improvement doctors observe after prescribing an antidepressant medication to a patient.

If what Kirsch claimed was, in fact, true, it would challenge everything I'd learned until then about these drugs and how they help treat mental health conditions. While Kirsch's findings remain controversial in the field, they made me think. I had never taken an antidepressant and still had recovered. Perhaps the reason why so many patients feel better when taking a pill—a pill that doctors say will bring them improvement—is partially driven by the expectation, or confidence, that it will work.

Kirsch's research questioned what I had been previously taught about depression, which is that it was a brain disease that needed to be fixed with a treatment plan that *should* include a prescription medication. However, the more I thought about the idea, the more I began to conceptualize the depressed brain as not so much the problem but as part of the solution. That is, if placebos work for depression, the mind, not the medicine itself, is producing the cure. And since hopelessness is a defining feature of depression, the real question is: *Is it possible for the belief in a cure to treat some illnesses even in the absence of the cure itself?* According to Kirsch, the answer is simple. Yes.

Over the next several years, as I graduated from medical school, completed specialty training in psychiatry, worked on a fellowship in integrative medicine, and began treating patients on my own, I thought about what Kirsch's ideas meant for both mental illness and mental health. After prescribing patients antidepressants, and watching so many of them get better, I couldn't help but wonder what role the drug was really playing in their improvement—not only from a psychological standpoint but from a neurochemical one. Was it the neurotransmitter changes, or was it the subconscious comfort of a drug that promised relief that supported their recovery? Could it be a little of both?

I wanted to hear the answers directly from Irving Kirsch. So, one day, I reached out to him to learn more about why placebos might be so effective.

"What we know about placebos is that for many conditions, including anxiety and depression, there is a substantial response that you don't get when you don't give any treatment at all," he explained.

He also said that the placebo effect works even when patients know the drug is a placebo. To my surprise, in such "open-label" studies, patients still see some relief from their symptoms. They know it's fake and yet it has a real effect. How can that be?

"When we give the placebo, we provide an explanation for why it might work anyway—the explanation is based in part on classical conditioning," Kirsch said.

You may remember learning about classical conditioning in a psychology class—probably because of Pavlov's dog. This form of conditioning is a simple learning process that pairs two different stimuli: one that elicits a biological response from an organism and one that is more neutral. For example, before feeding his hungry dog, Pavlov would ring a bell. The food would cause the dog to salivate. But, over time, as the dog associated food with the ringing bell, Pavlov could elicit that salivary response just by ringing the bell. The dog learned that the two stimuli were related, and they meant a good meal was coming his way.

Kirsch told me to think about an antidepressant pill as a conditioned stimulus, or that ringing bell. Since we live in a world where modern medicine is revered, supporting the need for shots, surgeries, and prescription drugs to cure what ails us, we have learned to believe these types of interventions are absolutely required in order to get better. Taking a pill, even when we know it's not supposed to work, can make us feel better because of those strong beliefs in modern medicine. How does such a belief translate to people actually feeling better, especially for those who are living with depression or anxiety?

"The pill itself can help mobilize your body's self-healing capacity. It can instill a sense of expectancy for improvement and a sense of hope," Kirsch told me. "This is particularly important for depression for which hopelessness is one of the defining characteristics."

When I confessed that his ideas, which he eventually expanded into a well-reviewed book, *The Emperor's New Drugs: Exploding the Antidepressant Myth*, were never discussed or formally presented during my years of medical training, Kirsch was not surprised. He acknowledged that psychiatrists, in particular, may have a difficult time accepting the placebo effect in mental health care.

"It's like taking away the only thing that they have [if they are only prescribing medications], so it's only natural that they would be resistant to it," he said.

If placebos are as effective as Kirsch hypothesizes, what I really wanted to know is if mental health practitioners like myself could somehow harness the placebo effect to help our patients heal. Kirsch immediately supported that idea.

"Even if you are prescribing medication, we know from research that you can increase the response by manipulating expectancy. If you induce positive expectations, you'll get a better response, and if you induce negative expectations, you'll get less of a response," he said.

This is apparent, he argued, when studies are designed to offer more than half the participants the active drug being studied. Some studies may split the participants down the middle: half will receive the drug and the other half the placebo. There are some study designs where two out of three participants would receive the active drug. That means each participant would have a two in three or 66 percent chance of receiving the medication. Kirsch said you'll see a stronger placebo response in the second scenario. Knowing there is a higher likelihood you will receive the drug means your expectations for relief are greater.

"People think, 'Okay, I'm more confident that I'm getting a real treatment,'" he explained. "So, they respond better to it."

Belief may be an unlikely healing power, but it is there. In fact, according to research reviewed in the *Lancet*, up to 35 percent of depressed adults will show improvement when given a placebo. That's a lot of people who could be helped if mental health practitioners can successfully instill a sense of expectancy for improvement and a sense of hope.

This remarkable placebo effect teaches us that hope is more than a feeling. It's an essential part of healing, provided it can be activated. You must believe that contentment, the state of being okay with who you are and what you have, is not only possible but inevitable. And that begins when you start to think beyond traditional medicine and add self-care to your mental health regimen.

The Power of Self-Care

Danae Mercer, a journalist and body positivity influencer, serendipitously found fame on social media, and she uses it to educate people about the tricks models and celebrities implement in order to look impeccable. Mercer, former editor in chief of *Women's Health Middle East*, said she was inspired to start posting about how the bodies in magazines were "filtered, posed, and perfected" as part of her pursuit of mental health.

Mercer has a personal stake in helping people see "behind the curtain" when it comes to all those seemingly perfect images. She was diagnosed with an eating disorder when she was a college student.

"I had dieted off and on since I was a teenager—the way, I'd say, most teenagers do," Mercer explained, "but when I was nineteen, my mother passed away. The way I found my control was through food. I developed anorexia and got very sick very quickly."

Luckily, Mercer's professors helped her get into treatment. She credits her university with providing a doctor, a therapist, and a nutritionist to help jump-start her recovery process, though she would be the first to tell you that meeting with a psychiatrist years ago was just the first step in a lifelong process of managing her mental health.

"Therapy is a powerful tool, and it gives you the resources to understand what's happening and gives you a safe space to deal with your issues," she said. "But self-love is a daily journey. And, for me, self-care practices are critical to maintaining my mental health."

In modern times, we have come to equate medicine with clinics, white coats, high-tech hospitals, and prescription drugs. We think about chemicals, molecules, and technology; however, we forget that self-care has been an integral part of healing for all of human history, even as some people try to downplay its benefits. What is self-care? Simply stated, it's utilizing adaptive and healthy ways to recharge. There's no one-size-fits-all answer. Some may approach self-care with a regular yoga practice, others through competitive runs or spending time in nature.

"When things are stressful, I need to make conscious self-care decisions again and again," said Mercer. "To ride the situation out, I am going to spend fifteen minutes journaling and meditate for ten minutes. I'm going to do these things no matter what. I often feel like we often skip [self-care practices] when we feel too busy or too stressed. But to be honest, that's when we need them the most; when we want to do them the least, that's when they usually are the most important."

Of course, self-care goes beyond yoga, exercise, or spending time with your friends and family. It also involves ensuring you are getting enough rest, eating well, and utilizing breath work as medicine. It provides some of the building blocks that allow you to optimize your mental health.

I understand that the term "self-care" often evokes images of spending a weekend at the spa or high-priced holistic medicines. Really, self-care is a healthy lifestyle where you are acting and living each day with the actionable intent to take care of both your body and your mind. You can practice self-care every day, and, most important, it does not have to cost a penny.

Self-care, truly, is the original form of preventative medicine. True students of history remember that Hippocrates, the Father of Medicine, was encouraging folks to eat right all the way back in 400 BC. He said, "Let food be thy medicine and medicine be thy food." Eating a nutrient-dense diet, with foods full of the vitamins and minerals that promote brain health, is an act of self-care.

Yoga classes, daily meditation practices, church services, taking a long shower, watching a movie with friends, or engaging in meaningful conversation with someone you trust are also acts of self-care. Staying hydrated by drinking enough water and prioritizing sleep are forms of self-care, too. It might mean turning off your cell phone at lunch, getting away from screens thirty minutes before bedtime, or taking time to focus on how you breathe when you start to feel overwhelmed. Really, any activity that is healthy, intentional, and supports your overall health and wellness falls into the self-care category. These small gestures can make a big difference in allowing you to become more resilient, less stressed, and more capable of weathering any potential emotional challenges the world throws at you.

We often have trouble incorporating self-care into our life because of our responsibilities at work, at home, or at school. Patients often tell me that making time to meditate or exercise "feels selfish."

Self-care is actually one of the most selfless acts you can do. That's because it's impossible to be all-in for those who need you the most when you're neglecting what your body and mind need to be at their best.

As we have discussed, self-care also has as much a role to play in healing as antidepressant drugs or other standard medical treatments. Scientific evidence demonstrates that these so-called lifestyle interventions can improve your mental health. It's like carrying a metaphorical shield with you that can block whatever complicated mess you are currently trying to manage.

Developing a mind-body practice like meditation, breath work, or yoga, regardless of whether psychiatric medications are part of the prescription, can lend stillness, balance, and tranquility to the chaos of the world around you. Physical exercise as self-care is not just good for the body, it's also good for the mind, and remember that food is medicine, too. These are the kinds of acts that can naturally increase the levels of different neurotransmitters in your brain, reduce your stress, help you weather challenging situations, offer you hope, and make you feel better all around. Even more important, they usually start to work immediately.

"For me, it's about doing things that make me feel strong in my skin," said Mercer. "That could be weight lifting, running, or going for a great yoga session. It's important to give yourself that time."

When I think back on my own experience with depression, while I never took an antidepressant medication, I did find ways to invest in my own self-care. I began a yoga practice. I found new purpose through faith. I found comfort in the connection I had with my family. These actions were antidepressants for me, as they are for so many of my patients. Unlike an antidepressant medication, they are self-sustaining. I never have to worry about them losing their efficacy over time. These seemingly inconsequential self-care interventions provided me with strength and hope, and the belief that I could be well again. In doing so, they triggered powerful changes in both my body and my mind. I've seen them do the same for my patients. There is healing beyond medicine. Self-care is its own form of healing, and it could be the fix you've been searching for.

CHAPTER 4

SURVIVAL OF THE FITTEST

The art of life lies in a constant
readjustment to our surroundings.
—*Okakura Kakuzō*

A few years ago, I received an invitation to attend a yoga workshop at a nearby studio. The workshop was called *Yoga for Men: Forging Resiliency*. I signed up because it was hosted by two friends of mine, Chris and Alec—and, as someone who enjoys yoga, it sounded like a nice thing to do on a Saturday morning.

I also admit that I found myself intrigued by the title of the class. In the days leading up to the event, I was turning over the idea of "forging" resiliency in my mind. I had never considered resiliency as something one could produce themselves, and I definitely hadn't considered the matter in terms of a person's gender. My experience—and my work—had suggested that some people were just naturally resilient. Whether by means of genetics or pure, good old-fashioned determination, they were able to bounce back with ease no matter what life threw their way. Others, unfortunately, were not blessed with such gifts. Even seemingly small obstacles had the power to flatten them, and it required an immense amount of effort for them to get back up again. I was curious to see what kind of information my two friends might present about resiliency in between vinyasas.

Chris and Alec are both charismatic men of color—faces that many are not accustomed to seeing in the yoga studio. They are decidedly not your stereotypical om-chanting yogis. Chris, a tall, muscular fitness guru with an inviting smile and Southern drawl, has one of those larger-than-life personalities that had the power to immediately captivate an audience. Alec, his counterpart, was partial to bright dashiki shirts and a 1970s style Afro. Despite that eye-catching look, Alec was a little more on the quiet side. Yet the combination of this Ivy League grad's voice and demeanor could easily usher others into the zone for a rejuvenating meditation session. They were both experienced and appealing yoga teachers, but I was curious about what they might have to say with regard to building a skill that most people believe you have to be born with.

The workshop began with a short vinyasa flow. The group was small, about twenty men in total with varying degrees of yoga experience. While we were all happy to move our bodies, it was clear that many of us were struggling to understand the connection between yoga and resiliency. Any seasoned yogi will tell you that mind-body practices, including yoga, are chock-full of symbolism, imagery, and metaphors that illustrate practical lessons that can be used off the mat. The link between those familiar movements and resilience's brand of emotional flexibility, however, remained elusive.

At the end of the flow, Alec and Chris moved to the front of the studio where a large white pad was waiting. Chris pulled out a marker and wrote the word RESILIENCY at the top of the page.

He turned to us and then asked, "What does resiliency mean?" He waited to write our responses on the paper.

I started to offer an answer but then stopped myself. I realized, in that moment, I wasn't exactly sure what resiliency was. But even if I could come up with some sort of partial definition, I was entirely certain I had no idea how to "forge" it. I decided I might be better off listening instead of talking. Maybe someone else had something more insightful to say.

After a few moments of silence, other members of the class eventually began pitching their own ideas about the concept.

"It means you don't break."

"Nothing gets in your way."

"It's all about strength."

"It's about grit. Pushing through no matter what."

As Chris scribbled these answers on the pad, it quickly became clear that no one else in the room had a secure sense of what resiliency was, either. Like me, they had a tenuous understanding of the concept and how it might help people overcome obstacles in their paths, but everyone kept getting stuck on traits like strength and grit.

Hearing those notes of uncertainty reminded me of a post I had recently made on social media that referenced California redwood trees. In the piece, I complimented nature's so-called skyscrapers for their rigidity and ability to stand the test of time. I suggested that humans could learn a thing or two from such strong and unyielding plants. I was surprised when a reader commented on the post to tell me I had gotten it all wrong. On a windy day, she wrote, these massive trees swayed like feathers in the wind. In hindsight,

I realized "rigid" wasn't the best choice of words. She was right: It wasn't strength that kept these trees standing for hundreds of years. It was something more than that.

As I listened to the men in my workshop continue to reference grit and perseverance—and pictured those mysteriously ancient redwoods bending in the breeze—it suddenly occurred to me that resiliency wasn't so much about sturdiness but adaptability. If resiliency was what gave some people the ability to endure life's hardships and heartaches while standing tall, forging resiliency must be about learning how to shift and move with the wind. At the very least, I thought, it meant creating space so you could better adapt to your environment, giving yourself the elasticity and grace to find healthy ways to overcome life's obstacles, whether they are big or small.

Resiliency: Nature versus Nurture

Resilience is defined by the American Psychological Association as "the human ability to adapt in the face of tragedy, trauma, adversity, hardship, and ongoing significant life stressors." Notice there's nothing there about whether this kind of adaptive ability is born or made. But that's the very question that many people in the mental health community have been asking for decades. Is resiliency determined by a person's genes or by the environment they live in? Like most nature-versus-nurture queries, it's not such an easy question to answer.

At first glance, it might seem like some people, by their very nature, are simply more adaptive than others. They are just built that way. For a long time, I believed that myself. I've worked with patients who have survived plane crashes and witnessed close friends die

during a military deployment. I've treated victims of human traf-
ficking and those who have survived years of domestic abuse. As I
listen to their stories, I'm often left in disbelief about how they are
still functioning, or even alive. Despite the horrible circumstances
they have lived through, many of them have not only survived but
thrived. They had managed to achieve graduate degrees and good
jobs, sustain deep friendships and happy marriages. They had
found ways to put the past behind them and find purpose and contentment. Frankly, you'd never know what they had been through
unless they told you.

Other patients I've worked with have endured similar hardships and not fared as well. They were not able to move past their
experiences—and, because of the trauma, they were dealing with
significant mental health challenges. Many of these patients had lost
their sense of purpose and struggled to find a reason to go on. They
had trouble maintaining a job and meaningful relationships. They
couldn't connect with other people, leaving them feeling misunderstood and isolated. Their pasts continued to haunt them, making it
harder and harder for them to overcome even those little obstacles
that we are all guaranteed to encounter in our day-to-day lives.

When you see such stark contrasts between two people who
have endured similar life adversity, you start to wonder what distin-
guishes them. Could it be the years of psychotherapy and trauma
processing that helped? After all, some patients had received professional therapy right away while others hadn't met a psychiatrist before walking into my office (sometimes to treat an issue seemingly
unrelated to the trauma). Was resilience about having the support
of family and friends? There were always some patients who had a
strong support network. Others didn't have that kind of home team
around to rely upon. Might there be some other factor at play when

it came to resilience? Try as I might to figure it out, there did not seem to be a direct correlation between any one thing and the people who were better equipped to adapt after facing adversity.

That's why it's all too easy to think that resilient people are just born with some kind of resiliency gene (or constellation of resiliency genes) that can help shield them from the mental health consequences of stressful life events. Sometimes, it seems like it's the only explanation that fits the data.

Certainly, research studies do support the idea that there are some genes, when it comes to trauma specifically, that may increase or decrease the possibility of someone developing mental illnesses like depression or PTSD after experiencing an adverse life event. Genome-wide association studies, where scientists look for associations between particular genes and traits, have identified a number of genes like catechol-O-methyltransferase (COMT), neuropeptide Y (NPY), and certain serotonin transporters that are strongly correlated with resilient behaviors. It makes some sense, because these genes are involved with different aspects of the way the brain processes information. Too much or too little of these specific neurochemicals may change the way you perceive and respond to different stressors, whether it's a breakup with your significant other or trying to survive a deployment to a war zone.

Several of these genes work on a specific brain network called the hypothalamic-pituitary-adrenal (HPA) axis, a special circuit that helps modulate our response to stress. Stress, simply defined, is anything that "exceeds the regulatory capacity of an organism, particularly in situations that are unpredictable and uncontrollable." Basically, it's those overwhelming feelings of discomfort in the body or mind when you encounter a situation that seems beyond your capabilities. It could be physical—like having to run a full marathon when you've only trained for a 5K. Stress can also be emotional or psychological, like the way you feel when you are working long hours to complete a big project at work, or involved in an argument with a close friend or family member.

Whether you are trying to trudge through mile sixteen or pulling yet another all-nighter at the office, your body responds to stress by producing chemicals like cortisol and adrenaline—sometimes referred to as the "stress" hormones. Feeling overwhelmed or "stressed out" can cause the body to enter into what's referred to as allostatic overload. This is when your body and mind are operating at full capacity and having trouble adapting. Sleep deprivation, not getting enough exercise, eating a poor diet, and smoking can all cause allostatic overload. It can also put the body into an inflammatory state that can end up increasing your risk for physical and mental illnesses.

Even seemingly small acts can trigger the release of cortisol, from getting out of bed in the morning to sitting in traffic on your way to work. Cortisol, by design, is released to protect the body and mind so it can manage whatever situation you may find yourself in. Its function is to get you prepared to face stress and deal with it in the most advantageous way possible.

Cortisol, however, is supposed to be a physiological solution to a short-term problem. While the amount of this hormone tends to fluctuate during the course of the day, the idea is that, once the stress passes, your cortisol levels will drop. If the stressor continues for long periods of time, those heightened levels of cortisol are eventually read by the body as a threat.

Although there isn't a way to determine feeling "stressed out" as a psychiatric diagnosis in the DSM, living in a stressed state for long enough can have devastating consequences to both your body and mind. Stress can, in fact, lead to changes in areas of the brain like the hippocampus, prefrontal cortex, and amygdala. Why is that? A surge in stress hormones causes your mind and body to remain on high alert, constantly trying to fight off a perceived attack, even if one isn't actually there. That may cause you to feel "wired and tired" with aching muscles, or make you feel foggy and have trouble focusing. This process leads back to the idea of chronic inflammation and its association with mental health. Inflammation has been reliably associated with both depression and anxiety, as well as PTSD.

Studies have shown that certain gene variants can make us more or less resistant to the body's cortisol response. That means the same stressful event could potentially trigger a greater spike in cortisol in one person and a smaller release in another. Over time, those differences can influence just how resilient someone may be as they are trying to navigate the obstacle course we call life.

That said, even though these genes exist, and have been shown to make subtle changes to the way our bodies react to tough situations, they are not solely responsible for our mental health. Genetics are not deterministic, even though we often talk about them that way. And more important, genes don't work in isolation. Our environment, as well as the choices we make, holds great sway over when, where, and how much a particular gene affects the way we act and the way we feel. Scientists call this idea epigenetics.

Think about it. You may come from a family of engineers, but maybe you'd rather be an artist—and just because engineering might come more naturally for you, doesn't mean you wouldn't enjoy art more. Or maybe you're five feet, six inches, like Spud Webb, but that didn't stop him from making it into the NBA. We can actually use epigenetics to make adjustments to how we live, so that we have more control over our life. If medical conditions like heart disease or diabetes run in your family, you can be proactive by being extra careful about your diet to reduce your risk. Similarly, if your mom, dad, brother, and sister all struggled with depression, it doesn't mean that you're automatically going to get depressed at some point, too, especially if you learn about the early signs and develop a good plan if you find yourself slipping. While genetics may contribute to resiliency—and we don't have much control over our genes—we have total control over our ability to adapt.

When I was a student at Juilliard, I met so many talented performing artists from all over the world. I was surrounded by some of the best actors, musicians, and dancers of my generation. Sometimes, it was hard not to be discouraged by how naturally good these folks were at their respective vocations. My roommate, for example, was one of the most talented violinists I have ever met. The son of two professional musicians, he had perfect pitch, rarely practiced, and could read through a Brahms score like it was a graphic novel. He could pull out his violin at a moment's notice and perform flawlessly in front of audiences of all sizes. I did not have those same natural gifts—my genetic blueprint did not shape that sort of effortless ability. But I'll let you in on a secret: Most of my peers at Juilliard didn't have that kind of predisposition to musical greatness, either. Yet we were all still there competing at the same level. Those of us without innate gifts were able to do so by focusing on the aspects of craft we could control: focus, self-discipline, and practice.

What you do matters, and it has the power to shape the brain's response to stress, too. One of the most remarkable features of the brain is its own natural capacity for adaptation. Scientists refer to this ability as neuroplasticity. The fact that your brain is so malleable explains how human beings are able to learn and store new memories, as well as recover after traumatic events. Our brain circuits can and do reshape themselves in response to what we encounter in our environments. What this means is that in times of stress, if one area of the brain isn't working as it should, a different region could potentially pick up the slack. Neuroplasticity shows us that what you do is just as important, if not more so, as how you are naturally hardwired when it comes to dealing with adverse events and stressful situations. Its ability to adapt and bounce back after physical or emotional stress means that you have the power to make your brain work for you and not against you as you progress in your own self-care journey. That's power.

While some people may have a particular gene variant that may put them at a bit of a disadvantage when it comes to managing stress, there are many ways to compensate for that neurobiological predisposition. As it turns out, thanks to neuroplasticity, you do have the power to forge resiliency. I think of it as something similar to the ten-thousand-hour rule popularized by Malcolm Gladwell—the idea that it takes about ten thousand hours of practice to master a task.

Even if you have the genes that promote resiliency, you still have to put them to work. Would musical geniuses like Mozart or Miles Davis have made their imprint had they never taken a music lesson? I'd venture to say no. You can have all the natural talent in the world but if you don't find a way to tap into it, it is likely to go to waste. Resiliency is no different. No matter what natural gifts your genes may have bestowed upon you, genetics will only take you so far. It's cultivating the right environment and taking the time to engage in practices that turn on those genes that make the real difference. Resiliency is a skill you can forge over time—and self-care plays an integral role in building that kind of competency.

Resiliency over Grit

There's been a lot of discussion about the power of grit over the past decade, especially, with the publication of Angela Duckworth's best-selling book *Grit: The Power of Passion and Perseverance*. During the *Yoga for Men* workshop, the guys were equating resiliency with "grit," but I eventually realized they aren't exactly one and the same. The difference between the two is important, especially when we are talking about preserving your mental health.

As I worked to better understand resiliency, I came across what many scientists believe to be the most resilient animal in the world: the moss piglet. These unique animals, also referred to as water bears or tardigrades, may be almost invisible to the eye but they are mighty in spirit. If you look at them through a microscope, you'll likely first be struck by their peculiar appearance. This eight-legged, stumpy-snouted micro-animal looks almost like a caterpillar wearing some kind of inflatable sloth suit. It's certainly not exactly the kind of strong, domineering look that brings resiliency to mind.

These little guys, though, are *tough*. They can survive ten years in a completely dry state—not to mention withstand temperatures as low as minus four hundred degrees and as high as three hundred degrees Fahrenheit. They are also equipped to endure radiation one thousand times higher than the level that would exterminate even the hardiest of other animals. Scientists have learned that they can survive in outer space, where other animals would almost immediately succumb to the cold, cosmic radiation, and lack of atmospheric pressure. Their ability to survive is remarkable. What I find most amazing, however, is that scientists theorize that moss piglets did not start out this sturdy. Rather, they evolved into their robustness because of their ability to adapt to their environment.

Consider their resistance to radiation. Moss piglets were often exposed to dry environments that were less than ideal for their genetic makeup. They had to learn how to live in these hot, waterless places in order to survive. "Survival of the fittest" wasn't about fighting against the environment. It was learning how to change in a way to protect them from it. By adapting to one problem, they grew to be protected from other potential threats as well.

What might this have to do with resiliency and grit? Although Duckworth's years of research dive much deeper into the relationship between the two, a simplified way of looking at grit is the ability to persist or to keep pushing through no matter what. The problem with grit is that eventually, regardless of how strong you are, you are going to break. Instead, resilience is about *adaptability*. Going back to the redwood trees, it's that ability to sway with the wind. When you can adapt and find a more deliberate and healthy way of addressing the stress in your life, grit becomes more of an advantage. You can more strategically put that effort, passion, and perseverance in a place that will help you achieve your goals, whatever they may be, without losing mental health in the process.

Take the story of Marcus Smith, a well-known defensive end for teams like the Seattle Seahawks and the Washington Commanders. I got to know Marcus initially through my work as a mental health adviser for *Men's Health* magazine, which offered the first opportunity for a series of conservations I would have with Marcus. He grew up in a middle-class family in Columbus, Georgia, and started playing sports at an early age. Unsurprisingly, it wasn't long before he found his way onto the football field. Once he did, he never looked back.

"Ever since I was five years old, I wanted to play in the National Football League," he said. "That's what I wanted."

While many kids dream of playing professional football, Marcus wasn't sure it could be a realistic path for him until his college coaches told him he had a real shot of making the pros. When he was later drafted by the Philadelphia Eagles as a first-round pick, he was thrilled—all the more so because he was relatively new to his position as a linebacker. He had entered college playing quarterback before his coaches moved him to defense.

"I got switched from a position I knew my entire life to a defensive position just two years before," he said. "I wanted to be great, but I didn't know if I would be great at a position that, at the time, I had no idea that I was going to be playing. I worried about it."

Marcus should have been on top of the world, but he was experiencing bouts of both depression and anxiety. It started, he said, after his parents divorced when he was just eight years old. Football, in the past, had provided an emotional outlet for him—a way to get out some of his negative feelings. Over time, however, he learned that while it was okay to let loose and lay it all on the line on the field, trying to tell others you were struggling was something else. "Being able to tell your brother in the locker room that you have a problem" was a completely different game.

"When I look back on it now, I had feelings of anxiety and depression for a long time, even when I was playing in Philly," he said. "But I just dismissed it. I just kept going along and hoping it would go away."

Unfortunately, as Marcus's successes grew, so did his anxiety. His own personal goals, as well as the expectations from coaches, management, and fans, were taking a toll on both his body and his mind. Yet talking about his struggles, even to his own family members, seemed nearly impossible. Marcus wasn't even talking to his wife about the way he felt, even though, in hindsight, he realizes she probably knew all along. The anxiety was getting so bad that he would wake up in the middle of the night, sweating and huffing, with suffocating panic attacks in his sleep.

From the outside, Marcus Smith was living the dream. Yet his career wasn't unfolding the way he had imagined it would. He tried to embrace the disappointments as just another part of the game. That's the perspective he'd been taught to take from his earliest days on the football field—to succeed in football, to weather whatever the game would throw at you, you needed an abundance of grit. Having grit meant you could find a way to overcome any obstacle set in your path. You could push through it and let nothing stand in your way. Grit was what made you strong, kept you moving forward, and allowed you to win. True champions brewed grit in their blood, sweat, and tears. They didn't talk about their emotional struggles. They found a way to persevere and succeed. That's why, Marcus said, he kept silent about the way he felt for so long. He feared that, in admitting his own challenges, others would label him as weak. Grit became an oppressing presence that only reinforced his beliefs that there was no point in seeking help.

That same grit, he now realizes, almost killed him.

"I didn't know what was going on with me," he said. "I didn't feel like there was a space for me to speak.

"It's a stigma in the National Football League," he said, explaining why players are afraid to open up about their personal issues. "They're oftentimes quiet about some of the things they deal with because they don't want the coaches to know . . . coaches will look at it as if he's not mentally tough, and they want people already mentally tough in the NFL."

As a result, Marcus kept quiet and tried to throw all of his energy into football. His game improved and, in late summer 2018, he signed a one-year deal with the Seattle Seahawks under famed coach Pete Carroll. He was finally seeing his career goals coming to fruition, and he believed he was in the right position to show his true worth on the field. Despite this career-affirming achievement, Marcus's mind was not at peace.

"I had no appetite, and I was out there literally on nothing," he said. "I remember one night I kept waking up. I was just trying to stomach through it. My wife was asking if I was okay, but I just kept it on the surface. That night, I didn't sleep at all. Every time I laid on my stomach, it just felt like my chest was caving in. I know now that was the anxiety. But I didn't want to feel like that anymore."

Early the next morning, as Marcus entered his car to make his commute to the Seahawks' practice facility, he came to a decision. Depression was speaking to him and it was telling him that he was incapable—of being a good player, a good husband, or even a good father. He felt like he couldn't go on and made up his mind that it was time to end his life. Even then, his ideas about grit kept him silent. He didn't share his plans with anyone.

A few miles away from the practice facility, he pulled off the road. There was a steep cliff just off to one side of the street, and he knew it was the right place. Marcus began to slowly inch his car toward the slippery slope in front of him with the plan to tip his car over the edge. Just before he hit the gas, moving the car to the point of no return, he was interrupted by a phone call. It was his wife.

There was really nothing extraordinary about the call. His wife often called before practice to check in and see how his day was going. That day, however, Marcus tried to rush her off the phone. She sensed something was not right, but he was still not ready to talk about the way he was feeling. Once he ended the call, Marcus tried to reengage with his plan to drive his car forward. Then his cell phone rang a second time.

This time, it was his mother-in-law. Receiving those two consecutive calls in that critical moment helped snap him back to reality. Marcus abruptly jerked the car back, overwhelmed with emotion.

"I was scared," he said. "She's talking to me and it just scared me. I realized I needed to get help because I couldn't believe I was just about to do that."

After he hung up, Marcus broke down in his car. He realized holding so tight to grit was not helping. In order for him to get better, he would have to let go of something that, up until this point, had been an inextricable part of who he was.

"I said I'm done with football—no more," he said. "I needed something to change."

This was the moment that Marcus Smith's life changed—when his grit evolved into resiliency. He finally understood that, to find contentment and live with peace, he would need to take his focus off the football field and put it back on his mental health.

"My mental health is way more important than just the game," he explained. "I had to go seek help. I had to go get the help that I needed, and once I started to see a therapist, I started to figure out where all my traumas, my anxiety, everything that I was dealing with, where it came from."

Marcus couldn't find a way to be more resilient unless he gave himself the time and space to heal—to take care of himself so he could learn the skills he needed to better adapt to the stressors he was facing in his own life.

Too often, the words "grit" and "resiliency" are used interchangeably. In some ways, it makes sense. They can both bring you to a similar destination: success. Both professional and personal achievements require determination and perseverance. Life can be challenging, on and off the field, and if you were to just give up anytime things felt uncomfortable, you wouldn't get very far in life. Is it any wonder that all the men in my resiliency workshop kept trying to define resiliency as grit?

While grit can be a valuable skill, it's no substitute for resilience. No one should have to white-knuckle their way through life, throwing themselves time and time again against insurmountable obstacles, damaging their bodies and minds in the process. Instead, you can find more success by adopting the skills that allow you to better adapt to life's stumbling blocks.

Over the years, I've heard many stories like Marcus Smith's. No, they didn't always involve pro football careers. But many patients share with me that they felt like grit was the only way forward. Yet, over time, like Marcus, they realized there was nothing strategic about grit. It will only tell you to keep trying harder. It won't tell you to try differently—or, perhaps, that a particular battle just is not worth your time or effort. It's going to tell you to keep pushing until you break. That's why grit can only take you so far. Eventually, if grit is the only tool you have in your mental health tool kit, you are only going to invite more storms and stress into your life—making it an almost guaranteed gateway to depression and anxiety.

Marcus Smith realized that walking away from football, in that moment, was necessary for him to redefine what it meant to be resilient in his own life. It could no longer work by just trying to keep quiet and soldier on. Today, he is able to protect his peace and purpose by actively confronting his feelings in a strategic way. This strategy can allow you to better adapt to whatever life may be throwing your way—and thrive despite its challenges. That's true resiliency.

The Resiliency and Self-Care Connection

As I continue to explore resiliency, I am inspired by the observation that it is a skill that can indeed be learned. It may take some time to get there, no doubt—but truly anyone can master it. In fact, I observe that, despite what you might think, many of my patients who have previously struggled with mental illnesses are actually the ones who fare the best during a time of loss and uncertainty. When I ask why, the response is almost always the same.

"I've been through this before," I am told over and over again. "I've learned what I need to do to get through."

Really, that's what forging resiliency is all about. It starts with self-care—giving yourself the tools that can help you become more self-aware and adapt to different challenges.

In my own life, depression has taught me to recognize those subtle changes that likely indicate I need to pay closer attention to my own mental health. If I'm spending more time alone, avoiding my friends, or feeling burned out, I now realize they could be early signs of a depressive episode before I even start to feel depressed. That's the time when I know I need to reach out to someone I trust, venture outside, take a break from work, move my body, or find other ways to create some balance in my life—I need to plug in to self-care. Over time, I've learned to adapt and confront my problems in a healthier way. It's a lesson, however, that I am still learning more about every day.

Remember that self-care means finding *adaptive* and healthy ways to recharge our mind and body so we can better face life's challenges. Notice the emphasis is on "adaptive." You, like Marcus Smith as well as countless others, can forge your own resiliency capabilities through the very skills that self-care teaches each and every one of us. Whether you feel most renewed by mindfulness techniques, a good night's rest, prayer, movement, or some other self-care practice, you are helping to protect your body and mind's reserves so you, like the redwood tree, can learn how to sway with the wind—or find some other way to manage stress.

Simply put, self-care is like taking a deep breath before you sit for a difficult test, face a panel of new faces at a job interview, or have a hard talk with your husband, wife, or child. It helps you to reduce stress, know when you need to ask for help, and learn from life's hardships. It's about practicing healthy and sustainable ways to manage our complex and ever-changing lives.

Active Coping

I remember working with one patient, Amanda, who was remarkably unhappy with her job. She understood, from our very first session, that it was the root of the depression she was currently experiencing.

"It's work," she told me. "But I'm not sure what might happen if I were to quit."

Amanda would spend her time off, vegging out on the sofa and watching television, trying her best to get lost in the stories played there so she wouldn't have to think about her inevitable return to the office. She was avoiding her friends and family. On the days she did work, she would commute with an ever-growing sense of dread.

Despite the fact that she was well educated and could have easily found a different job, Amanda was focused more on the symptoms of depression—lack of motivation, sleeplessness, negative thoughts—than directly addressing the source of it. Amanda thought if she just kept pushing through, she could find a way to regain her energy and joy.

After months of working on her mental health, she started to feel better. Yet nothing had really changed. She still hated her job, and she spent most of her free time fantasizing about finding a way out. Her emotions were no longer in a state of free fall, but she still wasn't happy. It wasn't until she started actively interviewing for a new gig that she found true relief. Instead of throwing herself against the same obstacle and expecting it to move, Amanda adapted and changed course. She moved herself to the place where she could live with contentment.

That's what we call active coping—it's a key part of resilience. It doesn't mean that you just jump ship when things get rough. It's not about avoidance or evasion and, as we learned from Marcus Smith's story, it's not about pushing through no matter what. Instead, active coping is about being deliberate and tactical about the way you face challenges. Active coping skills allow you to embrace life's tests and trials, including the most emotionally stressful ones, and give yourself permission to develop a strategy to overcome them. They encourage you to ask for help when you need it. Active coping helps you learn from your hardships and mistakes—and apply those lessons learned to new situations.

If I were back in that yoga studio with my friends Alec and Chris, I think I'd have a lot more to say about the power of resiliency. I could share my certainty that it is not just grit or strength. Rather, it's a skill we can all learn—a mindset that we can create by respecting who we are and what we need in order to protect our health and well-being.

Forging resiliency is a lifelong journey. It takes dedication and time to achieve. But it is a journey that you can start today—with some deep breaths, using your favorite vinyasa (yoga flow), having a long talk with a trusted companion, or finding some other self-care practice that will help you recharge, reset, and refresh.

One of the greatest benefits of self-care is how the very acts that bring you greater peace can help you better nurture your mental health over the long haul. No matter your genetic makeup, you have it within your power to change your environment, to find maintainable ways to address and manage the stresses you face each and every day. The practices you build today will help you learn how to better adapt in the future. It's not about resisting the impacts of stress in your life. No one can win that battle. It's about protecting yourself—mind, body, and spirit—when life challenges you, as it so often does. When you change your focus to adapting instead of conquering, much like the moss piglet, you'll find yourself learning more of the vital skills that can keep you living with purpose, balance, contentment, and hope.

CHAPTER 5

GIVING UP ON DEATH

Every day is a good day to be alive,
whether the sun is shining or not.
—*Marty Robbins*

As Kevin Hines boarded a bus that would take him to the Golden Gate Bridge, despite being just nineteen years old, he had already made up his mind that it was his time to go. Earlier that morning, he told his father that he loved him—apparently for the final time—and he had spent the day before revising a suicide note. While the bus maneuvered its way through the sluggish Bay Area traffic, Kevin began having second thoughts about his fate.

"It was the most devastating day of my life. I felt completely worthless," he said. "I sat on that bus, in the middle seat in the back row just crying my eyes out. And, as we are driving out to the bridge, it hit me. I didn't really want to die at all. I was hoping that just one person, anyone, would look at me and say, 'Hey, kid. Are you okay?

Do you need help?' I needed that, because I could not find a way to tell anyone I was in trouble."

Instead, another passenger looked over at Kevin, sobbing, before nudging the person next to him. "What the hell is wrong with that guy?" he sneered. It only made him feel worse.

As the bus arrived at the Golden Gate stop, Kevin paused at the door before stepping out onto the curb, wondering if even the driver might notice his emotional distress. Instead, the driver hastily urged him off the bus before abruptly closing its doors. Kevin then preceded to walk on the bridge for about forty minutes, when a woman finally noticed him and turned in his direction only to request that he take her picture.

Kevin thought, "That's it. Nobody cares."

The enormity of that feeling diffused any second thoughts he might have had about ending his life. So, he proceeded to the middle of the bridge and stared out over the four-foot railing at the dense blue water beneath it. After a few minutes of coming to terms with his decision, he stepped backward toward the traffic, then ran forward as fast as he could, catapulting himself over the edge.

He fell 220 feet at seventy-five miles per hour. Within four seconds, he hit the water, shattering his lower vertebrae on impact. Since the Golden Gate Bridge first opened in 1937, more than fifteen hundred people have jumped from its side. Fewer than thirty-five have survived. Kevin is one of them.

Regardless of how long someone contemplates suicide, it typically boils down to an in-the-moment decision. To live or to die. Of the few people who have survived attempting suicide on the Golden Gate Bridge, many reported that they regretted their decision, even in midair. This doesn't mean if they do survive, all of their problems instantaneously go away. In fact, Kevin had a long road of recovery ahead of him. His diagnosis of bipolar disorder meant that he would continue to have ongoing struggles with mental illness over the next two decades, including nine inpatient psychiatric hospitalizations. However, like the handful of others who *have* survived, Kevin said, "As soon as I let go of the railing, I felt instant regret. As I fell, I thought, 'What have I done? God, please save me.' I thought I had to die and I was wrong. And as I struggled in the water, before the Coast Guard came to rescue me, I worried no one would ever know I didn't want to die. No one would ever know that I regretted what I had done."

Kevin Hines is not alone in these kinds of feelings. The vast majority of people I speak with who have attempted suicide also report remorse after a failed attempt. In fact, nine out of ten people who attempt suicide and survive will *not* go on to die by suicide later in life. That's important, because it shows us that suicide really is an irreversible fix to a temporary problem. Most people do find a way to escape suicidal thoughts and ultimately move forward with their life.

When I spoke with Kevin Hines about that day, twenty years after his suicide attempt, he admitted to me that he still has days when a thought about suicide crosses his mind. But, that said, he's never again tried to take his own life. He believes he hasn't crossed that line again because of a profound change in his perspective— shifting his focus toward gratitude, even in moments of suffering, and never shying away from asking for help. Kevin writes candidly about his experience in his book *Cracked, Not Broken: Surviving and Thriving After a Suicide Attempt*. These days, he shares his story with others in talks around the world in hopes of convincing more people to share their pain if they are considering ending their lives. His intention is to inspire people to ask for the help they need so they have a shot at arriving at a better place. Kevin is quick to tell you that suicide is not the fix he once thought it might be.

"We're all going to die at some point," he said. "But it's important to give yourself time plus some hard work so things can change for you. Just because you are in a world of pain today doesn't mean you don't get to have a beautiful tomorrow. But you have to be here to get there."

If you're at the end of your rope and you feel like giving up on something, instead of giving up on life, give up on death. Self-care is an evidence-based healing process but you have to be here, present in your own life, to see how it works. Since thoughts about suicide can quickly become all-encompassing, until you take suicide as an option off the table, it's nearly impossible to make room for all the things you *can* do to promote resiliency and mental health. Giving up on death can help you clear enough space, no matter what you may be going through, to find the right tools that will support you as you move toward building a life full of purpose, balance, contentment, and hope.

A Story within the Numbers

According to the World Health Organization, we are in the grips of a global suicide pandemic. Over the past few years, it has become a true public health concern, with almost eight hundred thousand people dying by suicide each year—that's one suicide every forty seconds. In 2019, in fact, the Centers for Disease Control and Prevention (CDC) listed intentional self-harm as one of the top ten leading causes of death in the United States. While suicide often makes the headlines after a high-profile celebrity dies this way—think Kate

Spade, Junior Seau, or Anthony Bourdain—we don't often consider the fact that there are 130 suicides, on average, every single day in the United States alone. Each one of these people is someone's child, parent, spouse, friend, or neighbor—and a valuable person in their own right.

These statistics are alarming, but talking about suicide doesn't always have to be a downer topic, despite what the numbers suggest. That's because suicide is totally preventable, and self-care can play a significant role in that prevention. My work has allowed many people to open up to me about their own suicidal thoughts, and I can definitely tell you that just because you're thinking about suicide doesn't mean it's a foregone conclusion. Most of the time, acknowledging suicidal thoughts and opening up about them to someone you trust is an opportunity to make sense of your thoughts in the first place, figure out why you're having them, and then develop a good plan to move beyond them.

I understand that suicide is something no one wants to talk about, because talking about it can feel weird or awkward. It's not unusual for a friend to send me a text or give me call about someone they know who just opened up to them about having thoughts about not wanting to be around anymore. I typically get the story, followed by a line that says something like *I'm not sure what to do*. No doubt, suicide is a complicated topic and people have some pretty deep-seated feelings about it. What we all can do is at least listen and show support where we can. It's not a conversation we have to be afraid of because usually when someone is opening up to you about unwanted thoughts, it's because you're someone they trust. They may be trying to process their thoughts in a supportive environment. It's never a bad idea to recommend a mental health professional, like me, but sometimes a little support rather than closing the door on the conversation altogether can go a long way. As we all strive to promote strong mental health, it's something we need to discuss more openly.

In a day and age when men and women are receiving more psychiatric medications and less talk therapy, it's important to understand what we know—and what we don't know—about suicide. If we can better identify the true risk factors (and avoid the pitfalls inherent with long-standing myths regarding suicide), we are in a better position to bring this pandemic to heel—both inside and outside the psychiatrist's office.

Who Is Really at Risk?

Open up a basic psychiatry textbook, or just do an online search, and you'll find the following "typical" suicide risk factors.

- White or Caucasian race
- Male
- Over sixty-five years of age
- Unmarried (or family conflict)
- Has been diagnosed with a mental illness
- Is dealing with substance misuse issues with drugs or alcohol
- Has attempted suicide before

Some of these you can obviously modify (like cutting back on substance abuse) and some you can't change, like how old you are. You'll notice that, as previously discussed, most people who have attempted suicide in the past will not ultimately go on to die from suicide in the future, but a previous suicide attempt still would place someone at higher risk for a future suicide attempt compared to someone who had never before tried to take their own life.

These types of lists are misleading, though, because they give the impression that only people who fall into these categories ultimately attempt or die from suicide—and that's just not true. The list notably excludes racial minority groups, young people, and women, who are at risk as well. No one is totally immune from suicide. So, to shrug off signs of depression in someone like a young Asian American woman who is married with kids and goes to church every Sunday with her husband would be a bad move. It's not just the older white men with a diagnosed mental illness we'd need to pay attention to. People of all ages, races, genders, and backgrounds have the potential to lose their life in this tragic way.

When it comes to suicide attempts, the list of risk factors broadens. Again, a previous suicide attempt tops the criteria but, as we noted earlier, the vast majority of people who attempt suicide once do not go on to die by suicide. This presents somewhat of a conundrum. While, as doctors, we take any suicide attempts seriously, and many people who have attempted once may at some point try again, it's not a foregone conclusion that they will. Ultimately, it's hard to know which patients who attempt suicide will ever try again. As a psychiatrist, I often have to look over a patient's medical history and search for particular patterns in impulsivity or self-harm that may help me determine how much at risk a person may be, but it's still not cut-and-dried.

We also see, as with completed suicides, that untreated substance use disorders (like drinking too much alcohol or abusing drugs like cocaine) certainly don't help prevent suicide attempts from happening. It's tempting to turn to drugs like alcohol or cannabis when you're feeling down or depressed because, in the moment, they may help you feel better; however, drug abuse can make it more likely you'll engage in self-harm behaviors that you will later regret. Additionally, adverse childhood experiences, social isolation, job-related stress, sexual violence, barriers to health care, and easy access to firearms or lethal medications can also create a higher risk for a suicide attempt. While the risk factors for a completed suicide are quite specific, the ones here provide an inventory that is almost too expansive. I have worked with many patients who have met one or more of these criteria. However, I still find reason for hope in that most of them have never contemplated suicide in the first place.

This is one of the reasons why it is so challenging for psychiatrists to know which patients are at most risk for attempting suicide, especially since, more often than I'd like to admit, it's the people you didn't think you had to worry about.

Take one of my own patients, June. This thirtysomething financial wunderkind had always been a mover and shaker. She graduated at the top of her class from an Ivy League university and then worked her way up the corporate ladder to a senior analyst position at a big firm in Austin. She felt tremendous pressure from her family to excel, and often felt like she was in the shadow of her older brother, a successful orthopedic surgeon. She was, in fact, so career-oriented that even dating had taken a back seat in her life, and friendships were few and far between as well. But even as we discussed her worries about her job and personal life, June was always warm, vibrant, and funny—she just always seemed to be laughing.

She was also a dreamer. June recognized that, perhaps, she wasn't maintaining the best work-life balance, because she was working toward something bigger for herself.

"You see, I want to retire by the time I'm in my mid-forties," she told me once. "I can at least do something I like then."

June is one of the last patients I would have ever expected to try to end her life. Then, one weekend, I received a voice mail from her mother telling me that June had been hospitalized after trying to end her life by overdosing on medications. Thankfully, she survived. As I listened to her mother's quivering voice on the recording, I thought about my last meeting with June not even two weeks earlier. At that time, she seemed calm, content, and at peace. I couldn't get my mind around how this could have happened, and I was so relieved that she wasn't hurt. But I also couldn't help but think: *What did I miss?* I've thought about that situation again and again, about what warning signs might have been lurking under the surface as we talked. Years later, the incident remains with me.

For years psychiatrists, epidemiologists, and other public health experts have been trying to find a way to forecast suicide risk. There are simply too many complex factors at play. There's no formula, no diagnostic workflow, and no checklist to reliably make clear which patients are most likely to end their own lives.

Not that we haven't tried, as a field, to come up with some kind of predictive tool kit. Mental health professionals are constantly looking into it, and there are seminars about suicide prevention at almost all of the conferences I attend. The National Institute of Mental Health (NIMH) puts millions of dollars into different studies to help us better understand mental illness—and this includes ways to prevent suicide. A few years ago, a group even looked toward using machine learning algorithms to help them better identify at-risk patients. In 2018, researchers at the Kaiser Permanente Washington Health Research Institute designed a unique computer model to help them pinpoint which patients might be more likely to attempt suicide. While they found some success with the system, it was still only able to predict suicide attempts or deaths from suicide about 85 percent of the time.

Even an artificially intelligent tool that can go through a patient's medical records dating back several years to calculate a suicide risk score can only do so much. Having that type of score available, of course, could let a doctor know that certain patients may need treatment or outreach. However, even with some savvy computer assistance, about 15 percent of people that the system would've considered to be at a lower risk still attempted or completed suicide.

Understanding Suicidal Thoughts

Despite the difficulty in identifying people who are at highest risk for suicide, it's part of my job as a psychiatrist. It's why, at every visit, I ask my patients about suicide. Questions like: *Are you having any thoughts about wanting to hurt yourself or wanting to die?*

Usually, the answer is no, but every once in a while, the conversation leads in an unexpected direction and the answer will surprise me. In fact, I was caught off guard when a longtime patient of mine who I'll call Tom reluctantly admitted, "If I'm being totally honest with you, yeah. I've had thoughts about not wanting to be here anymore off and on for years."

He had never mentioned them to me before. When I asked him why, he said, "Well, I would never hurt myself. They're just thoughts, I wouldn't act on them—what's the big deal?"

Suicidal ideation, defined as thinking about or planning to die by suicide, is a packed term that can be interpreted in many different ways. While it's always a big deal, and never "normal" to be thinking about suicide, it's not terribly uncommon for a person at some point in their life to speculate about the "what-ifs." There are different types of suicidal ideation, or ways to characterize thoughts about suicide. The first are passive suicidal thoughts—like: *The world would be a better place without me*, or *I'd be better off dead*. These were the kinds of thoughts Tom was having.

Then, there are thoughts that use more explicit phrasing—what mental health professionals call active suicidal ideation. Some who are experiencing active suicidal thoughts are contemplating specific ways to harm themself. They may even be forming a suicide plan to carry out. That's when time is of the essence and a little intervention, like making sure a family member or friend is close by for support or, in severe cases, arranging for a few days in a hospital, can go a long way. It can ultimately save a person's life.

The reasons people are afraid to talk about suicidal thoughts, especially with a psychiatrist or other mental health professional, are multifaceted. There's definitely some degree of shame involved, because no one wants to be perceived as not having it all together. There's also a perception of weakness—the idea being that strong or "mentally fit" people are impenetrable to thoughts about suicide or can easily stave them off if they were to occur. None of these perceptions are true. In fact, the more we talk about suicide, and the more we understand its causes, the better equipped we are to prevent it.

To answer Tom's question, the big deal is that suicide is always preventable, and thoughts about it are usually our mind's way of communicating with us when it's overwhelmed. Tom noticed that his mind shifted to suicide when he felt overworked and underappreciated. He thought about it late at night, when his family was asleep, or when he was alone, and speculated about whether he would be missed. But if in these very moments you can learn to give up on death—by totally taking it off the table as an option—then there's an avenue to listen and to understand how thoughts about suicide might actually help you use self-care to improve your mental health.

In Tom's case, our work together helped him understand that when passive suicidal thoughts began to enter his mind, he should spend more time with his family, not less time. He also learned that setting boundaries by closing his work laptop at 6:00 p.m. every evening allowed him to focus more on things he knew were good for him, but hadn't prioritized, like spending time outside taking walks or cooking dinner with his family. The first conversation was definitely the hardest for him, but eventually Tom learned that opening up about his suicidal thoughts to me was a good starting point to improve his mental health. While it wasn't an overnight transformation, eventually Tom's suicidal thoughts became a thing of the past.

Thinking about suicide is never normal per se, but it's not entirely uncommon, either. That's yet another reason why I advocate that we switch our focus away from mental illness to that of overall mental health and well-being. When we normalize mental health, we can let go of common myths and misconceptions about suicide. We can encourage people who may be having suicidal thoughts to speak up or ask for support, instead of relying on guesswork or computer models to try to find the proverbial needle in the haystack. And we can remind people, as Kevin Hines does when he speaks to an audience, that things not only *can* but most likely *will* get better in time. We can point people toward hope.

Sometimes, I will end a session with a patient by saying, "I truly believe that you will get better." I certainly did so with Tom. I don't do this because I'm overly optimistic. I do it to help give direction to our work. I do it to emphasize the importance of giving up on destructive thought patterns, like suicidal thoughts, that may get in the way of the person's overall health and healing. And I do it to remind my patients that as long as they are living with hope, suicide doesn't stand a chance.

Tackling Tough Conversations

When we move away from a focus on mental illness—and to one that supports overall mental health—we can make space to listen to and support people who may be experiencing suicidal thoughts. While these are not easy conversations to have, they are important. Many people are afraid to give voice to any thoughts about self-harm. There's the stigma to consider, to start with, and many are afraid they'll be labeled crazy or just have their feelings dismissed outright. The problem, however, in staying silent is that it allows these thoughts to fester and, over time, that's what makes them so dangerous. When you can open up about suicidal thoughts, you can learn to make sense of them. It's the first step to finding a way to move beyond them.

Kevin Hines, for example, still struggles with suicidal thoughts at times. He agrees that it's important to give them air to help take away their power.

"Our thoughts don't have to become our actions," he said. "Imagine—if all of our thoughts became our actions—how many of us would be in jail for road rage right now. We need to be able to recognize that our thoughts do not define what we do next."

Of course, not all conversations about suicide are going to happen in a psychiatrist's office. Maybe you've never even met with a mental health–care professional, or you don't plan to. It may be that you've heard a friend or a loved one expressing some form of suicidal thinking in the past. That raises a critical question: *How should you handle it?*

Conversations about suicide are tough. It can be hard for people who may be experiencing suicidal thoughts to talk about it. Kevin Hines said, even as he hoped just one person would reach out and help him, he had trouble articulating how he was feeling. He couldn't find the words to describe his pain. Yet even people who do mention suicidal feelings may find that they are easily dismissed by others. A common suicide myth is that people who talk about suicide aren't serious about it—they only talk about ending their life as a way of seeking attention. I think it's important to change the framing there. Most people who mention suicidal thoughts are not seeking attention. They are asking for help.

In other cases, if a friend or family member tells you they are having suicidal thoughts, you may feel uncomfortable—and, frankly, overwhelmed. You may not feel like you have the knowledge or experience to deal with it. In fact, you may walk away from the conversation just because you are so afraid of saying or doing the wrong thing.

So, if someone does confide in you about having suicidal thoughts, don't panic. Instead, try to actively listen to what they have to say—and then direct them toward help. Encourage them to reach out to their primary care provider, make an appointment with a mental health professional, or call the National Suicide Hotline at 1-800-273-TALK but at the very least, just be human, show empathy, and listen as best as you can.

When people who are feeling hopeless open up about suicidal

thoughts with someone they trust, they can better learn to manage their thoughts by using the power of self-care. It's a process that can allow you to emerge even better and stronger than before.

Feeding the Right Wolf

There is a traditional Native American story about wolves. The tale describes a grandfather telling his grandson how, inside each person, two wolves live. One is a wolf that is full of sorrow, regret, and lies. The other wolf embodies goodness and light. He brings love, hope, and compassion. Each day, the grandfather explained, these two animals battle, fighting desperately for dominance. When the grandson asked which wolf would win the fight, his grandfather replied, "The one you feed."

When you choose not to open up about suicidal thoughts, it's like feeding the dark wolf, because you can't move beyond suicidal thinking by pretending like it doesn't exist or avoiding it altogether. You have to first acknowledge what you are feeling, no matter how dark those feelings are, and then talk about them with someone you trust. These types of conversations are a way to feed light, love, hope, and compassion. It ultimately takes suicide off the table, and by doing so, you're no longer feeding the dark wolf; you are feeding life. In Part II, I'll introduce instructions about how you can utilize self-care to improve your mental health, which can also help you develop specific strategies for dealing with suicidal ideation.

In yoga, there's a commonly referenced Sanskrit term, *drishti*. Translated, it means "focused gaze." Some yogis also say it's a point of view—a form of wisdom that comes from letting go of the busyness of the world and concentrating on what really matters. I think about *drishti* as gravity, or a pulling force that can give direction when you feel lost. It's what keeps you grounded. Everyone has a different *drishti* that can "bring them back" to the moment and allow them to shift away from feeding their dark wolf. It could be reflecting on your commitment to being a good father, thinking about your role as a son or daughter, or even acknowledging that as long as you are alive you have a purpose even if you don't know what that purpose is.

Meditating with intentional mantras—or simple phrases—like "I am worthy" or "Be as kind to yourself as you are to others" can help ground you. These practices, paired with relaxing breath work, can help you refocus negative thoughts as well. In fact, studies that looked at the effect of mantra meditation on mental health suggested it can improve negative thoughts and feelings in those who regularly practice it. Similarly, the foods you eat, how physically active you are, and the way you breathe all have the power to interrupt cycles of negative thinking, including suicidal thoughts. Reshaping negative thinking ultimately promotes improved well-being.

There are countless stories supporting the idea that you have to claim success in order to realize it. This doesn't just apply to becoming wealthy or climbing the corporate ladder. It also works for your mental health. Your mind is a powerful tool. Own it, train it, and love it. Feed the good wolf by embracing hope, inviting optimism, and appreciating that negative thoughts are temporary and will pass in time. You can give up on the ideas that don't benefit your mental health and focus on the acts, feelings, and thoughts that do.

Kevin Hines understands the value of self-care in his own journey.

"I work hard to balance myself mentally, emotionally, and physically—and my self-care plan has kept me alive for twenty years," he said. "It involves developing a peer support network. It includes things like exercise, eating non-inflammatory foods for most meals, and educating myself on coping strategies I can use to stay stable. I do breathing exercises every day. I take my medication and I make sure to sleep. Every single aspect of that self-care is as pertinent as the last."

You don't have to do the same things Kevin does to support your own mental health, because there's no one-size-fits-all approach to self-care. However, you *can* banish the idea of suicide so you can make space for the techniques that can help you feed the light, hope, and compassion inside you.

It's time to give up on the myths and misconceptions that tell us suicide is the natural endpoint of mental illness. Instead, let's take death out of the equation and work toward living a life filled with purpose, balance, contentment, and hope. That is the destination we all seek. Suicide is a way out, but what I am suggesting instead is a way through. If we focus on living with mental health as the natural endpoint, we're much more likely to get there.

Buying Time with Self-Care

Suicidal thoughts usually emerge from situations where you feel like there is no other way out or like your back is against the wall, when everything you have tried to do to make yourself feel better has failed. In these moments, the best strategy is to slow down and to give yourself time to explore other possible ways to react besides the one reaction you can't reverse. Buying time might mean getting out of your house or apartment, calling a friend, or just making plans for tomorrow. At least giving yourself a chance to talk to someone first about the way you are feeling can often help you realize that even in your deepest moments of despair, you still have reasons to live.

I am not by any means suggesting that slowing down, especially in critical moments when you are considering the prospects of life versus death, is an easy process. I understand that it's difficult. Anxiety can place an unbearable hold on your body and your mind, making you feel like there's no escape. Psychosis can produce derogatory voices that will lie to you and tell you that suicide is the best option. Depression may make you believe that there's no hope moving forward with your life. Although mental illness can potentially cloud your will to live in the moment, usually over time the intensity of suicidal thoughts rises and falls in alternating waves.

This is where self-care turns into a potentially lifesaving medicine. Time to reconsider the decision, to explore other options, or to get professional help—even if just giving yourself a few minutes, hours, days, weeks—can allow an opportunity for the intensity of the moment to pass. More often than not, that's exactly what happens.

In my practice, I have worked with patients who have struggled with the idea of suicide as an option for years, sometimes even decades. But many of these patients, even those with the most severe forms of mental illness who once spent years of their lives consumed by the idea that they would one day die by suicide, were able to give up on death by buying time. The longer they lived, the more they had to live for, even if they hadn't yet found contentment in their lives. Most important, time gives you the best opportunity to get treatment and to heal.

When a group of Golden Gate suicide survivors were asked

how they felt about the construction of a suicide barrier on the bridge, some reasons they supported it included just allowing people more time to wrestle with the experience before making a final decision. Although for at least forty minutes, Kevin walked across the bridge in his own state of ambivalence, would he still have jumped if he had had one or two hours to consider what he was *really* about to do? No one can know for certain. However, time *can* be a deterrent that may help some people change their mind about decisions that involve suicide. More time may have allowed a man or woman on the bridge that day to eventually notice Kevin in distress and offer a sincere hand, or for him to change his mind on his own.

If you are experiencing suicidal thoughts, self-care will likely be the furthest thing from your mind, but it can be the very thing that can buy you the time you need for negative thoughts to pass. It can extend the fuse, so you are not moved to act on destructive thoughts before it's too late.

The suicide spark may eventually fizzle out if you can give it a longer fuse. One of the easiest techniques is taking deep, grounding breaths. There are different ways to breathe that can produce different effects on the body and the mind, as we'll discuss in the next chapter; however, during critical moments, focusing on your breath can quickly reconnect you to your body and offer clarity.

It can also give you a sense of stability and control. Even if you are unfamiliar with specific exercises that utilize breath to calm the body and the mind, just taking some time to stop what you are doing, count your breaths, and be in the moment can help you buy additional and potentially lifesaving time.

It's safe to say that we would all do whatever we can to prevent suicide from happening. We've already established that it's hard enough for psychiatrists and other trained mental health professionals to predict suicide or to truly comprehend the depths and complexities of someone else's mind, so it's potentially even more challenging if you haven't had years of mental health training. That's why it's so important that you voice what you are feeling to someone you trust if you find yourself in a situation where suicide is an option that you're considering. If you can't find someone who is immediately available, just talk to anyone—whoever you can. And keep asking, because eventually you'll get a response.

While it may sound too good to be true, especially when you are feeling hopeless, the simple act of focusing your attention on what you might do if you were well, whether it's meeting a friend, participating in an activity you once enjoyed, or checking out a new band, may help reduce the likelihood of a suicide attempt by giving you something to look forward to. It's one of the reasons why being future-oriented, making plans for tomorrow, and next week, and next year, can keep you alive, oftentimes long enough to see your life eventually get better.

Functional MRI studies have shown that anticipating positive events can activate brain regions like the bilateral medial prefrontal cortex—the same area of the brain that is implicated in feeling a sense of well-being. This means that not only imagining that your life will improve but actually claiming that it *will* get better, and making plans for what you'll do as it gets better, can ultimately translate to feeling better. If you feel like you don't have anything to look forward to, then give yourself something to look forward to, even if it means looking forward to the day when you'll truly find peace and contentment in your life.

When you can start to incorporate more self-care practices into your regular routine, you are doing more than just buying time when things aren't going well. You are proactively engaging in different techniques that can promote overall mental health and well-being, all but ensuring that you are in a better place to give up on death. These acts will give you the time, space, and capacity to delay, if not altogether prevent, suicidal thoughts in the future.

PART II

THE
FIVE PILLARS
OF SELF-CARE

Now that you are ready to let go of those old, outdated notions of mental health, as well as put brain-based explanations of mental illness into proper perspective, you better understand why it's possible to proactively engage in different practices to help shape, support, and protect it. I call them the five pillars of self-care for mental health.

You may be aware that some religious practices, particularly the Islamic faith, rely on their own five pillars: faith, prayer, alms, fasting, and pilgrimage. These pillars provide its members a strong foundation for their values and beliefs. They also serve as the blueprint for living a good life. In a way, the five pillars of self-care are not that different. But instead of providing direction for deepening a relationship with a higher power, these pillars are there to help you build a strong foundation for your mental health.

The five pillars of self-care—breath, sleep, spirituality, nutrition, and movement—are essential for achieving mental health, which means living with purpose, balance, contentment, and hope. When you can adopt healthy practices around these pillars, you are in a better position to live with mental health. In the following pages, we'll discuss why these pillars are so important, as well as different self-care practices you can adopt to help you live your best life.

CHAPTER 6

BRINGING ATTENTION TO BREATH

Your breath is medicine.
—*Michael Stone*

Every day, we take an average of twenty thousand breaths, and unless you have a medical condition like asthma or chronic obstructive pulmonary disease (COPD) that can make breathing difficult, you may never pay attention to yourself breathing. That's why it can be challenging to fully appreciate how the simple act of taking one or more breaths really is one of the most powerful self-care strategies for mental health. We've all had those experiences when we're really stressed about something, and there's that annoying person who peers over our shoulder to say, "Just relax, calm down, take some deep breaths and you'll feel fine." But if you're anything like me, it's actually the last thing you want to hear. Minus the intrusion, however, it really is solid advice, because when we focus on our breath, especially in moments of emotional distress, the mind and the body have no choice but to respond generally in a positive way. Heart rate and blood pressure drop, and the brain is flooded with calming neurotransmitters like GABA.

You can extend beyond the idea of simply "taking deep breaths" by developing a breath work practice, which elevates the concept of breath as medicine to an entirely new level. Breath, for example, is a quintessential component of yoga, which combines breath with movement. This is one of the many reasons why I'm so passionate about yoga. Breath and movement are both self-care modalities that are essential for mental health.

Years ago, when I began speaking publicly about the therapeutic benefits of yoga in treating mental illness and promoting mental health, some people automatically assumed I was a yoga teacher instead of a psychiatrist. A reporter even came to my clinic where I meet with patients to write a story about my work and appeared befuddled before asking, "Is this enough space to teach yoga classes? Where's the yoga studio?"

You don't need to be a yoga teacher or have mastered your Downward-Facing Dog to benefit from breath work. In fact, as I learned early on, even during the most challenging yoga practice, breath is what allows balance, stability, and flexibility. You can begin to utilize a breath work practice while sitting in your office, watching TV, or taking a shower—these are good places to start. My office doesn't have a yoga studio, and I'm much more of a yoga practitioner than a yoga teacher, but that doesn't stop me from teaching patients how to breathe, even in my office. Eventually, like many of my patients, you may find yourself wanting to combine breath with movement. Maybe you'll want to give yoga a try if you haven't already; however, sometimes people will tell me, "I get that yoga is good for me, but I just don't like it."

Truth be told, at first, I didn't like it, either.

When I was a junior in high school, I attended a music camp in Florida. We spent most of our days rehearsing for concerts, going to the beach, and enjoying time away from home. The scheduled yoga class seemed an aberration. One afternoon, I found myself led into a humid room with about thirty other disgruntled teens. The floor of the crowded space was covered in squishy pastel-colored mats. The teacher, a middle-aged woman dressed in tights and flowing scarves, was a living caricature of the 1970s "woo-woo" yogi. She drifted between our mats like a prancing goddess, advising us to stretch, breathe, and open our minds in a singsongy voice, accompanied by an instrumental soundtrack full of ambient tones, Buddhist oms, and the crashing of ocean waves.

Honestly, it was just a little bit much, and after all the activity of the week, her hummed mantras combined with the darkened room put me into a blissful sleep. I don't think I managed even one complete vinyasa, or flowing yoga sequence. I just dozed, occasionally roused when the teacher chimed a castanet-style bell between her thumb and forefinger to emphasize one of her yoga-isms. Once the hour ended, I, like many of my fellow campers, left the class wondering why anyone would ever bother with yoga when they could just go home and take a nap instead. What was the point?

Despite an unremarkable first experience, I gave yoga another chance and it would be several more years until it really clicked. That was during a time when life felt burdensome, I was overwhelmed by transitions, and I was alone quite a bit. Looking back, what I was feeling were classic signs of depression, but at the time

I didn't realize it. I was just looking for something—anything—to allow me to feel better.

It was a rainy evening in the middle of Houston's midtown district. The small waiting room of the studio was full of vibrant colors—there were splashes of yellow, fuchsia, and tangerine just about everywhere you looked—which reminded me more of a nightclub than a mindfulness space. The energy did as well. Since it was only my third time trying yoga, I was open to learning about a new experience. After waiting for class to begin, we crowded into the tiny room. Others were leaving, saying their goodbyes and cracking jokes while sipping Voss water and high-end green juice. This was nothing like what I expected.

When the teacher beckoned us in, the first thing I noticed was that it was immensely hot and noticeably muggy. The instructor, an athletic-looking woman wearing designer yoga pants and a tank top, stood on a wide box at the front of the room. As the class settled onto their mats, she commanded, "If you feel tired during the class, don't leave. Just lie down and focus on your breath."

Is this some sort of posh yoga boot camp? I thought.

I had no idea what I was in for, but I'd soon see that she wasn't joking. Some of the newcomers would, not even halfway through the class, try to creep for the exit as the heat and exhaustion started to overwhelm them. A few managed to successfully escape. The others were stopped with the teacher's halting sneer. "Stay in class, yogis! Discomfort is only temporary!" Whether they came back to their mats as a consequence of motivation or embarrassment, I couldn't tell you. I was too busy just trying to keep up.

Even as I moved my body from posture to posture, the sweltering temperature made it difficult to think about anything other than the task at hand, which was making it through that class.

As we flowed, the teacher instructed us: "Breathe into the posture, breathe into the pain and it will pass." Between the warmth and the challenge of contorting my body into these new and challenging poses, I really had to pay attention to the way I was breathing. There was no way to manage the class without continuing to breathe in deeply—not unless I wanted to pass out or, like some of the other newbies, cry uncle and make a break for the door.

Anyone who has had to take a deep breath on a hot, humid summer day knows that it's not always pleasant. It can feel a bit like you are sucking drops of water directly into your lungs. Now imagine being in the middle of a dimly lit, hot room, surrounded by twenty people who are all trying to one-up each other with gravity-defying arm balances. The process can quickly go to your head. Despite being a regular on the basketball court, I was gasping for survival almost the entire class. I quickly noticed that my breath was intrinsically tied to my body, and yoga had very little to do with how "in shape" I perceived I was. When my breath was not deep and regular, my balance and focus were off, making it more likely that I would fall out of a posture. When I could tie the two together, my movements, as peculiar as some seemed, felt much more natural.

"Breath to movement!" the teacher bellowed. "Inhale through your nose and exhale through your nose. Slow, deep inhales and audible, cleansing exhales!"

At first, my body bristled at her directions. The experience felt more than a little weird, as trying to coax myself into stilted loops while the sweat formed a puddle around me was totally foreign. Yet when I regulated my breathing, adhering to her guidance—even releasing the odd *uhhhhh* sound with my exhale—I was able to follow through, allowing my breath to carry me in a way that matched my movements, all to the thump and pulse of Bob Marley's "Three Little Birds" playing on the loudspeaker.

When I walked out of the studio that evening, bewildered by what had just transpired, my body was sore, as I expected, but remarkably my mind was clear. In fact, I felt better than I had felt in a long time. Those good vibes lasted, too. Even hours later, and into the next day, I felt a profound sense of calmness and ease. Although I was still confused about what yoga was (and what it wasn't), after a handful of very different class experiences, I was definitely curious to learn more about it. I didn't know how or why that particular yoga class gave me the mood-boosting buzz it did—whether it was the no-nonsense affirmations or the endorphin rush of moving my body in a hot room with a good sweat. What I did know, however, was that it was a different feeling than I was used to experiencing from other types of workouts. Perhaps it was the unrelenting demands to "pay attention to your mind, pay attention to your body, pay attention to your breath" that penetrated through the fog hanging over me, but somehow, that day the message got through. That was the day I became a yogi.

Breath to Movement

Ask ten different people about what yoga is and you'll likely get ten different answers. That's to be expected, because there are so many different types of yoga classes and practices. You may have one friend who is gung ho about Ashtanga yoga, a type of practice that focuses on flowing from posture to posture. A coworker may be a hot yoga aficionado, where he keys in on deepening a sequence of postures in a 105-degree room. Still others may find their groove with kundalini, which includes postures, meditation, and a little group chanting for good measure. You also can't forget laughter yoga, goat yoga, or aerial yoga. Going outside the box of a traditional yoga practice may seem like sacrilege, but I'm encouraged by the fact that people are finding ways to modify yoga and also have a little fun with it. A study by *Yoga Journal* and Yoga Alliance actually showed that there's an upward trend in the number of people who regularly practice yoga. No matter who you are, or what preconceived notions you may have about yoga, there's likely to be one type that will work for you. Yoga, truly, is for everyone, regardless of gender, age, color, size, or shape. That's another reason why I love it so much.

Despite all the wild variation you see in the yoga landscape, what all of these different types have in common is a focus on bringing the mind and body together through breath. In fact, the word "yoga," in Sanskrit, means "to yoke." It represents the union between breath and movement. And while many people likely associate different yoga practices with gravity-defying handstands or post-marathon stretching for uber-fit yuppies, the emphasis should really start with the breath part of the equation. That's what can offer you one of the biggest benefits to your mental health.

When I first talk to patients about yoga, I usually hear two somewhat predictable responses. First, *I enjoy practicing yoga*. In fact, their love of yoga may be why they sought me out in the first place. The second category of response is usually something like *I don't know much about it*, or *I've tried it already and I hate it*. Either way, usually by the time someone books an appointment with me, they already know I am both a psychiatrist and a yogi. Some want to learn more about how a mind-body approach can change their life. Others are just hoping that I can give them a prescription to help them feel better without having to hear about my Crow Pose journey.

Either way, learning to train the mind to combat depression, anxiety, or anything really that affects mental health is much like going to the gym to build muscle. It's a skill that must be developed. When I recommend yoga, it is partly because the breath work involved has strong mental health benefits; it can reduce emotional stress, it can increase the release of mood-boosting neurotransmitters, and, most important, it *really can* make you feel better. What I've found, more and more, is that the lessons learned from developing an individualized yoga practice, including how to yoke your breath to your movement, can be carried and leveraged well beyond the confines of the yoga mat.

Introducing Mindfulness

The easy part is telling someone to *relax, take deep breaths, or calm down*. Of course, generally speaking, these words tend to ensure that the person they are addressing will do the total opposite. Think about the last time you felt overwhelmed and someone told you to "Get over it. Just calm down." I'm guessing it didn't go very well.

Taking control of your breath is a great way to help your body relax. That said, it's important to understand that relaxing, by itself, is not a treatment for anxiety, depression, or even stress, per se. That's probably why being told to relax doesn't do much. Relaxation is what happens to the body and mind after we effectively treat conditions like anxiety, depression, or stress, whether it's through breath work or through other means.

Breath is the world's oldest medicine. It's available to all of us at all times, and it doesn't cost a penny. Not only do we need our breath for survival, it also has a calming effect. Yet it doesn't work if we just try to breathe more. It's not that simple. Deep breaths on their own, without method or awareness, don't allow you to reap the full benefits for mental health. Breath as a mindfulness-based intervention allows you to do just that.

You've heard about mindfulness. Certainly, there's a lot of talk about it these days. Wellness experts put a high premium on "being mindful," whether you are practicing yoga, doing a guided meditation, or heading to the park for a tranquil walk alone. You probably have some of your own ideas about mindfulness, too. When I've spoken about its importance, I've heard responses like "Isn't mindfulness for rich people who don't have any *real* problems?" or "I think people who have time to meditate probably have less stress to begin with." I even had one patient tell me, "Doc, I'm not going to be that guy who goes all-Buddha and starts chanting on a hill."

It's fair to say that mindfulness may not be what you've envisioned it to be. All stereotypes (and influencer hype) aside, mindfulness is all about conscious awareness. This means paying attention to yourself, including the way you breathe, and also paying attention to your environment. We spend a good chunk of our lives on autopilot, letting our reflexes and habits guide us, without much thought about what we are doing or why we are doing it.

Think about the last meal you ate. Did you eat because you were hungry? Because it was noon and that's when you usually have your lunch? Or did you sit down and really savor your meal, enjoying the taste of every bite, as well as the company of the people you were having lunch with? It's the latter example that really embodies mindfulness. What's interesting is that as the human brain evolved, instinctual behaviors, like eating a meal, evolved alongside mood centers in the brain like the amygdala and the cortex. As a result, eating wasn't just about quieting hunger pangs or giving our body nutrients it needs in order to survive; it also was coupled with our mood, feelings, and emotions.

Simply put, mindfulness means really being plugged in to your life. It's paying attention to your surroundings and actions. Breath work, yoga, and meditation are all considered mindfulness-based practices, because to truly reap their benefits, you need to have an awareness of your mind-body connection as you engage in them. That's how these activities might be different from lifting weights or going for a run. It's also why yoga, in particular, is more than just a workout—despite what I thought the first few times I tried it. The truth, however, is that it's possible to do just about anything with conscious awareness. Many people do experience running or lifting weights as a form of moving mindfulness, especially when they are able to focus on their breath during a rep or the pattern their feet make as they hit the ground while racing along. When you are practicing mindfulness, regardless of what you happen to be doing, you focus on being aware. You pay attention to what you are sensing, feeling, and experiencing in the moment, without shackling yourself to unnecessary judgment.

Yoga can cultivate that kind of awareness. The focus on your breath, for example, inhaling your body into an Upward-Facing Dog Pose, and then exhaling your way into Downward-Facing Dog, may help you learn to be more present in the moment by keying in on how your breath and body are working together. Over time, those breaths do more than just move us through a yoga flow. They help us interact with our environments more intentionally with the same type of mind-body awareness.

During times when you feel anxious, when your palms are clammy, your thoughts are racing, and your heart feels like it's pounding out of your chest, pay attention to your breath. Feel the rise of your belly as you inhale and the air passing by the back of your throat as you exhale. Imagine that in the moment your breath is cleansing your mind of tension, worry, and stress. Pay close attention to how your body relaxes and your heart rate slows down. You may notice that after a few minutes you feel just a little bit better. That's the power of conscious awareness, and that's also the power of breath.

The Anatomy of a Breath

Remember that every day, you take about twenty thousand breaths without having to even think about it. Each breath holds a powerful ability to bring a sense of calm, focus, clarity, and contentment. When we breathe, nitrogen, oxygen, carbon dioxide, and small amounts of helium, neon, argon, and hydrogen enter the respiratory tract. Carbon dioxide is filtered out by the lungs and expelled when we exhale. Oxygen-rich blood then travels throughout the body to provide nutrients to our vital organs.

To understand how breath is linked to mental health, you need to understand its role in the autonomic nervous system (ANS), or the part of the nervous system that controls involuntary actions. The ANS regulates important bodily functions including maintaining your core temperature, blood pressure, respiratory rate, and heart rate. It's why your body keeps breathing even when you are not expressly telling it to do so. The ANS essentially keeps the body in working order by making sure those vital activities are happening even when you may be focused on other things. It is also important to note that the ANS governs two other key parts of the body's nervous system: the sympathetic nervous system, which helps to direct our response to fear, anxiety, and emotional stress;

and the parasympathetic nervous system, which promotes rest and relaxation.

Breath is what fuels the ANS. Consider this: If someone were to tell you to try to slow your heart rate, you would automatically take a deep breath. You might even, if you are really into it, close your eyes and imagine yourself in a peaceful place to help hasten that relaxation. This is a powerful example of how the mind and the body are connected. When you slow your breath, inhaling and exhaling more deeply, your heart rate will soon slow down. It really has no choice. The body is wired in such a way that breath gives the ANS its marching orders. Speed it up, the heart rate goes up and you may find yourself hyperventilating as your mind moves to a more anxious state. Slow it down and you can move the body into a more relaxed state—reducing any stressful feelings.

When you dig a little deeper, you can also see how breath powers the sympathetic and parasympathetic nervous systems, too. We need these two systems working together to maintain physical and emotional balance, as well as to help ensure our survival. When one isn't working properly, it knocks our entire being out of whack. We can be overcome by stress, letting our emotions get the better of us, ultimately leading to problems that affect both our physical and mental well-being. Or, alternatively, we can lose all motivation and also lose the impetus to live full and intentional lives.

Imagine you're on a camping trip in Yellowstone with some friends. You are all sitting by the fire one night, enjoying s'mores and good conversation, when you spot a grizzly bear approaching your campsite. You've been amply warned about the risks of hungry bears in the park, maybe even seen the video in the visitor center that showed a local bear effortlessly pulling the door off a car in order to get at a cooler of hamburgers. Anyone would expect to experience fear in that moment. Your breath will start to quicken, becoming more and more shallow as you consider what you should do. Your sympathetic nervous system is going to kick in, accelerating your heart rate and raising your blood pressure. Your pupils will dilate to expand your visual field. Blood will rush to your brain, as well as to the muscles in your arms and legs. After all, to effectively deal with a hungry bear, you need to not only think fast but move fast. Basically, with this threat upon you and the people you care about, your body is being propelled into a state of heightened awareness to ready yourself for fight or flight—and, in doing so, increase your chance of survival.

You may have heard people say that a little bit of stress or anxiety is a good thing. This is exactly the kind of situation they are talking about. You need at least a little stress to get you motivated and moving—and to help you determine whether you are better off fighting the bear or finding your way to a safe place. Those lower levels of anxiety and stress help promote survival and, depending on the situation, may also help you thrive in the face of different kinds of adversity.

The idea that stress can, in some cases, offer a beneficial advantage becomes clearer when we think about situations outside the hypothetical grizzly scenario. You will find that the sympathetic nervous system is also activated when you are about to give a big presentation at work, take an important exam, or work up the courage to ask someone you are attracted to out on a date. Whenever you feel your heart beating a little faster, it usually means that your sympathetic nervous system is at work. It is what keeps us stimulated, sharp, and ready for whatever is coming our way. It's when that response starts to overwhelm us, letting those anxieties inhibit our motivation, focus, and capacity for survival, that it becomes detrimental.

Sympathetic overdrive, or when the sympathetic nervous system is overstimulated, can feel suffocating. Many people who have medical conditions that result in sympathetic overdrive report feeling like they are drowning or unable to catch their breath. Situations that affect your mental health can lead to sympathetic overdrive, too. Whether it's ongoing arguments with your partner, dealing with the little aggressions that come from a micromanaging boss, or just feeling like you are constantly disconnected or under pressure can also lead to a sympathetic nervous system response. Even though these things may seem like just part of a normal life, they signal both the body and the mind that your safety is being compromised and, to save yourself, you need to do something about it. In effect, the mind perceives these everyday stressors in a similar way that it would that hungry bear. Practically speaking, it's not always plausible to challenge your annoying boss to a fistfight or run away from a partner with whom you are struggling.

While fight or flight helped keep us alive and kicking when we were searching for food and evading predators on the vast plains thousands of years ago, it's not always as applicable to managing the minutiae of our modern lives. That means there is often discord between what the mind is telling us to do and the socially acceptable response. It's no surprise that such a disconnect can often lead to a feeling of emotional discomfort as your heart pounds out of your chest, your palms sweat, and your temperature rises. You may even feel trapped, your breath coming in fits and starts, when your brain needs all the oxygen it can get to help you deal with the situation happening in front of you. When you put it all together, and this mix of sympathetic responses continues to happen over and over again, what you have is the physiological recipe for anxiety.

Breathing through Anxiety

Anxiety, or the mental health condition characterized by intense, excessive, and persistent worries that can interfere with daily living, affects over 40 million people in the United States alone—and approximately 280 million people worldwide. This means that you likely know someone who has suffered from anxiety, or there's even a good chance you may have experienced it yourself.

As stated above, a little anxiety is not always a bad thing. While it is definitely uncomfortable, if we can learn to recognize it, breathe through it, and potentially take advantage of it, it can help motivate us to put ourselves out there in the world and go after the things we want most in life. For example, I've worked with several patients who hated their job. Every morning, they would wake up in a state of panic and dreading having to drive into the office. While it's not always easy just to walk away from a career you hate, recognizing that maybe it's time to plan a transition to a different work environment could be a way to listen to what anxiety is trying to tell you rather than allowing it to control you. The problem comes when all those worries become persistent, turning your anxiety into a chronic state. When ruminating thoughts are interfering with your ability to do your job, connect with friends and family, or leave the house, you can assume that your sympathetic nervous system has moved into overdrive, and you may need some help to return it to baseline.

Anxiety disorders are actually the most commonly diagnosed mental health conditions in the United States—and, as discovered in a survey by the American Psychiatric Association, each year people report becoming more and more anxious. While it's easy to speculate about why this may be happening—the world, these days, does often seem to be moving at a faster pace than in generations past—it is an alarming trend that needs to be addressed. That increased anxiety is not only bad for your mental health; new studies demonstrate that, over time, it can have a significant impact on your physical health, too.

If you ever find yourself with racing thoughts, persistently brooding over different worries, having trouble catching your breath, finding it difficult to sleep (and never quite feeling rested, even when you manage some shut-eye), or constantly feeling tension in your shoulders, neck, hips, or other parts of your body, you may be experiencing anxiety. If you continue to have those symptoms daily, for a period of at least six months, you might have generalized anxiety disorder.

Although there are several medications that may reduce anxiety, among the most familiar are a class of medications known as benzodiazepines (or benzos)—you may recognize the trade names Valium and Xanax. At one time, these were the most commonly prescribed drugs in the United States. Benzos were the Mother's Little Helpers that Mick Jagger and the Rolling Stones talked about in their seminal 1966 song of the same name. In the 1960s and '70s, the country even experienced a benzodiazepine craze of sorts; doctors handed out these downers like candy, with the goal of helping those anxious housewives and overworked businessmen dampen their sympathetic nervous system response and, in theory, better manage their busy lives. Of course, at the time, the medical community did not understand or appreciate just how addictive these drugs could be. Even with this knowledge, benzos are still commonly prescribed by doctors and sought after by patients.

Benzos produce antianxiety and sedative effects that can have a dramatically noticeable effect on mood. They work by binding to a special receptor in the brain that allows the increase of an important neurochemical called gamma-aminobutyric acid (GABA). This neurotransmitter is an inhibitor, meaning it decreases activity in different parts of the nervous system. The aftereffect is the promotion of feelings of calmness and relaxation. These drugs are still prescribed because not only do they work well but they work quickly. Doctors prescribe them to provide immediate relief for patients who are experiencing anxiety so severe that they are in a constant state of panic. Because they are highly addictive drugs, however, they are only meant to be used in the short term. It only takes a couple of weeks of regular use for someone to develop a dependency—and withdrawing from these drugs can be extremely uncomfortable and sometimes even deadly. No one should try to withdraw from these drugs without talking to a physician first.

Anxiety can be incredibly uncomfortable, and it is easy to think that the only solution when confronted by its related symptoms is to reach for the quick fix of a drug like Valium or Xanax. There is something else, however, that can increase GABA in the brain to help you get to a calmer, more relaxed state—something that doesn't require a prescription or a risk of addiction, something that doesn't cost a thing, and something that everyone can easily access whenever they need it. That's right: your breath.

When you employ a mindful breathing technique, you can help to increase the levels of inhibitory neurotransmitters to stop sympathetic nervous system overdrive in its tracks. While it may seem too good to be true, numerous studies now support the notion that practices like yoga, which focus on intentional breath, can lead to an increase in GABA levels, reduce anxiety, and improve mood. When you bring conscious awareness to your breath, you can quickly and easily harness your body's natural antianxiety capabilities. It's really an underutilized intervention that can work for everyone.

A few years ago, I was covering a weekend shift at an inpatient psychiatric hospital when I received an urgent page from a nurse on the unit. An elderly woman, who had just been admitted a few hours earlier, was experiencing significant emotional distress.

"She's having a really hard time and is extremely anxious about being here," the nurse explained. "Can I get an order for 1 mg of Ativan for her?"

Ativan is another benzodiazepine, and it's often used in hospitals to help calm down anxious patients. More often than not, it's immediately necessary, especially, if you haven't tried self-care strategies first. You can get the same effects with targeted breathing exercises. I think the nurse was surprised when I said that, instead of putting in the order for the drug, I'd just come and talk with the patient first.

When I went to the patient's room, I sat on the end of her bed and we talked for a few minutes. Then we did a few rounds of 4-7-8 breaths, sometimes called "relaxing breath." This is a technique where you inhale for four seconds, hold your breath for seven seconds, then exhale for eight seconds—and it can be very effective at reducing anxiety, calming racing thoughts, as well as lowering heart rate. Sure enough, within a few minutes, the patient told me she felt more relaxed and was able to settle in at the hospital. All without the need for a benzodiazepine.

While there are definitely times when anxiety medications are necessary for patients, breath is a tool that we all have at our disposal, right there waiting for us when we need it. You can employ breath to help calm yourself before that big presentation at work, during a heated discussion with your partner, or even when your three-year-old is having a massive tantrum in the grocery store's cereal aisle. You can try it right now and take note of the effect it has on your body, mood, and overall outlook. I continue to use 4-7-8 breathing every day, and it works. Breathing, truly, is the oldest form of medicine—and it's an act of self-care that can benefit us all.

Breath Work as Treatment

Treating anxiety isn't always straightforward, and sometimes it can be difficult to immediately determine the best course. A patient I'll call Jessie, an African American man in his early twenties, came to my office one morning and I immediately recognized that he was unsettled. He couldn't bring himself to sit down and I watched as he restlessly paced across the room.

"Listen, Doctor. I can't sleep. I can't eat. I feel like there's something electric shooting through my body and my brain," he said, cradling his head in his palms as he continued to agitate back and forth across the room.

Jessie went on to tell me he had originally seen his family physician about recurring stomach issues.

"I felt like there was a knot stuck in there," he said, clutching both fists and jabbing them into his abdomen. "I was also getting these spells, man, where I just couldn't catch my breath."

In the weeks since, he had been referred to a gastroenterologist for his symptoms, and then, when they did not abate, to me.

"I think there's something wrong with my stomach, like irritable bowel syndrome or Celiac disease; I've been reading a lot about them lately," Jessie told me. "Both my family doctor and the GI doctor said I need to see you, too. Can you give me an antibiotic or something? Maybe something else? The past few days have been absolute hell."

As he talked more, he also told me he had been taking Xanax for the past two months.

"I just ran out of the Xanax, too—so I need a refill on that," he said. "Can you also sign a medical leave of absence for me? I really can't go back to work like this. I feel so messed up."

Spending more time with Jessie allowed me to learn that he had been in a minor car accident shortly before he started experiencing his symptoms. At first, he was only experiencing the stomach pain and shortness of breath when he was driving, but soon he found himself feeling nervous, gasping for air, and feeling like his heart was beating out of his chest a few times a day. There seemed to be no rhyme or reason to why these episodes kept happening.

"I'm avoiding getting in my car whenever I can because I don't want to lose control," he said. "I'm surprised I even made it here today."

His other doctors couldn't find anything wrong with his stomach or lungs, but they had given him Xanax to help him relax. It helped him at first, but like many others who have developed a dependency on this powerful benzodiazepine, Jessie found, over time, that it took more and more of the drug to achieve the same calming effect he needed just to stay balanced. When he ran out of the prescription, his anxiety symptoms worsened, and the fact that he was also withdrawing from Xanax didn't help, either.

Over the next few months, I worked with Jessie to wean him off Xanax and teach him how to utilize breath work to help him manage anxiety. At first, it was hard for him to make the transition from viewing breath as a frightening symptom of his anxiety to something that could help him control it. In time, though, Jessie improved. He learned to identify what was causing his anxiety (his fear of another accident) and then use self-care techniques, including breath work, to temper his sympathetic response to those triggers. No benzos needed.

It's important that we acknowledge that anxiety, at least in small doses, is a natural thing—there's no getting away from it. We all need at least a low level of underlying anxiety to get us up and moving every day. Ultimately, when utilized appropriately, anxiety is the thing that helps us not only survive but thrive in the world around us. It's only when anxiety festers and becomes uncontrollable that it is destructive. By focusing on our breath—and using it to help bring us to a natural state of calm—we can help ensure that our anxieties never reach that point. We can use our breath, powered by our lungs and our own self-awareness, to help us slow down, think more clearly, and see the world as it truly is. It really is a super power.

Breath beyond Yoga

It took a few classes, but eventually I was sold on yoga. Those few hours of levity were intoxicating and only seemed to become more frequent as I deepened my yoga practice. I didn't understand it at the time, but learning how to better yoke my breath to my movement was working to help stabilize my mood. Over the next few months, I'd do whatever I could to feed my yoga practice—all on a student's income. I would do the free trial classes at new studios in town. I'd invest in Groupon deals when I found them. I even, at one point, passed out flyers for my favorite local studio on the weekends so I could be compensated in complimentary classes. To this day, you'll find me practicing yoga several times a week. I'm not always in a studio. Often, I'll just move through some sequences at home, in the park, or even when I have a few minutes to myself in the office. It is not just therapeutic for me—it is a form of therapy. As I move through vinyasas, breathing from one posture to the next, I know I am doing what I can to better protect my mental health.

You have likely been introduced to yoga as a form of physical exercise. Movement, too, is a form of self-care that we will talk more about later in this book. However, what often allows people to take full advantage of yoga as a self-care strategy for mental health is its intentional focus on breath. In yoga, the benefits of breathing into a posture are twofold: It helps to reduce the physical discomfort a particular pose may have on the body, and it also helps limber up an inflexible mind. Yogis take deep inhales to prepare the body for movement, and deep exhales to stretch and strengthen. These breaths also can significantly reduce anxiety by dampening the sympathetic nervous system response and quieting the mind.

Despite my deep appreciation for yoga, I know it's not everyone's cup of tea. Luckily, it is not the only form of mindfulness that can teach you how to harness your breath to optimize your mental health and well-being. You may appreciate the slow, intentional dance of Tai Chi—or the ability to relax into a guided meditation. You can find what works for you. All you need are conscious awareness, deep inhales, and cleansing exhales—no complicated classes, studio memberships, or spandex pants required.

Your Self-Care Playbook: Tested Breathing Techniques to Calm the Body and Mind

You, too, can utilize your own breath as medicine. Different disciplines and practices have different methods to help you harness your breath for relaxation. These are techniques I recommend to my patients to help them better manage unwanted anxiety. While you may want to start with coherent breathing as you learn to bring (and keep) conscious awareness to your breathing, any of these methods, with regular practice, can help you reduce anxiety and stress and restore your body and mind to a calm state.

Coherent Breathing

While this type of breathing can be done either seated or lying down, beginners will benefit from lying down in a private place. Close your eyes and let yourself feel the weight of your body pressing against the ground and the sensation of the ground pushing back. Position your feet hips' width apart and let your palms face upward. Then pick a point of focus to send your gaze.

Bring awareness to your focused gaze, your *drishti*. It can be a spot on the ceiling, a light fixture, or, if you are outside, a cloud in the sky. You can even close your eyes and imagine a focal point in your mind's eye.

Once you have your gaze set, bring attention to your breath. Even though we take over twenty thousand breaths each day, we rarely bring attention to them. To help you focus on your breathing, place one hand on your belly, palm down, and the other on your heart. Feel the rise of your chest, your belly expanding, with each inhale. Experience the fall of your abdomen with your exhales.

You don't want to breathe from your chest; this is a common rookie mistake that can lead to a gasping or choking sensation. Rather, let the air make its own space within your lungs, and pay close attention to your body as it brings in oxygen and then expels carbon dioxide, which will fuel your body and bring you peace.

While coherent breathing is not likely to extinguish severe anxiety or panic, it is an excellent place to start learning how to become aware of your breath and help ensure that you are not taking it for granted.

Resistance Breathing

Once you've mastered coherent breathing, you can move on to resistance breathing. This is a popular approach in yoga, known as *ujjayi pranayama* (or victorious breath), and involves allowing a soft restriction at the back of your throat to foster an audible breath. Place the tip of your tongue behind your teeth and slightly tense your glottis, the opening between your vocal cords. When you start, take a few inhales through your nose and then let them go through your mouth with a whispering sound. As you progress, seal your lips. Simply inhale and exhale through your nose.

Like with coherent breathing, it helps to focus on the rise and fall of the belly to keep you grounded as you master resistance breathing. The physical sensation of resistance breath is similar to the feeling of sucking in air through a straw. You'll know you are doing it right when you hear an ocean-like sound coming from your vocal cords as you exhale each breath. Think ocean waves crashing onshore or the wind whispering through the trees.

Yogis may use resistance breath as they move through different postures, but you can do this breathing technique while sitting in a chair or just finding a cross-legged position on the floor. It's entirely up to you. Sitting on the floor, however, especially when you make use of a meditation cushion, can help you maintain an open posture that also helps you breathe from the diaphragm in order to get the most out of these restricted breaths.

As you master this technique, the intention is to do no more than two to four sets of *ujjayi pranayama* per minute. You may find yourself getting a little dizzy at first because this type of breathing rushes oxygen into the lungs and brain. More quickly than you may realize, you'll find that this rush is accompanied by a distinct sense of calm thanks to vagal nerve stimulation.

When you create this kind of resistance in your breathing, you stimulate the vagus nerve, a vital cranial nerve that connects the base of the brain to important organ systems including the heart, the lungs, and the gut. When you practice *ujjayi pranayama* breathing, you activate the parasympathetic nervous system, which, in turn, tells the nervous system to relax the body and mind.

You don't have to practice resistance breathing long to feel a calming effect. I often set a timer for sixty seconds and incorporate a couple of sets of *ujjayi pranayama* breaths to give me a sense of peace—and the clarity I need to continue my day.

Alternate Nostril Breathing

Alternate nostril breathing is a specific type of resistance breathing, and it works in similar ways. As part of a yoga practice, you might perform alternate nostril breathing by placing your thumb on your right nostril and then exhaling completely through your left nostril, immediately followed by placing your ring finger of the same hand on your left nostril and inhaling through the right nostril. You then alternate, exhaling through your left nostril and inhaling through your right. After the third cycle, begin exhaling through your right nostril, inhaling through your left, and so on.

This kind of breathing may be a bit uncomfortable at first, especially if you are experiencing any sort of nasal congestion. It's okay to slightly open your mouth if that makes it easier to breathe. You can practice alternate nostril breathing while sitting either in a chair or on the floor with your legs crossed. Some studies report improvements in parasympathetic tone (the rest-and-relax portion of the nervous system) after just five minutes of alternate nostril breathing. Studies also report that with a little training (fifteen minutes per day), after just six weeks of honing this breath work practice, the impact can be more dramatic. It can even help to boost mood.

I find alternate nostril breathing most effective when I'm about to give a talk or a big presentation. I like to do a couple of rounds to ground myself and bring a sense of calm, really, in any situation that may cause me to feel nervous. If you're ever needing to step away from a stressful situation to collect your thoughts, practicing alternate nostril breathing is an effective way to use your breath to calm your nerves.

Box Breathing

One of the best benefits about box breathing is that it's easy and you can do it almost anywhere, including at work or relaxing at home. I recommend starting by sitting down with your back supported in a comfortable chair where you can place your feet on the floor. You can also try box breathing while standing up.

Close your eyes and then breathe in through your nose as you count to four. Feel the air fill your lungs and notice your belly as it expands. Then, at the top of your inhale, hold your breath while counting slowly to four. Resist the urge to be too forceful as you hold—that's uncomfortable and can make you feel like you're suffocating. Instead, simply make a conscious decision that you're going to neither inhale nor exhale for about four seconds. Finally, exhale slowly as you count to four. Repeat this pattern of breathing for several minutes until you feel your body and mind relax and a sense of calm descend upon you.

Box breathing has been used by Navy SEALs and Army Special Forces Operators for years. That's for good reason; it works fairly quickly and can help reduce symptoms of physical and mental stress, which can keep you feeling sharp.

4-7-8 Breathing

Find a comfortable seat, either in a chair or cross-legged on the floor, and close your eyes. If it is close to bedtime, you can do this lying down in bed. Once you've gotten comfortable, inhale through your nose as you silently count to four, hold your breath for a count of seven, and exhale as you silently count to eight. You can either exhale with your mouth open or exhale through your nose. Then repeat over the course of several minutes.

The 4-7-8 breathing technique can be thought of as a modification of *pranayama* breathing and has been largely popularized by Dr. Andrew Weil—a guru of integrative medicine. Think of 4-7-8 breathing as a natural tranquilizer for the body and the mind. While the science is still catching up to prove exactly how and why 4-7-8 breathing works for anxiety and insomnia, it's a popular practice that I personally find beneficial, as do many of my patients. It's also important to note that the exact numbers are a bit arbitrary. What's most important is that the exhale component is longer than the inhale. A long exhale is thought to better stimulate the vagus nerve that's so important in telling your brain and body that it's time to relax. It may take a few tries before you feel comfortable with 4-7-8 breathing, so it's okay to start out with box breathing if you need to and then, with time and practice, work your way up to the 7 and 8 counts.

Breathing with Awareness

Developing an appreciation for breath as medicine may not come naturally. As you adopt these practices, the calming effects may happen more quickly for some than others. It's important to understand that not all techniques will work equally as well for everyone. With patients, I recommend picking one option, spending some time with it, and then taking it from there.

Once you learn to become more aware of your breath, you'll find you can use your favorite technique just about anywhere you might need a calming parasympathetic boost. That said, the first step to understanding the power mind-body medicine has on your mental health is being keenly aware of the healing power you already have within you—and, as I learned from my early days in the yoga studio, it all starts with your breath.

CHAPTER 7

THE SLEEP SOLUTION

*A good laugh and a long sleep are the
best cures in the doctor's book.*
—*Irish proverb*

Kenny was a natural-born storyteller. When he first came to see me, this flamboyant sixty-something semi-retiree regaled me with stories from his youth. To hear him tell it, he spent his twenties and thirties "living it up with sex, drugs, and rock and roll." Of course, there was a lot more to him than his past misadventures. He had traveled the world, saving every penny to squire himself to Europe, India, and even to live for a spell in New Zealand. A self-described adrenaline junkie, he embraced new experiences, no matter how dangerous, whenever the opportunity arose. He had even recently married a much younger woman—and laughed sarcastically over the unexpected headaches that arose from their significant age gap. When I finally got the chance to ask him why he came to see me, Kenny was blunt. "I feel like I'm losing my juice, man."

During that first visit, given Kenny's natural swagger and his comment about "juice," I assumed he was just having some sort of late midlife crisis he needed help working through. As we talked more, though, diving a bit deeper into his different stories from past and present, I learned that he was feeling deflated. He was snapping at his wife more and more—they were fighting over little things. They had just moved into their dream home, but instead of enjoying their new place, he found himself annoyed at all the projects needed to fix it up. Kenny said just about everything, even things that used to bring him immense joy, now just irritated him. He felt off-kilter and wanted to find a way back to his happy-go-lucky self.

When I asked Kenny about sleep, he was candid. He had always been a night owl, with just enough sleep to get by, but he also admitted that since scaling back at the office, he had developed an affinity for online poker that was keeping him up later. That also meant he wasn't sleeping as much or even as well as he used to, and I suspected that his terrible sleep was taking a toll on his mood.

Sleep problems, like sleeping too much or not enough, or even just feeling tired all day even though you were in bed for eight hours, is a common occurrence with most mental illnesses. If you page through the *DSM*, you'll quickly see that sleep disturbances are associated with bipolar disorder, major depression, and generalized anxiety disorder, just to name a few. Really, any mental illness can affect sleep. When you aren't getting enough rest, both the body and the mind suffer—and that lack of restorative sleep can wreak havoc on your mental health.

Benjamin Franklin's famous quip "Early to bed, early to rise, makes a man healthy, wealthy, and wise" is remarkable in its neuro-psychiatric prescience. Anyone who has tossed and turned all night knows that too little sleep can make you feel cranky, foggy, and inefficient. What you may not know is that long-term sleep deprivation, which many people living with mental illness suffer from, can influence the very same neurotransmitters implicated in mental illnesses like depression and anxiety. Too little sleep, over time, can impact expression of the brain's serotonin receptors, as well as interfere with serotonin production. Coincidentally, it does so in a manner analogous to depression. Sleep deprivation can become a vicious, self-perpetuating cycle. The less you sleep, the more depressed you feel. Conversely, the more depressed you feel, the less you sleep. It's no wonder that according to some studies over 80 percent of patients with depression have sleep problems.

It makes sense, because sleep is a vital part of health—as important to our overall well-being as air, food, and water, although most of us, including myself at times, do not put as high a premium on sleep as we should. It can be especially difficult to create time and space for some good shut-eye when there's so much we have on our to-do list: planning for work, taking care of the kids, or staying up late to finally enjoy some alone time. In fact, some of us view it almost like a badge of honor to be able to get through the day with as little sleep as possible. When I was in college and medical school, I'd actually hear other students brag about pulling all-nighters before a big exam. That's a problem—and studies now show that insufficient sleep can lead to health consequences affecting cognition, mood, concentration, and a hampered immune response.

The good news, however, is there are many ways to support

healthy sleep, even when you aren't feeling your best. In fact, keeping good sleep hygiene is a self-care practice that makes a huge difference to your overall mental health and well-being.

Dissecting the Sleep Cycle

In many ways, sleep is easier to do than to explain. If I asked you what sleep is, you might say it's a form of rest—or that it's the thing we do when we close our eyes at night. Certainly, scientists and medical doctors have spent decades trying to determine exactly what sleep is, why it's so important, and what's happening in the body when we do it. The truth is that many researchers are still hard at work trying to figure it all out. What science can say, with some certainty, is that nearly every species undergoes this naturally occurring, regular form of rest. We can also say that, when we do fall asleep, the body undergoes significant physiological changes. Your heart and respiratory rates slow. Your temperature drops. Your muscles deeply relax and you lose consciousness for a while. Your senses, like your hearing, smell, and touch, are inhibited. Basically, your body moves into a sort of shutdown-and-recharge mode, all while disengaging from the outside world so that some important internal housekeeping can occur.

Sleep is not just one single state. Rather, it's a complex restorative process that goes through a series of different stages throughout the hours you lie down to rest. There are two distinct types of sleep: rapid eye movement (REM) sleep and non-REM (NREM) sleep. REM is a form of light sleep that derives its name from the quick movements the eyes make behind closed eyelids. This is the type of sleep where most vivid dreaming occurs, breathing patterns are irregular, and the brain paralyzes the muscles in the body so you don't act out your dreams. NREM, on the other hand, is generally absent of the characteristic rapid eye movement. This stage is also further divided into three distinct substages: N1, N2, and N3. As you progress through the stages of NREM, your sleep gets deeper, and by the time you reach N3 it would be difficult for someone to wake you up. It's also in the deep stages of sleep when your body is in total recovery mode, repairing muscles, sharpening the immune system, and consolidating new memories. During NREM sleep, receptors in the brain involved in firing neurotransmitters like serotonin, histamine, and norepinephrine—all of which are involved in supporting mental health—are, in a sense, "turned off" so that they, too, can rest and work more effectively when you're awake.

While we could stop the discussion by just explaining the differences between REM and NREM sleep, in order to really understand what's going on in your brain when you're trying to catch some z's, we need to dive a little deeper. A typical sleep cycle usually works like this. Just as you drift off to sleep, and hover in that sort of in-between state of drowsy but partial consciousness, you enter the first stage of NREM sleep. A few minutes later, the body further relaxes into light sleep, the second stage of NREM sleep—most of the night is spent here. In light sleep, you are unconscious, and your heart rate and breathing have slowed down, but it's still pretty easy for someone or something to wake you up. As you move deeper into your rest, you enter into the last stage of NREM sleep. What sets this last stage apart is that if you were to hook someone up to an electroencephalogram (EEG)—a device that measures brain activity using electrodes placed on the scalp—you'd see a very distinct pattern of low-frequency slow waves. Because of this, the last stage of NREM sleep is sometimes referred to as slow-wave sleep. Once you reach into NREM sleep, it's total lights-out.

After you move through the three stages of NREM sleep, you'll shift into REM sleep. Ironically, even though your eyes are moving at breakneck pace, the rest of your body remains immobilized. In fact, during the REM stage, you *can't* physically move because your muscles are paralyzed. If an EEG were recording your brain waves at this point, you'd actually see activity that looks very much like what you'd see in an awake person. There are several different theories about the purpose of REM sleep, including its potential role in brain development, consolidating memories, and even dreaming as a subconscious way to purge yourself of undesirable behaviors like aggression. Its exact function remains a mystery.

During a healthy night's rest, you'll go through the sleep cycle, and all its stages, between four and five times—about once every ninety minutes or so. As the night goes on, however, you will spend less and less time in deep sleep during each successive pass through the cycle. This is important, because having adequate deep sleep is key to maintaining optimal health. It's during deep sleep where your body goes through the essential processes that help to restore energy, strength, and well-being. When you cut back on overall sleep time, you reduce the amount of time you spend in deep sleep. This, in effect, shortchanges you of the crucial minutes your body and mind need to recover and recharge.

What Gets in the Way of Sleep?

Insomnia, or having a hard time falling or staying asleep, is more common than you might think. According to the American Sleep Association, nearly 30 percent of adults report having insomnia in the short term—with 10 percent experiencing ongoing sleep problems.

We've all had the occasional sleepless night, but it becomes insomnia if it's happening at least three nights per week for at least three months. There are also different types of insomnia, as well as causes for it. Initial insomnia or sleep onset is when you're having trouble falling asleep—the feeling of lying in bed for what seems like forever, tossing and turning. Middle insomnia means trouble with so-called sleep maintenance or staying asleep through the night. A number of things could cause middle insomnia, including sleeping in a room that's too hot, sharing a bed with your husband or wife who's snoring like a chain saw beside you, or drinking too much water before bed and needing to get up several times to use the bathroom. Late insomnia—you probably guessed—is when you wake earlier in the morning than you'd like. This can happen more frequently with senior adults, but stress, anxiety, or depression can cause it as well. If three categories aren't already enough, there's even mixed insomnia, where a person's disrupted sleep pattern fits into multiple types of insomnia. Unfortunately, whether it's sleep onset or sleep maintenance insomnia, the result is the same—less time in quality deep sleep and more feelings of sluggishness and brain fog throughout the day.

It's undeniable that insomnia is a complex and multifaceted condition. There are many reasons why someone might have trouble sleeping, and it's not always immediately apparent what those reasons may be. That's because insomnia has a bidirectional relationship with many common health problems. Keep in mind that the vast majority of mental illnesses have sleep-related symptoms, but there are also a variety of physical illnesses that can interfere with a good night's rest as well.

When a patient like Kenny comes to see me, one of my first steps is to determine whether a medical condition like an enlarged prostate or obstructive sleep apnea could be present. Other conditions like gastroesophageal reflux disease (GERD) or perimenopause have the power to downgrade healthy sleep.

There are also natural changes to sleep that occur just as a product of healthy aging. Some evidence suggests that as we age, we can expect to sleep anywhere from eight to ten minutes less per night on average with each passing decade until that stabilizes at around age sixty. After age sixty, expected changes would be: less time spent in deep sleep at night—which means waking up a bit easier—and spending more time napping during the day; especially if your schedule allows for it. Even if sleep problems are caused by healthy aging or by a medical condition, it's still possible that because of sleep's hold on the mind, non-restorative sleep can still adversely affect your mood, feelings, and behavior.

That's why it is so important to include sleep as a pillar of self-care for mental health. Good sleep is medicine. Struggling with chronic insomnia, whether it's caused by a stressful job, worrying about your kids, or a medication you're taking that's interfering with your sleep, can wreak havoc on your body, both physically and mentally. The good news is that there are tons of evidence-based ways to improve sleep. And the most beneficial and sustainable strategies for achieving your best sleep usually don't involve a prescription for Ambien. Improving sleep hygiene is often a huge part of what it takes to rest easy at night for some deep restorative z's.

I've seen, firsthand, just how quickly sleep can work in the inpatient setting. Remember Orin? He was experiencing suicidal thoughts after he separated from his wife and was admitted to the hospital for depression. While he was prescribed antidepressants for his mood when he came into the hospital, he started feeling better within a day or two, well before the medications even had a chance to start working. One of the reasons why Orin's healing occurred so quickly was because, within the confines of the hospital, he had social support, three meals a day, and a place away from any outside stressors that could interfere with his ability to rest well. As he struggled with his depression at home, his sleep had suffered. Once admitted to the hospital, he was sleeping at least seven hours or more each night. When you can have a much-needed reset on a basic biological need, you will see fairly rapid results. The sleep helped him to return to a baseline, and to a point where he could start addressing his other symptoms.

I've seen similar stories related to sleep play out with many of my patients. Someone comes to the hospital in a state of crisis and, more often than you might think, after a night or two of good sleep, they're feeling better prepared to address the challenges that brought them to the hospital in the first place. It works the same way in the outpatient setting, too. When Kenny, that sixty-something-year-old adventurer, started turning off his computer earlier in the evening and adopting a sleep hygiene routine, he began to notice incremental improvements in how he felt. Time and time again, we see that sleep matters—and it matters a lot, especially for mental health.

Sleep and the Brain

You may wonder why sleep can have such a powerful effect on our health. There are many reasons for it, but one of the most important is its role in helping to keep our brain working at its best. When we aren't getting enough rest, it takes a toll on basic brain operations. That, in turn, has a profound effect on our mood and behavior.

For example, sleep deprivation has also been shown to hijack different brain regions involved with mood regulation. These include the amygdala, which is linked to fear and aggression, as well as the ventral anterior cingulate cortex, an essential part of the brain's reward system. Because these important areas are not operating optimally, if you're sleep deprived, you might become highly sensitive to negative stimuli. The result? You are super irritable. You lose your temper over small things. You have trouble shaking off any worries. After days or weeks of sleep deprivation, sometimes referred to as a "sleep debt," you may find that your emotional buffer has all but vanished. Comments or actions that might sting a little if you were at your best now have the power to upend your life.

Mental health and sleep are so tightly linked that struggling with a mental illness, like major depressive disorder, has actually been found to produce alterations in sleep architecture—those distinct stages of sleep we talked about earlier. Generally speaking, if you're depressed, it takes longer to fall asleep after your head hits the pillow, but once you're asleep you get into the dream-producing REM stage more quickly. Depression is associated with an increase in the amount of time spent in REM sleep and less time spent in deep, slow-wave sleep compared to people who aren't depressed. This means less restorative sleep even if you're spending all night (and all day) in bed. It can make you feel exhausted, as if you haven't slept at all.

Stress can also affect the production of cortisol, glucose, and adrenaline. When you don't get enough restorative sleep, your body requires more energy to stay alert, and that puts stress on the whole system. As a consequence, your body is more likely to produce stress hormones like cortisol. Remember that in the short term, a little bit of cortisol goes a long way and helps the body to prepare to fight, run away from, or generally manage whatever obstacles are in its way, especially during a day that would be best punctuated by an afternoon nap. Over the long haul, your body will read all that extra cortisol as a problem, activating the immune system, and a lot of unnecessary inflammation, to deal with it. That same inflammation, in turn, has been associated with conditions like major depression and fatigue.

That's not the only problem with the additional hormone release. All of that extra cortisol produced during times of heightened emotional stress is associated with being in a perpetual state of alertness, which can make getting a good night's sleep nearly impossible. Between that and the glucose and adrenaline release that accompanies cortisol, you have a body that is primed and ready for action. You are vigilant, and your body is tuned into the environment to anticipate an approaching threat. Your muscles are tensed, poised to move—and to move fast. It's just not a state that's conducive to getting some relaxing shut-eye. The extra cortisol, in effect, is creating an internal environment that's like being amped up on espresso, making it even harder to rest. You can see why it becomes such a vicious cycle so quickly unless you make some significant changes to your sleep habits.

A Little Bit of Housekeeping

Sleep has yet another vital role in health: It provides the right environment for the brain to get rid of detrimental debris and other cellular waste products. It's like the body's own deep cleaning service. The lymphatic system comprises vessels, fluid, and lymph nodes. This unique system collects and then carries toxins and other wastes out of the body. Sleep is a process that is fundamental to health because when it fails, your kidneys, liver, heart, and lungs can become damaged over time.

The brain is a high-value organ, supporting the function of every other organ and tissue in the body. It also creates a fair amount of cellular and molecular waste—busy organs will do that. Understanding how the brain managed to rid itself of all this debris was a huge neurobiological mystery until researchers at the University of Rochester imaged the brains of mice as they slept.

Lo and behold, as the mice slumbered, the scientists looked on in awe as special brain cells called astrocytes, a type of support cell for neurons, created unique channels to help move cerebral spinal fluid—the clear, colorless substance that resides in the brain— through the organ. These sleep-related changes were, essentially, washing the garbage that had collected through the day out of the brain and into the outside lymph nodes. The researchers named it the "glymphatic" system.

What might the brain's waste removal process have to do with its relationship to mental health symptoms? Quite a bit, actually. The University of Rochester researchers were initially interested in the glymphatic system and its role in removing protein plaques associated with Alzheimer's and Parkinson's disease. If the glymphatic system isn't working, it's not just the buildup of plaques and tangles that matter to overall brain health. When you don't sleep enough, the brain can't do its everyday housekeeping. The resulting abundance of debris in the brain can lead the immune system to send in the troops, resulting in excess inflammation. Inflammation, as seen in study after study, exacerbates depression, anxiety, and a host of other mental health conditions.

As you can see, good sleep works to promote mental health on several different fronts.

The Right Amount of Sleep

When I start to talk to patients about sleep, one of the first questions I'm asked is how much sleep is enough to reap the mental health benefits. Certainly, we've all heard that eight hours is the sweet spot, but it isn't a hard-and-fast rule. Some of us need more sleep than others, due to our age, genetics, or health status. A healthy amount of sleep for a newborn could be up to seventeen hours a day, while a senior adult could potentially get by on six. While it's a good rule to aim for seven to eight hours of sleep per night, it's not a magic formula. What's more important to feeling rested and well is the quality of your sleep. This, truly, is a case where quality—or the amount of time you spend in deeper stages of sleep—is more important than quantity.

The good news is, even without a definite measurement of your slow-wave sleep times, your body can tell you when you are rested enough. Just as you know when you haven't slept well, your mood and demeanor can give you a fairly accurate idea of whether you've had enough z's. If you can wake up without an alarm, don't immediately reach for your coffee fix, and generally feel refreshed, you are probably managing enough rest.

That said, today it is easy to track your sleep using a variety of different wearable devices. These trackers will monitor your sleep patterns throughout the night to provide insights on how much sleep you are getting and, perhaps more important, whether it is of sufficient quality. Some will even map out your sleep stages for you. Wearable devices can help you learn more about your personal sleep experience, which can help you develop a game plan for how to optimize sleep for your mental health.

Can't I Take a Pill for That?

Many patients who are having sleep troubles ask me to prescribe some sort of sleep aid to help them get back on track. Depending on the situation—and if the person is in severe distress—taking out the prescription pad might make sense. In those cases, however, a pill to help you sleep isn't the best long-term fix.

Traditionally, not unlike in severe cases of anxiety, medical doctors sometimes prescribe a benzodiazepine to help someone catch up on sleep. If you recall, these drugs are sedatives that work by inhibiting certain processes in the brain to the extent of allowing you to slow down. Benzos work well—and they work fast—but they are highly addictive. People who come to rely on benzodiazepines, like Valium, to help them fall asleep every single night may eventually find that they need a higher dose of the drug to produce the same sedating effect, but that pales in comparison to the fact that these drugs can also be lethal. If someone is prescribed a benzo who has undiagnosed sleep apnea, for example, taking the drug at bedtime may lead to death by suppressing respiratory drive. Benzos can also increase the likelihood of falls, especially in older people. While some patients who see me with sleep problems hope that they'll go home with a prescription for a benzo like Valium, Ativan, or Restoril, I write prescriptions for these types of drugs sparingly.

When so-called Z-drugs like Ambien and Lunesta entered the scene, they quickly eclipsed benzodiazepines as some of the most prescribed sleep medications on the market, but long-term use of Z-drugs can also lead to problems, including next-day drowsiness, cognitive impairment, and, in severe cases, suicidal thoughts. I've also heard patients tell me about all sorts of weird and potentially dangerous Ambien stories, including walking, cooking, or driving in their sleep. Like with benzodiazepines, people taking Z-drugs can develop a dependency and experience withdrawal once they stop taking the drug.

For doctors, writing a prescription for a sleep medication is the easy part. Sometimes it can be hard not to, because we know how distressing sleepless nights can be. When it comes to sleep medications, some are just safer than others; however, the vast majority of these drugs don't actually address the underlying problem that may be leading to sleep disturbances in the first place. Additionally, medications like benzos may ultimately disrupt sleep architecture, resulting in less time spent in deep, slow-wave sleep, even though you might feel more tired at night or actually be sleeping longer. And they, too often, lead to a self-perpetuating cycle where you take a drug to sleep, wake up groggy and uncomfortable, and then over-indulge in caffeine or other stimulants during the day, which then, in turn, interfere with your ability to fall asleep later that night.

There are alternatives to common sleep aids that are not habit-forming. Some people like to use melatonin supplements. Your brain naturally releases melatonin, a hormone, from the pineal gland. This release occurs later in the day, usually a couple of hours before bedtime as daylight starts to fade. Melatonin works by helping the body regulate its natural sleep cycle—stay awake and alert during the day and sleep during the night. Studies show that melatonin can be useful for helping blind patients—who navigate the world in the absence of light—get on a regular sleep schedule. Unfortunately, bright light, or even the blue and green lights that emanate from your television, cell phone, and computer screen, can hamper the production of melatonin. That's one of the big reasons why you'll hear about recommendations to stay away from laptops and smartphones an hour or so before bedtime. If you don't, you're literally working against your body's natural sleep mechanics.

It's also worth noting that alcohol is not your friend when it comes to supporting healthy sleep habits, even if you think it might be. I'm not that doctor who's going to tell you that you can't ever have a couple glasses of wine or enjoy a beer after work. If you overdo it and find that you can't fall asleep without a couple of drinks, you might want to think about the long-term implications of alcohol on your sleep stages and ultimately your mental health.

What's interesting about alcohol is that it can give the perception that you've had restorative sleep because you've fallen asleep quickly, but the alcohol is really hijacking your sleep architecture. While the first half of the night you may experience more of that deep, slow-wave sleep, you experience less of it during the second half of the night. Alcohol can also cause you to wake up more during the night. You might find that you sleep hard and fast after a few drinks, then you're up at 3:00 a.m. tossing and turning. It's like tricking the mind and body into thinking that you had really great sleep when in fact you didn't. Long-term alcohol abuse can make obtaining restorative sleep challenging, even if you're spending eight or more hours in bed. Alcohol and some sleep medications can ultimately make sleep worse.

That's why, when patients like Kenny come to see me, I'm careful about providing a prescription drug for sleep right away. And when I do, I would offer one with very minimal, if any, potential for tolerance or addiction. In Kenny's case, we focused first on self-care, and that meant taking a hard look at his current sleep habits. After a few weeks of implementing a sleep hygiene routine, which meant going to bed at the same time every night, shutting off the laptop earlier, keeping his room dark and cold, and reserving his bed for nothing more than sleep and sex, he found that he was sleeping better than ever. Not just that, because within a few months, not only was he sleeping better; he was *feeling* better. He had his "juice" back.

Given the impact sleep has on the body and mind, you can see why improving sleep can be a vital part of improving mental health. Just a few nights of good sleep can provide dramatic results on your mood—and the best part? There are many different ways to make sure you are getting the most out of your time in bed.

Your Self-Care Playbook: Optimizing Sleep

Sleep is an essential bodily function, a restful state that helps to restore and recharge both the body and the mind. When you are not getting enough, it can have detrimental effects on your physical and emotional well-being. That's why managing sleep is such an important part of self-care. As people look to find ways to optimize their mental health, improving sleep, curiously, is often overlooked. Luckily, there are a variety of ways you can put a premium on your downtime and help ensure your sleep schedule is set up to nurture your mind, body, and spirit.

Practice Good Sleep Hygiene

Very few of us can go to sleep based solely on will alone. Most of us have to find a way to invite relaxation in, and then make it feel comfortable enough to stick around. We can do this by practicing good sleep hygiene, which means adjusting our behaviors and our environment to optimize sleep.

First, you'll want to take a good look at your bedroom. Then ask yourself: *How can I create an environment that is most conducive to relaxation and sleep?* That means turning off your screens an hour or so before bedtime, lowering the temperature in the bedroom to 65 to 67 degrees Fahrenheit, and turning off all lights. In fact, it doesn't hurt to put in some blackout shades if you need to so that you can make sure the room can be as dark as possible.

When I talk to patients about sleep hygiene, I recommend removing televisions from the bedroom. Remember that exposure to blue and green light can interfere with sleep—also, watching television right before bed can amp you up when what you really need is a calm and relaxing environment. Use your bed for sleep and sex only. Your work laptop and any other hobby supplies can stay in the living room. Since you want to associate your bed with relaxation, remove anything that gets in the way of that.

If you're waking up multiple times every night to go to the bathroom, try to limit the amount of water you're drinking right before bed. Avoid long daytime naps if you can, so that you're tired at night. Make sure you have a comfortable mattress. If your bed partner snores like a bear, earplugs are effective, and they don't have the same side effects as Ambien. It's fun and informative to see how much control you have over your sleep environment—that's what sleep hygiene is all about. Improving sleep hygiene is the easiest self-care strategy to get better sleep and improve mental health.

Create a Bedtime Ritual

We all have our rituals. Chances are, you already have a morning ritual, a series of regular habits or activities that help you start off the day right. Maybe you turn on the coffee maker, take a shower, or do a few push-ups straight out of bed to get your blood pumping. Having that kind of ritual helps wake us up and gets us moving, especially on those mornings we'd prefer to hit the snooze button.

When you consider your morning habits, it becomes easy to see why so many people benefit from creating a soothing bedtime ritual to end the day as well. Just as you need some time to get yourself going in the morning, you need time to relax at the end of the day. Give yourself that time. For some, this bedtime ritual may include a nighttime meditation. Others may take a hot bath before bed. Still others might read a chapter from a printed book while sipping on a cup of caffeine-free herbal tea. Some might get a jump on the next day by setting out their clothes, preparing some breakfast, and doing whatever they need to do so they can ease into their morning (and make sure they aren't worrying about forgetting anything). Your ritual should be what works for you and helps you wind down and set the mood for sleep. Whatever that ritual ends up being, make it part of your daily routine so it lets both your body and your mind know that it's time to wind down and prepare for rest.

Progressive Muscle Relaxation

Some people may find it challenging to fall asleep because of anxiety that physically manifests itself as tension somewhere in their body. In these cases, I recommend progressive muscle relaxation.

To start, get in bed and stretch out so you are comfortable. Then, as you breathe in, tense a muscle group for about ten seconds. As you breathe out, completely let go of those muscles, allowing them to fully relax. Take a few breaths and then move on to the next muscle group. Most people start with their hands, move to the arms, and then work progressively up to the shoulders. Then repeat with the feet, legs, and hips. Don't forget your chest, back, and stomach. Of course, many people also see benefit when they clench and then release the muscles in their face and neck.

After tensing and releasing each muscle group, it sometimes helps to focus on the difference you feel between the two states. If the muscles are still tense, you can always repeat the tension and relaxation a second or even a third time—whatever it takes to help your body release extra physical anxiety or stress.

Breath Work

You likely remember 4-7-8 breathing from the breath work chapter. To help you harness this natural breath-induced tranquilizer, lie down in bed and shut your eyes. Then, inhale through your nose for a count of four, gently hold that breath for a count of seven, and then exhale through the mouth over eight beats. Repeat as many times as you'd like.

While 4-7-8 breathing is easy to remember, you can help move your body into a more relaxed state, even an hour or two before bedtime, with any breath work that focuses on extended exhales. When you exhale for a longer period of time, it helps to activate the parasympathetic nervous system and put the body into a calmer state.

Yoga Nidra

Yoga Nidra is thought to have originated in India thousands of years ago. It was later developed in the 1970s by Indian guru Swami Satyananda Saraswati and adapted in the United States by psychologist Richard Miller as iRest Yoga Nidra. Nidra is a yogic meditation practice that can help your body prepare for sleep. It's not the type of yoga that involves Downward-Facing Dogs or Crow Poses. During a Yoga Nidra practice, you lie on your back in *savasana*, or Corpse Pose, the entire time while an instructor leads you through a dreamlike guided meditation.

Many yoga studios offer a Nidra session, and it's usually the last class of the night. But you can also practice this form of yoga at home using an app. There's some evidence that completing just an eleven-minute Nidra meditation before bedtime can reduce overall stress, improve sleep quality, and enhance general well-being.

If you try Nidra once, and it's difficult for you to settle in, I get it. My first Yoga Nidra experience, which I assumed would be easy—no handstands required—was more challenging than I expected. I was still a psychiatry resident and at the end of a long day had rushed over to the studio, in traffic, to meet my wife there for the class. As I walked in, minutes before the session started, I already had a million things from the workday on my mind. Shortly after the session began, I was lying on my back *trying so hard* to relax.

Since I wasn't physically moving my body, and the guide suggested that sleep was for after the class when we got home, I really felt like I was trapped there with my anxious ruminations and had nowhere to escape. I had to make a conscious effort to acknowledge that a little anxiety wasn't going to hurt me. So, using my mind's eye, I envisioned everything I needed to do as a cloud in the sky, and although my imaginary sky was initially clustered with clouds, I watched as they just floated on by. Before I knew it, I had the sense that I was in a dream but still awake. It was bizarre, but one of the most blissful feelings I have experienced.

It may take a few Nidra experiences to feel like you're really getting the most from it, so stick with it. Even that first night, as torturous as the class initially felt, I slept like a rock.

CHAPTER 8

TAPPING INTO YOUR SPIRITUAL SELF

*We are not human beings having a
spiritual experience. We are spiritual
beings having a human experience.*
—*Pierre Teilhard de Chardin*

What do you think about spirituality?

It's one of those questions I love to ask my patients, because it almost always leads to deeper discussions about connection, purpose, and the meaning of life. Conversations about spirituality can be rich, thought-provoking, and challenging. Usually, the way we understand ourselves as spiritual beings depends largely on our background and our life experiences.

When I suggest that spirituality is an important pillar of self-care for mental health, it's not uncommon for the person sitting across from me to smile politely and affirm, "Oh, but I'm not religious."

It's undeniable that religion is a form of spirituality that resonates with a lot of people, but it's just one manifestation of it, and that's important to keep in mind. Maybe religion resonates with you and maybe it doesn't. Whether you are religious or not, spirituality can be useful because it helps us appreciate the interdependent nature of the human experience. It allows us to understand that none of us is navigating life alone, and it helps foster a sense of connection. Some people find that connection in church every Sunday, in the company of a community of believers; others find it at a meditation center. One of my patients told me that going on long hikes and being in nature helps him tap into his spiritual self.

That said, spirituality and medicine have a complicated history. Go back in time and you'll see that spirituality and healing have evolved since the dawn of man. Ancient Greek physicians wouldn't just give you a poultice for a festering wound, they'd also make sure you prayed and sacrificed to the right gods to allow for a quick and painless return to health. Fast-forward a thousand years to the Middle Ages and you'll find that doctors had traded polytheism for one all-knowing God, at least on the European continent, but they still relied on prayers as much as the latest bloodletting practices to treat patients. Even today, with advances in medicine giving us remarkable new treatments and drug therapies, most medical doctors believe there is a spiritual element to healing and wellness. In fact, in a survey of physicians, the vast majority stated they were religious or spiritual, and 20 percent of respondents said that their spirituality was part of their reason for pursuing a career in medicine. Spirituality and health care have been, and continue to be, intricately intertwined. These overlaps are seen in mental health care as well.

In this chapter, we'll discuss how spirituality can help bolster your mental health. Tapping into your spiritual self isn't just about finding God. It's about learning how to appreciate the necessity of spirituality for mental health in a way that works for you. It's also important to note that spirituality as a self-care practice doesn't have to be about any kind of organized religion, but it certainly can be. You'll hear about my experience growing up in the Christian Church, and how faith has been an important factor in helping me find my own purpose. I don't want you to become hung up on the idea that if you aren't religious then spirituality isn't for you. Rather, as you'll see, there are distinct advantages to embracing spirituality even for the most secular mind. Such gains are threefold: Spirituality can offer a sense of community, a feeling of purpose, and a stronger connection to the world around you—all things that we know can help improve mental health and well-being.

What Is Spirituality?

Because spirituality can mean so many things to so many different people, it can be challenging to figure out exactly what we're talking about. Merriam-Webster's take is that the word "spiritual" means "relating to, consisting of, or affecting the spirit; incorporeal." Go down a little farther and you'll see that "spiritual" is also defined as "concerned with religious values" or "of or relating to supernatural beings or phenomena." Even within a trusted international reference guide, spirituality has a fair amount of fluidity. From my perspective, that's a good thing, because it means that spirituality is a tool that everyone can use, regardless of their belief system.

How spirituality connects with mental health, however, requires a closer look. Maya Spencer, MD, a member of the Royal College of

Psychiatrists, was able to take that flexible definition and home in on it. "Spirituality," she writes, "involves the recognition of a feeling or sense or belief that there is something greater than myself, something more to being human than sensory experience, and that the greater whole of which we are part is cosmic or divine in nature."

Embracing your spirituality means accepting that you have value and that your life matters. It also means acknowledging that your life is part of something bigger than yourself. Spencer says that spirituality embodies universal themes like love, compassion, altruism, wisdom, and truth—the attributes that contribute to our greater humanity. Living with spirituality is not just about appreciating a higher purpose as is taught in many religious faiths, but perhaps a broader purpose that may not exist above but around you. When I asked Anoop Kumar, MD, an emergency medicine physician and thought-leader in mind-body medicine, about the importance of spirituality, he said that it can be a loaded term but that spirituality is really about living with conscious awareness. "It's living with a broader range of experience with regard to one's identity and the world, and the relationship between the two. It's what connects the physical and mental, crossing the boundaries of other and self," he said.

The word "spirit" comes from "breath," and Kumar explains that breath is very unique in that it connects the body with our inner selves. The breathing techniques we discussed in Chapter 6—coherent, resistance, alternate nostril, box, and 4-7-8—offer pathways to make this connection. You can see how the pillars of self-care are interdependent; using one strategy may help you with the other. During an inhale, the diaphragm moves to make way for air, but that's not all that happens, because breath triggers more than just air exchange.

"When we breathe, there is dramatic physiology and anatomy involved—the chest size actually changes," he said. "But breath also affects mentality. Patients who are breathing fast and shallow are more likely to be anxious than those who are breathing slowly and deeply. Our breath is kind of this in-between space that connects anatomy, physiology, and mentality. That's exactly what spirituality is, too; it crosses the boundaries of other and self, physical and mental, and anyone who is sensitive to that is, in a sense, spiritual, whether they subscribe to that word or not."

Many spiritual practices also have a strong social component. Sharing a particular set of beliefs, whether in the form of an organized religion or a specific mindfulness practice, can bring like-minded people together in ways that can help them connect and support one another. That sense of belonging also offers some protection to mental health. It can help to assure people that they are not alone, as well as give them a sense of purpose in terms of their role in helping others within their community. Spirituality helps to enforce the idea that we are all part of something bigger than ourselves.

When I delve deeper into conversations about spirituality with my patients, it soon becomes clear that those quick "not religious" responses aren't the end of the story. Most people find unique ways to cross the boundaries Kumar speaks about and, in doing so, they garner extra protection for their mental health. One of my longtime patients, a man with over thirty years of sobriety under his belt, found a like-minded community in his weekly Alcoholics Anonymous meetings. He also discovered faith in the process.

"My relationship with God has been so important when it comes to staying sober," he told me, "but it's also the community, the people, and the church, because they hold me accountable. I don't want to let them down."

Another patient, a woman in her early fifties, doesn't believe in God in the traditional sense, but she was introduced to yoga during a team-building retreat for work and found developing her own yoga practice to be a spiritual experience for her. The combined acts of self-awareness, breath, movement, and community helped her find purpose.

When you take a closer look at what religion, in particular, offers to mental health, it's that scripture, prayer, and faith with a promise of salvation are ideas that people who are religious connect with in a deeply personal and profound way. That connection can offer a sense of calm and a sense of peace. It can also help some religious people live and act with purpose.

So many of the conversations I have with men and women who are struggling with mental illness center around the idea of "feeling lost" or trying to sort out what they're *supposed* to be doing with their life. I understand, personally, that it can be a troubling feeling to have. What makes matters more complicated is that even if you do believe that you understand your purpose, you may feel incapable or ill equipped to carry it out—whether it's a career change or a decision to start a family. With this in mind, religion *can* create an environment where accepting your purpose is a little easier, because many religious faiths ascribe to the belief that purpose is what's given to you by God. You wouldn't necessarily have to find it on your own, or even know what that purpose is in order for your life to have value. Instead, you'd listen to what God is telling you to do, and find comfort in knowing that you are living and acting in accordance to His will, all while trusting that He will provide you with the resources and skills you need. It's the unequivocal belief that life will ultimately be okay, regardless of what you are feeling today.

When I was a teenager, I received an unexpected and beautifully handwritten letter from a family friend—a woman of profound Christian faith. At the bottom of the letter, she had penned a Bible verse, "For I know the plans I have for you, declares the Lord, plans to prosper you and not to harm you, plans to give you hope and a future." Those words resonated with me, because they shifted my thoughts about purpose, which I began to understand as a pulling force, similar to gravity. Purpose pulls us in the direction it's supposed to, rather than a self-fulfilling prophecy that we create by ourselves. We can create turbulence in our life when we fight our purpose, ignore it, or stand in the way of it.

How many times have you scratched and clawed for something that you didn't even really want? Or done what you thought was expected of you rather than what you were meant to be doing? I began to see purpose as the process of finding acceptance and peace in my unique path, whatever that may be, and I truly believed that acceptance would lead to happiness.

On those mornings when self-doubt was ravaging my mind, and I struggled to find the will to even get out of bed, I would repeat the verse out loud, or write it down, or meditate on it—anything I could that would allow me to live with the words, inviting them to change the way I thought, and felt, and behaved. Those words helped me understand that as long as I was alive, I had value. There was a reason why I was still around—and my life had purpose, even if I didn't wholly understand what that purpose was yet. Over time, the verse emerged as a personal mantra of sorts. It helped inspire me to keep moving forward instead of accepting the mistruths that depression was telling me.

Eventually, yoga, too, helped me understand how breath and movement are a conduit for spirituality as a form of self-care for mental health. Especially when practicing yoga with others, there's a rhythm involved—the synchrony of movement and breath helped me experience a sense of community and allowed me to see how I fit into that community. It's my experience in the yoga studio as well as the countless stories I have heard as a psychiatrist that have helped me understand that religious or not, spirituality is important for mental health. It may offer a form of scaffolding that can help give direction and meaning to your life.

While I find spiritual connections in faith and yoga, there are many other ways to nurture your spirit and find your own purpose. You may find it in a rewarding career, the comforts of family, or the richness of volunteering your time. You may even find that you feel an uncanny connection to your inner self and the world around you when you are in nature. I get it. I took my first trip to South Africa in my early twenties, and standing in the breeze on Cape Point, gazing out into the milky blue abyss of the Atlantic Ocean, was one of the most spiritual experiences I have ever had. Some people find that immersing themselves in the latest scientific quest for meaning allows them to feel connected to themselves and the broader universe. You may find a spiritual connection in the unrestrained energy of a live music scene in your town. There really isn't a one-size-fits-all approach. There's what works for you. What's important is that you are consciously aware of how whatever you choose to do allows you to focus on connecting with yourself and the world around you—that's what spirituality is all about.

Science versus Spirituality

It's easy to brush aside spirituality and not count it as a legitimate self-care intervention for mental health. After all, we have so many innovative tools and techniques to probe the mind. Why incorporate an intangible concept like spirituality? It almost seems like science and spirituality are two parallel categories that, like oil and vinegar, do not mix.

Kumar suggests that science and spirituality have more overlap than people realize.

"Generally, we think science is referring to the objective range of experience and spirituality refers to the subjective," he said. "But spirituality is a process of hypothesizing, experimentation, and integration. We are given beliefs, we turn them into hypotheses that we then test, and, after those tests, we accept them or reject them. Frankly, I don't see a lot of difference between science and spirituality as they both refer to the quest of the human being to understand what the heck is going on—how am I interfacing with this smorgasbord of experience and what does it mean? This is a way of investigating the world except you use your mind and instruments of perception instead of microscopes, telescopes, and other devices."

Your spirituality, through those hypotheses and experiments, can help guide you as you look for your own purpose and place in the world. It can help you weather the little bumps and bruises in life—as well as the bigger things—and make you more sensitive to the consequences of your ideas, choices, and experiences. It can also help you develop more resilience in the face of stress.

"Often, we're taught in this modern world culture that there's you and then there's the world around you. These are two distinct entities," said Kumar. "But you have to figure out how to navigate this world. That's a lot of what life is about. Spirituality can help to show you that these are not two different entities but an expression of the same thing. When we can explore deeper ranges of our identity, you can integrate you and the world in a much more fluid way, which allows you to be more open, more creative, and not so afraid of trying new things."

Accessing your spirituality allows you to have greater resources at your disposal to help you navigate the world, regardless of whether or not you are struggling with a mental illness. By making a spiritual practice part of your self-care regimen, you are likely to find that you have a wider range of tools in your tool kit to help you feel more at one with yourself as well as with the world around you.

The Astonishing Power of Prayer

Several years ago, a young woman named Cara came to see me in my office. Cara was a military veteran who struggled with PTSD after several deployments in Iraq. Despite her past traumas, ironically, Cara was often the one who was *encouraging me* that her recurring nightmares were eventually going to go away. When I asked her where that certainty came from, she always told me it was her faith—her belief in God as well as her belief in the power of prayer that gave her complete confidence.

I also hoped that she would soon be able to sleep through the night without waking up—or enjoy a trip to the grocery store without flinching every time someone behind her dropped their keys. I had prescribed a medication for nightmares as well as an antidepressant to help with those symptoms. She was also on a wait list for cognitive processing therapy at the local teaching hospital, a twelve-week intensive program for patients with PTSD.

Although she told me that the medications were helping her a little bit, she always attributed the most benefit to her spiritual life. That's important because remission rates for PTSD from taking selective serotonin reuptake inhibitors—SSRI antidepressants commonly prescribed for PTSD—are quite low, on the order of 20 to 30 percent. Scientific evidence does in fact support that spirituality can potentially serve as a buffer against developing PTSD and depression, but it's a complex relationship and not all studies have reached the same conclusion. Medical doctors and researchers also don't know exactly what it is about spirituality that is so beneficial, which leaves lots of room for speculation.

High levels of spirituality may help protect against mental illness because it instills a level of hope that may be difficult to find without a deep spiritual connection. Spirituality might also increase the likelihood of engaging in adaptive coping strategies (like developing a yoga practice, engaging in meditation or prayer, or participating in a weekly religious service) that add additional mental health benefits. I can't help but notice that several patients I've worked with have also credited their faith for optimizing their mental health—whether it be Christianity, Islam, Buddhism, Hinduism, or another religious practice.

To better understand the intersection of religion, prayer, and mental health, I reached out to Blake Wilson and his wife, Dr. Ronique Wilson, both of whom I've known for decades. They form somewhat of a power couple in Houston, Texas. Blake is the pastor of the Crossover Bible Fellowship and Ronique is a licensed psychologist and ministry director of the Wise Women Project. The two have worked tirelessly to make mental health a priority in the ministries they lead. When I asked them why religion might be an advantage to some people who struggle with depression and anxiety, Ronique said that a structured belief system offers the believer several important benefits.

"First, religion provides a sense of control. Often, when people are dealing with mental illnesses, they seem to come on suddenly, which can give you a sense of being out of control," Dr. Wilson said. "A person's faith practices often give them guidelines for how to navigate life. They tell us how to handle difficult situations, and give us a framework on how to handle and view positive situations we have in our lives. When we apply those practices during a mental health crisis, it gives us back some of that sense of control and a way to cope."

In addition, Dr. Wilson said, organized religion provides a strong framework for outlining ways to live a good life. When conditions that adversely affect mental health may lead to more destructive behaviors, that framework is there to empower you to move toward more constructive living. For example, if a person's faith dictates that they participate in religious events and interact with others within the church, they may find that ritual can potentially overcome falling into a ritual of isolation, or maladaptive coping like heavy alcohol use or negative ruminations. It may seem inconsequential, but sometimes it's those little things that end up making the biggest difference in finding a path toward healing.

Another powerful ritual that religion may encourage is developing a prayer life. Growing up in the church, I was introduced to prayer early on as a way to communicate with God, as well as a way to relinquish physical or emotional pain. Many churches teach that prayer not only deepens your relationship with God but can provide answers to your most pressing questions. The idea is that by communicating directly with God and asking for help, letting go of worry or anxious ruminations becomes a little easier.

Outside of a religious construct, the idea of "letting go" is seen in conventional mental health care as radical acceptance—an idea popularized by esteemed psychologist Marsha Linehan. It's often used as a central theme of dialectical behavior therapy, an evidence-based methodology for treating impulsivity, depression, and borderline personality disorder. Radical acceptance means wholehearted acknowledgment that there are some things you can control, like how you react to what's going on in your environment, while there are other things you can't, like the actions of the people around you. Rather than investing all of your time and energy trying to control the things you can't, spend that energy focused on controlling the things you can.

Religious prayer offers a direct way to radically accept the things we can't control by offering them to a higher power. We also see similar ideology in yogic philosophy. Yoga itself is not a religion, but it is a practice that does incorporate elements of Hinduism, Buddhism, and Jainism. The Sanskrit term *aparigraha* is often used in yoga. It's the final Yama (or moral guideline) in Patanjali's Eight Limbs of Yoga—a set of instructions from the ancient yoga texts on how to live with meaning and purpose. *Aparigraha* translates as "non-hoarding." I think of it as the process of "letting go" of anything, including materials, thoughts, feelings, or emotions that don't serve our greater good—like jealously or harboring a revengeful spirit. The Bhagavad Gita, the traditional Hindu text, goes on to state, "A yogi should constantly concentrate his mind by staying in a solitary place, alone, with mind and body controlled, free from expectations, and free from acquisition."

Prayer is a foundational element of many religions as a way to connect your inner self with a higher power and to let go of things that don't serve you. Prayer isn't only practiced in a physical church or confined to the walls of a temple. It's a daily practice that can help people who are religious manage the ups and downs of daily life. Many people will tell you that prayer is what helps them to get through the most challenging times in their life. Pastor Wilson explained how Christianity addresses the relationship between prayer and mental health. "The Bible says in Philippians Chapter 4, 'Be anxious for nothing, but in everything, through prayer and supplication with thanksgiving, make your requests known to God,'" he explained. "The issue of anxiety is brought up by the apostle Paul in Philippians Chapter 4—the issue of people feeling anxious and worried. But Paul says one of the things that we should do, instead of worrying, is engage in prayer and depend on that higher source in our life."

According to the Christian faith, prayer may bring a sense of comfort and peace that comes directly from God. But, as it turns out, science may also offer an explanation. Scientists have discovered that religious prayer has the power to make actual changes to your body's physiological processes in response to stress.

Researchers from Aarhus University in Denmark investigated the relationship between prayer and physical pain. They recruited both religious and nonreligious participants in a study where subjects were exposed to a painful stimulation and asked to rate the intensity of pain, desire for pain relief, and anxiety on a standardized scale. The investigators were interested in learning about the effect that prayer might have on those ratings. In one condition, participants were told they could pray internally to God during the stimulation, provided they included the phrase "Dear God, I pray that you will help to relieve the pain and give me good health" at least once as they did so. In a second condition, participants were asked to pray again, except this time in a secular way addressing their prayer to a random guy named Mr. Hansen.

As you might imagine, praying to Mr. Hansen, religious or not, seems a little silly, and as expected, it didn't do a whole lot for reducing the perception of pain. But when researchers looked at the effects of religious prayer, they saw that pain ratings, as well as participants' stress responses, were reduced. In fact, religious prayer decreased both pain intensity and unpleasantness ratings by more than one-third for those who identified as religious. Notably, prayer-induced reductions in pain were corroborated by a drop in respiratory rates, suggesting that prayer was helping to promote physiological changes that made it easier to manage an unpleasant experience.

In a later study, the Danish researchers decided to look at what might be happening in the brain when a person who is religious prays while experiencing pain. Twenty-eight devout Protestants who registered for the study received painful electrical stimulation of varying intensity while they were simultaneously examined with a special type of brain scan—functional magnetic resonance imaging (fMRI)—that measures oxygen metabolism in the brain. In a sense, fMRI allows us to see which brain regions "light up" in response to particular thoughts, feelings, or physical sensations like pain. Researchers found that ratings of both pain intensity and unpleasantness were reduced when the study participants engaged in religious prayer—that they already knew from previous work. But when they looked at brain activation patterns, they saw reduced neural activity in the brain's parietofrontal network, an area implicated in modulating the pain experience. What this means is that prayer can potentially make changes to the way the body responds to pain, and ultimately result in the experience being less painful altogether.

We've done a lot of talking about physical pain, but there's also evidence that prayer works in a similar manner when it comes to emotional pain and trauma. Those same physiological changes that have the power to diminish a physically painful experience can also offer benefits for the mind with regard to stressful emotional experiences. In fact, several studies have also shown that prayer has positive benefits for mental illnesses like anxiety and depression—and that engaging in prayer is associated with increased optimism about getting better and overall mental health coping skills.

What if you're not religious? Do religious people have an inherent mental health edge over people who aren't? The answer to that question is no. Religion does not automatically protect against developing a mental illness, and it doesn't presume that if you do develop a mental illness, you'll have an easier time treating it. It's undeniable that some religions do encourage using tools like prayer that may help, but it has to be accessed in order to work. There's also a complicated relationship between religion and mental health, and not all churches prioritize mental health like Pastor and Dr. Wilson. Just like any other medicine or self-care tool, you have to be invested in order for the mental health advantage that religion may offer to work. Spirituality and religion are not one and the same. If you aren't religious, you just have to find other ways of tapping into your spirituality.

One way to do this is by practicing mindful meditation. It's a form of spirituality that has been found to offer similar benefits for reducing perceptions of physical and emotional pain. Although Buddhist monks may get the same kind of mental health bang for their buck with meditative practices, a study based in Taiwan also demonstrated that mindful meditation without religious strings attached produced similar changes in the brain when compared to the changes we spoke about with religious prayer. Practicing mindful meditation can reduce perception of physical pain, as well as mitigate the types of anxious ruminations that can be characteristic in mental illnesses like depression. Small studies and conflicting results limit experts' unequivocal stamp of approval for utilizing mindfulness for mental health self-care, but the risks are low and the potential rewards are abundant. I recommend it to all of my patients, and it's a practice that I encourage you to explore as well.

Mindful Meditation

Contributing to both prayer and mindful meditation's effectiveness is that they both require conscious awareness. The act of prayer itself is typically practiced in a quiet or sacred space, and it requires that we are plugged in to our experience in the moment—without outside distraction or interference. During prayer, a person is totally focused on how they are connecting with God. Essentially, prayer can then induce a heightened state of consciousness.

Similarly, during a meditation practice, you would sit quietly or lie down on your back. Certain types of meditation, like transcendental meditation, make use of silent mantras—that could be a word or phrase, similar to the verse I found meaningful in my own life. It's what gives you the kind of sensitivity, as Kumar put it, that allows you to better connect with the world around you. It's one of the reasons why spirituality, in whatever form most speaks to you, can help you better manage your mental health day to day.

As we discussed briefly before, meditation can also make distinct changes to the way your brain works. When researchers at Carnegie Mellon University compared brain activity of Tibetan monks who practiced regular meditation with people who had never meditated before, they saw that the monks' brains worked a little differently. Decades of meditation had decreased activity of what's referred to as the default mode network, which I like to think of as the "mind's mind."

The default mode network consists of areas of the brain like the medial prefrontal cortex, the posterior cingulate cortex, and the angular gyrus—areas that are implicated in mood and emotional regulation. When you are awake but not really doing anything, like if you're daydreaming or taking a walk, the default mode network is most active. It is believed that problems with the functioning of the default mode network contribute to mental illnesses such as Alzheimer's disease, depression, anxiety, and ADHD.

The longer monks had been actively engaging in meditative practices, the less active their default mode network was. This means that when you first start meditating, your mind's mind may be more distracting, or outright annoying—similar to my first Yoga Nidra experience. With more time and practice, however, that pesky voice in your head and the anxious ruminations may become quieter. Appreciating the importance of spirituality, religious or not, as a self-care practice for mental health can help you develop greater resources to navigate the world, manage stress, and reduce physical and emotional pain.

The Elephant in the Room

As interlaced as spirituality and medicine are, some churches and religious practices have historically suggested that mental illness can only be dealt with in the church itself. Conventional medicine isn't without blame, either, because sometimes it may seem like science and faith contradict each other, and medical doctors may be hesitant about having conversations about faith with their patients. One common myth is that most medical doctors don't believe in

God. Numerous surveys have suggested that a majority of physicians actually do believe in God and most medical doctors also consider themselves religious.

You can still find areas where medicine and religion seem to clash when it comes to what causes mental illness and the best course of treatment. Dating back to medieval and early modern periods in western European history, demonic possession was widely attributed as a cause for mental illness. During the Middle Ages, exorcisms were generally thought of as the accepted treatment for the erratic behavior of demoniacs. Today, many faith leaders are pushing back against misinformation that claims mental illness is the result of sin. Academic centers like the Muslim Mental Health Lab at Stanford University are also incorporating programs to help better understand the unique relationship between religious faith and mental health. Moreover, the American Psychiatric Association houses a Mental Health and Faith Community Partnership to help foster a dialogue between religious leaders and psychiatrists.

"For too long, the Church has not viewed mental health as a legitimate concern," said Dr. Wilson. "We discount it and make it a faith issue. If you interacted with a person who had high blood pressure, diabetes, or a cancer diagnosis, you wouldn't tell them to stop taking their medication. That's because you believe that medication has a purpose in helping to address whatever the medical issue is. But when you have a mental health issue, too often people hear they don't need medication, they don't need therapy, they don't need inpatient treatment because if you just will your mind to be better, then you will be better."

Both she and Pastor Wilson agree that religious leaders have a unique opportunity to educate their congregations about mental health. They can reach people from all walks of life to explain why, in times of crisis, prayer can help, but many people will also benefit from seeking out the care of a qualified mental health professional.

I have personally witnessed the importance of mental health professionals and churches working together. A young African American woman who was experiencing a psychotic episode was once admitted at an inpatient psychiatric facility where I was working. She was extremely ill, experiencing delusions of persecution—she felt unsafe and she was hearing voices. Although she wanted the medical team to help her get better, she was adamant that we communicate with her pastor first. It wasn't until he came to the hospital, met with the medical team, and prayed at the bedside with the young woman and her family that she made the decision to take medications. Eventually she recovered.

Spirituality can be a powerful self-care practice for mental health because it can offer community, hope, and purpose. It can provide direction when it seems like your life is going nowhere. Religion is only one of many spiritual paths. These kinds of spiritual self-care practices don't always come easy—you need to make room for them—but when you do, you'll see they can offer a host of benefits that will bolster your mental health even during the most stressful of times.

Your Self-Care Playbook: Accessing Your Spirituality

Many people rely on faith to guide almost every aspect of their life, but it's easy to consider the advantages that spirituality has to offer as limited to people who are religious. We are all spiritual, we just have to access our spiritual self so that we can harness its benefits for our mental health. Your spiritual self can be used to reduce stress, connect with people around you, and find purpose. Here are a few ways to tap into your spirituality for your best mental health.

A Beginner's Guide to Meditation

Simply put, meditation is a practice to help transition your body and mind into a calm and relaxed state. The bells and whistles (or, if we are going to play true to stereotype, gongs and water fountains) that we often see in movies—or hear about in podcasts—are completely optional. All you really need is the ability to quiet your mind and focus so you can train yourself to be more mindful and aware.

I recommend starting out by sitting quietly in a room free of distractions. Sit in a chair or on the floor, you pick—but make sure your back is straight. Pick a point of focus, your *drishti*. Once again, it can be a spot on the wall or an imaginary star that you visualize with your eyes shut. When you are ready, close your eyes and sit in stillness, bringing attention to your breath. Eventually you may want to meditate on a meaningful mantra—a word, sound, or phrase—that encourages you.

To make sure my meditation is not just a gateway for a nap, I like to set a timer for several minutes so I can be intentional about my practice. If you feel like you need to be guided through your meditation, there are plenty of excellent apps you can download to help keep you focused and consciously aware during your meditation practice. That said, there's no one *right* way to meditate. The most important part is just allowing yourself the time and space to sit in stillness. That way, your parasympathetic nervous system can do its job by calming the body and the mind.

Prayer

The important thing is acknowledging, as we have discussed, that religious prayer does have mental health benefits. This means that if you do happen to be religious, consider your time spent communicating with God as a self-care technique for your mental health. What's important is that you are consciously aware, plugged in, and invested in your prayer. In my own journey, I found that developing a personalized prayer was more effective than praying something I had memorized. However, I often combined mantra meditation in the form of focusing on my favorite verses in addition to my personal prayer practice. In some cases, depending on your religious faith, you may find the most comfort in reciting a prayer that has been prepared specifically for finding comfort during challenging times. Prayer is a deeply personal but effective strategy for supporting mental health.

Connection

Another benefit of adopting a spiritual practice is the community that comes along with it. Whether you belong to a church, an ashram, a meditation group, an outdoor meetup, or even a twelve-step program, being able to gather with others who share your beliefs can be a powerful way to buoy your mental health.

Like prayer, so much of finding a spiritual connection with others depends on your personal beliefs. Even if you may be more of a loner at heart, consider finding ways to share your practice with others—whether it's making the extra effort to get to the 11:00 a.m. Sunday service, signing up for a meditation workshop, or joining a local meetup group for a hike out in nature.

Selfless Service

Altruism, or selfless service, is widely accepted as an adaptive coping strategy for overcoming mental health challenges. Even small acts of kindness have been shown to increase feelings of being in control as well as general optimism. Engaging in selfless service—whether it's walking dogs at the local shelter, delivering meals to the elderly, or volunteering at the soup kitchen—is a spiritual practice in its own right, because it can foster a sense of connection with the people around you. It also just feels good, and those good vibes can definitely give your mental health an extra boost.

CHAPTER 9

THE MEDICINE ON YOUR PLATE

The bottom line is you should have an intentional
diet that feeds your mental health.
—*Drew Ramsey, MD*

Not long after I opened my psychiatry practice, a man named Cory came to see me. He was an aspiring entrepreneur and amateur musician, who had recently moved to Austin to make a name for himself in the live music capital of the world. Although Cory quickly found a good job in a competitive market and secured a regular performance gig at a busy coffee shop, he acknowledged that his mood was sliding into a serious and inexplicable funk.

"I know a lot of people have *real* problems," he said. "I had this audacious goal and I made it happen. I'm where I thought I wanted to be. I should be happy, but I'm just not."

Cory's depression was taking its toll. He wasn't *feeling* his music like he used to, and he was making careless mistakes at work. Although he wasn't completely sure he even liked his job, he was afraid that he'd be disciplined for poor performance. He just felt like he was letting everyone around him down. In addition to that, he was also frustrated because he had put on nearly twenty pounds in less than six months. Not taking care of himself made him feel, as he put it, "unhealthy and pathetic."

Any mental illness can affect appetite, it's not just the eating disorders like anorexia or bulimia. The *DSM* lists changes in appetite as a diagnostic criterion for several conditions including major depressive disorder and generalized anxiety disorder. An increase or decrease in appetite, as well as a notable weight loss or gain, often coincides with a drop in mood. It makes logical sense, because when you are feeling down, it can be hard to find the motivation to go grocery shopping or spend time in the kitchen cooking your favorite meal. What's especially true when we are stressed is that we lose ourselves in our favorite carb-loaded comfort foods like burgers and beer or a pint of ice cream. For some people, however, food is the last thing on their mind when they're feeling depressed, stressed, or anxious. When I asked Cory to talk to me about his eating habits, he was circumspect.

"I just don't have time to eat," he said. "I've been so tired and stressed that I've been shoving my face full of whatever takes the least amount of effort. Lately, that means microwavable meals, packaged ramen, and fast food."

Numerous studies have highlighted the importance of a balanced diet for overall health and well-being. At this point, we all know that we should be eating more fresh fruits and vegetables, and that overdoing it with the processed foods is a bad idea. Even though food lies at the bedrock of medicine, you might be surprised to know that most medical doctors don't get a lot of information about nutrition during training. Moreover, what we do receive tends to lean heavily on promoting a heart-healthy diet. Historically, psychiatrists have left discussions about food and health to primary care physicians or cardiologists. As mental health professionals, it was hard to feel like we had that much skin in the game. I didn't consider a potential relationship between food and mental health until years after I had finished medical school. Without additional training in integrative medicine, which takes on a holistic approach to health and wellness, I probably wouldn't have thought to ask a patient like Cory about what he was eating or how he was eating it.

In some ways, this oversight is understandable. For as long as I can remember, much of our discussion around food and health has been about a certain kind of dieting—what to eat (and what not to eat) in order to maintain a certain weight. Outside of eating disorders, weight control doesn't fit that well in the mental health wheelhouse. Even as I began to recognize the importance of self-care modalities like yoga, breath work, spirituality, and movement for maintaining strong mental health, nutrition fell lower on the list because of how I personally thought about food: Eat for physical health, not for mental health.

It can be challenging making sense of guidelines recommending which food is healthy because the recommendations seem to change by the day. Studies contradict each other, and the conflicting science can get in your head. Even today, some mornings while making breakfast I'm toiling over whether I should scramble an egg white or toss the yolk in there, too, all while my coffee is on the counter getting cold. For a very long time, eggs were considered a healthy and nutritious way to start the day. Then, studies suggested eating eggs would lead to high cholesterol and heart disease— avoid them at all costs. Now eggs are back on the good food list once again. In fact, the latest studies show they're one of the most nutrient-dense foods on the planet.

There was a similar trend with fats. For years, common wisdom held that people should only eat low-fat or even fat-free foods. Now newer studies demonstrate that the body, particularly the brain, needs a certain amount of fat, albeit the monounsaturated and polyunsaturated types, to stay in tip-top shape. Even with the latest evidence suggesting that olive oil and foods with good fats, like avocados, yogurt, and nuts, are incredibly beneficial to overall health, many people have trouble moving away from the notion that fat, in any form, isn't acceptable.

Instead of thinking in terms of "good foods" and "bad foods," appreciate food, in general, as sustenance that supports mental and physical health. Food is good for us when approached in a balanced way. Let's also acknowledge that many of the loudest voices sounding off about the idea that an entire food group is terrible for you are typically those with some sort of agenda, whether it's to sell a diet plan or get more likes on social media. So, as you can imagine, talking about nutrition as an essential part of mental health self-care can be a little complicated. Is it any wonder that so many medical doctors, psychiatrists included, have found it better to ignore food-related conversations as much as possible?

In recent years, more psychiatrists are adopting the "food is medicine" motto, and they're right to do just that. Our bodies need certain nutrients in order to grow, flourish, and thrive. Nutrient-dense food really is the foundation for how we work, play, look, and feel. When we don't consume enough vitamins, minerals, and other key nutrients, it can take a detrimental toll on our mental health.

Thinking intentionally about your best food choices can nourish your body and your mind.

This Is Your Mood on Food

Remember that as the human brain evolved, the regions of the brain responsible for drives like hunger were intertwined with our emotional and mood centers. You know from your own experience that eating is about much more than satiation. As it turns out, our brain, like the rest of our body, thrives on nutrient-dense foods. These nutrients provide the building blocks to keep our cells, neurotransmitters, and other molecules in the brain working optimally. Food matters for supporting mental health and well-being. In fact, food is one of the most effective forms of preventative medicine available to us. That's why it's important that we focus on what foods we eat and how we eat them as part of our self-care regimen for mental health.

Specific nutrients, including omega-3s, B vitamins, and other plant-based molecules, can have a profound impact on your mood. Several studies have shown that targeted dietary changes not only help prevent conditions like depression and anxiety; they can also treat them if you've already been diagnosed.

You may already be aware of how food can influence your mood. Remember in Chapter 6, when we talked about mindful eating? Think about the last meal you ate. Maybe you sat down to eat because you were hungry, or just because you always eat at that particular time. Did you eat with friends and family or alone? Did you find a way to take your time and savor both the food you ate and the company you kept? Or was it a quick meal on the go? These are all factors that can contribute to how food can affect our mood.

Now let's use that same mindful approach to think about the

way you feel when you skip a meal or haven't eaten enough. If you are like me, missing meals can make you feel anxious, irritable, and "hangry" pretty quickly. What about the morning after a night of heavy drinking? That hangover does more than just give you a headache—it makes you feel groggy and slow. It also affects your mood. Think about how you feel when you eat too much. It makes you feel tired and sluggish, right? That's why it's important to understand how making small changes to the way you eat can potentially improve your mental health.

The Food Shrink

Several years ago, I flew to Washington, DC, to attended a conference for the American Psychiatric Association. At the time, I was finishing up specialty training in general psychiatry. As part of a fellowship I had received from the APA, I was sitting on its Council on Communications—a committee that focuses on how psychiatrists can help shape public discourse about mental health.

While I was waiting for the committee meeting to begin, reading the agenda and poking at my breakfast, a tall, charismatic man walked through the door and made his way to the front of the room. I asked a friend sitting next to me who it was.

"That's Drew Ramsey, the chair of the committee," she replied. "He's the food shrink."

Now that was interesting; I had never heard of a food shrink before.

This was to be my first (but definitely not my last) encounter with Drew Ramsey, MD, a well-known psychiatrist and author of books including: *Eat Complete*, *50 Shades of Kale*, *The Happiness Diet*, and *Eat to Beat Depression and Anxiety*. Ramsey is the face of nutritional psychiatry, part of the Food Is Medicine movement, and he's on a mission to educate about how we can harness nutrition to improve mental health. After that meeting, I returned to my hotel room and began reading about his work that focused on how food affects the brain, which in turn affects our mood. The idea that food could actually help someone beat depression or anxiety was a new concept for me—and the whole idea was intriguing.

A few months later, I started a fellowship in integrative health and medicine with the Academy of Integrative Health and Medicine (AIHM) based in La Jolla, California. It was during that course of study that I started to learn some fascinating ideas about the connections between the gastrointestinal system and the brain. For example, there is more serotonin, the so-called mood neurotransmitter, in the gut than in the brain. That means that what is going on in the digestive tract could potentially impact our mood. At the time, emerging research was suggesting that probiotics, or live bacteria and yeast found in fermented foods like yogurt and kimchi, could help reduce symptoms of depression. Other research has since supported the idea that a fiber-rich diet may be associated with better mental health.

As I was learning about these groundbreaking studies, I noticed how easy it was to become lost in the contradictory information. There was the old egg debate, to start, but I had many more questions than that. Should you eat beef or not? Was it better to go plant-based? What's the deal with gluten? Any issues with Beyond Beef? It seemed like these were questions that only a food shrink could answer.

Within the year, I had reached out to Ramsey for some guidance. In fact, the more I spoke with him, the more I understood how essential nutrition can be to supporting your mental health. One of my questions was how he first got interested in nutritional psychiatry in the first place. Given scant training in nutritional psychiatry in medical school, how did he know that food would be such a powerful intervention for mental health?

"It was an inevitable merger of all the things I was interested in at the time," he explained. "I had been a college athlete and, in medical school, started eating vegetarian. I was very interested in how food affected my health, and I hoped that the foods I chose would improve my physical well-being."

That made sense. One of my best friends in medical school was vegetarian. During our late-night study break conversations about life, including his decision not to eat meat, "because it's bad for you," I was persuaded to ditch steaks and turkey bacon clubs for a while, too. I made it about three months, until my dad invited me to a Super Bowl party. I can't remember who was playing that day, but I clearly remember succumbing to sausage gumbo and beef fajitas.

During Ramsey's training, the STAR*D was published, a study indicating that only about one-third of patients entered remission after being prescribed a therapeutic trial of an antidepressant medication. Around the same time, the first studies looking at the intersection of food and mental health, particularly about the importance of omega-3 fatty acids—a type of polyunsaturated fat found in cold-water fish like salmon, mackerel, and tuna—for mood, also came on the scene.

"As I started to practice, I saw that antidepressant medications took a while to work, and even when they did, there was often an incomplete response. Some symptoms improved but patients didn't feel all the way better," he said. "It occurred to me that we weren't really considering food in how we approached mental health. As the data started coming out, it became more and more clear that food matters; it's probably the most powerful preventative tool in mental health and brain health. We should be using it with patients."

That's why I asked Cory about what he was putting on his plate. Unfortunately, the fast-food-centric, overly processed Western diet has been shown, time and time again, to get in the way of optimal mental health. It not only lacks the nutrients our brain needs to work its best, but it can promote inflammation, which has been associated with a number of mental illnesses including depression, anxiety, ADHD, bipolar disorder, and schizophrenia. The way most Americans eat may actually be creating an environment within our body and our mind that increases risk for mental illness. That's the bad news. The good news is that there are easy ways to make adjustments to what you already enjoy eating, without giving up entire food groups, to give yourself an opportunity for your best mental health.

Feeling Mediterranean

In the 1950s, an American physiologist from the University of Minnesota, Ancel Keys, noticed a fascinating trend regarding health and longevity. Certain people living in small towns in southern Italy, many of whom were impoverished, somehow experienced better health outcomes than wealthier constituents in the United States. He could not pinpoint the exact reason for such a profound difference between these groups. Keys hypothesized that diet could offer an explanation. He then published the famous "Seven Countries Study," conducted in the United States, Italy, Greece, Finland, the Netherlands, Japan, and Yugoslavia, where he investigated the role of lifestyle factors, including nutrition, in the development of cardiovascular disease. The study determined that those who adopted a Mediterranean diet, rich in fresh fruit and vegetables, whole grains, legumes, nuts, fish, and olive oil, as well as fermented dairy products like yogurt, were more likely to live a longer, healthier life.

In the decades since, large-scale studies have supported the idea that eating a Mediterranean diet has multiple health benefits, especially as you age. It's been linked to not only reduced risk of heart attack and stroke, but also a decreased risk for developing specific types of cancers. The same studies have shown that the Mediterranean diet is also neuroprotective, meaning that it helps protect our neurons, helping us to stay sharper as we age. When you put all these findings together, it reinforced the idea that the foods that are good for the heart are also good for the brain. But they raised an important question that hadn't been investigated yet: Could a Mediterranean-style diet perhaps help with the prevention or treatment of mental illness?

The answer appears to be yes. Researchers at the University of Navarra in Spain followed twenty thousand former students, documenting their typical diets over a number of years. They found that what people eat has a tremendous impact on their physical and mental health. At the beginning of the study, and then every two years after, the participants filled out a lifestyle questionnaire where they were asked to list the kinds of foods they ate on a regular basis. They also completed a basic health inventory to note any medical illnesses they had. Researchers scored participants' dietary patterns based on how closely their food choices aligned with a Mediterranean-style diet. After a two-year follow-up period, they found an interesting relationship between food and mood. A Mediterranean diet, as expected, played a protective role, helping the study participants avoid cardiovascular disease, type 2 diabetes, and cognitive decline. But, intriguingly, adhering to a Mediterranean diet was also found to act as a buffer against depression. The folks who ate in the Mediterranean style were significantly less likely to develop depression later in life.

Since then, dozens of other studies looking at the food-mood relationship have been performed, and several show a strong correlation between a Mediterranean diet and reduced risk for developing depression and anxiety. Coincidentally, many of those projects also have found that eating more of a Westernized diet, full of processed foods and refined sugar, works in the opposite fashion; it may increase the risk of developing or exacerbating a mental illness. You can see why Ramsey was allured by the emerging data.

Where many of the studies fell short, however, was answering questions related to whether or not a Mediterranean diet might be an effective treatment for mental illness. That question was tackled head-on in a seminal 2013 study where researchers from Monash University in Australia conducted the first ever trial to see whether prescribing food for depression could help treat it. Involving coaching by a licensed dietician on how to make the right swaps for a more Mediterranean-type diet, the idea was that dietary modifications that helped people eat in a more Mediterranean style could help reduce the severity of their depressive symptoms.

The trial, which was aptly named Supporting the Modification of Lifestyle in Lowered Emotional States (SMILES), yielded remarkable results. After six months on a modified diet, depression scores were reduced by about 30 percent. That's in line with the success of antidepressant medications. When researchers looked into other factors like weight loss, exercise habits, or other healthy lifestyle changes that might be responsible for improvement in depressive symptoms, it was still concluded that nutrition provided an independent and direct effect on mood. Eating for brain health made a difference.

The SMILES trial introduced the idea that diet can potentially treat mental illnesses like major depressive disorder, and the fact that people who are in the thick of a depressive episode can still find ways to incorporate healthier foods even when they aren't feeling their best. Since then, the trial's results have been replicated in other studies. The medical community is gradually beginning to accept that changes in the way we eat can lead to improvements in mood. The Mediterranean diet is a great foundation as we look to improve the way we eat as part of a self-care playbook for both physical and mental health.

"One of the biggest issues, before, in helping patients adopt healthier eating practices was that there was no structure or framework to show them how to do it," said Ramsey. "Knowing that the Mediterranean diet works in both preventing and treating depressive symptoms can really empower people to take more control over their diet. We now have a way to guide people on how to include more foods that will nourish their mental health."

How Food Works for Mental Health

You may be asking yourself how fruits, vegetables, fish, and olive oil manage to have such mighty effects on mental health. The answer is actually quite simple. It's not only that what's good for the heart is also good for the brain, although physical health and mental health are interdependent. The answer lies in the vital nutrients contained within a Mediterranean diet.

To better understand which nutrients are the most important, Ramsey and his colleague Laura LaChance, MD, from the University of Toronto, scoured the scientific literature to understand which foods you might prescribe especially for depression. As a result, the two published an Antidepressant Food Scale, a nutrient profiling system that highlights foods that are packed with nutrients thought to play a significant role in treating depression. The highest-scoring foods on their list were seafoods (like oysters), leafy greens, berries, and cruciferous vegetables (like kale and broccoli). Why? Because these foods all contain a variety of the essential vitamins, minerals, and phyto-molecules the brain needs to keep itself in top working order.

"The nutrients in these foods help decrease inflammation, they improve diversity in the microbiome, and they help boost the brain's ability to grow and repair itself," said Ramsey. "That's why the Mediterranean diet works so well. When you eat in that way, you are getting more of these vital nutrients to your brain. You are also eating less of those unhealthy, processed foods that lead to inflammation and brain fog. It's a win-win."

Let's break that down a little more, starting with the importance of decreasing inflammation. There's been a lot of talk about inflammation and health lately, and for good reason. Inflammation, or the protective immune response that helps to fight off injury and infection, is great, but only in small doses. Inflammation is the cornerstone of our body's immune system and helps protect us from illness; however, if you are living in a perpetually inflamed state, health problems may develop over time. Leafy greens, seafood, and fresh fruit are considered to be high in anti-inflammatory nutrients. Since there's a positive association between inflammation and mental illness, you want to do what you can to reduce inflammation in the body. Anti-inflammatory nutrients from food can help.

Then there's the microbiome, composed of the trillions of

microscopic bacteria residing in our guts. The gastrointestinal tract isn't just responsible for digesting food; it also works to regulate our immune system. That means that the brain and the gut are in near-constant communication, sending important molecules back and forth to keep tabs on what's happening in the body.

Many conditions that affect mental health are also accompanied by gastrointestinal symptoms. Consider that irritable bowel syndrome (IBS), a medical condition that can cause alternating bouts of constipation and diarrhea, is prevalent in about 11 percent of the general population compared to between 54 and 94 percent of people who pursue psychiatric treatment. Think about how many times you've had a queasy feeling of butterflies in your stomach when you're nervous. There's obviously a connection between our mood and our gut. These symptoms are most likely related to the body's stress response. In fact, chronic stress can reduce amounts of healthy bacteria in the microbiome. This is important: Under normal circumstances, these bacteria help the gut and the brain communicate, passing important messages between the two. There's research indicating that abnormal changes to the microbiome are associated with mental illness like bipolar disorder, major depression, and generalized anxiety disorder. And it also likely explains some of those pesky related gut problems like nausea and upset stomach that often accompany these conditions.

This led to another question: If you could get more of the "good bugs" back into the microbiome by consuming fermented foods like yogurt, kefir, kimchi, or kombucha, could you then restore the gut (and, as a consequence, the mind) to proper working order? Perhaps eating probiotic-containing foods could reduce the body's stress response and result in a calmer mindset and improved mood. While the research is still emerging, it looks like the answer is yes.

People who regularly eat fermented foods, as well as ample fiber (which is what those good bugs like to eat), have bodies that are better equipped to manage stress. They also show less inflammation in the body. Both of these factors are associated with better mental health and well-being.

When it comes to mental health, you will hear a lot of talk about neurotransmitters like serotonin, dopamine, and norepinephrine, to name just a few. Brain-derived neurotrophic factor (BDNF), however, is a different type of chemical that's abundant in the brain. It helps to promote cell growth and connection. Some scientists refer to BDNF as "brain fertilizer," but I prefer to think of BDNF as a natural way of giving the mind a warm cuddly hug. It plays a key role in helping our brain cells develop, grow, connect, and communicate with each other. BDNF just so happens to also protect the brain from the effects of stress. In essence, it allows the brain to adapt more easily when things aren't going so well. You can think of it as a form of cellular resilience. Having more BDNF means that your brain cells are stronger, fitter, and better able to form new connections when needed. That makes it easier for you to learn, remember, and better navigate the world around you—even when the going gets tough.

When your brain does not make enough BDNF, its cells can't communicate with each other as efficiently. Patients diagnosed with mood and anxiety disorders tend to have lower BDNF levels than the general population. Experts aren't completely sure why, but mental illnesses can impact BDNF production in a negative way. Here's the good news: A Mediterranean diet that includes nuts has been shown to increase BDNF levels and reduce symptoms of depression. That's why I often suggest that my patients try to include more nuts in their diet. It's an easy and accessible snack, as well as a great addition to salads, smoothies, and stir-fries. While some people might worry about the amount of calories found in a serving of nuts, their nutrient density makes them a no-brainer (forgive the pun). They are easy to carry with you, extremely filling, and, once again, turn up that BDNF to help make your brain more resistant to stress.

"There's been a cascade of data in the past decade, with studies consistently showing that food matters to mental health," said Ramsey. "And food, for the most part, is a factor that is under everyone's control."

Small Changes, Big Effects

Making a spinach and Swiss chard salad when you're struggling to get out of bed in the morning can seem pretty ridiculous, and maybe even impossible. It's important to understand that changing diet alone probably won't cure mental illness, just as taking an antidepressant alone, and doing nothing else, probably won't cure depression. Nutrition as a self-care strategy for mental health works best when you're utilizing it alongside the other skills in your self-care playbook. Since we've already reviewed the evidence together, you know that science supports the idea that nutrition is medicine for the mind. Believing in the healing power of food is all that's needed to start implementing small changes to what you put on your plate.

I understand you may be hesitant to change the way you eat. It's not easy because we all have specific food preferences, things we like to eat and things we don't. What if you don't like nuts, or you're repelled by the smell of fish? What if you're a vegetarian or a vegan? What if you have certain food allergies or sensitivities? What if you don't have time to cook? It's important to acknowledge that we don't all like or tolerate the same foods. That's okay. You can make any type of diet more Mediterranean with a little bit of effort.

The best way to start is by taking a hard look at your current diet. I recommend, for a week or two, keeping track of the foods you eat. I might even put a star by those meals that you really enjoy or eat on a regular basis. Then you can estimate how Mediterranean your diet already is.

The Mediterranean Diet Food Score is a quick and easy way to see how closely your diet follows the typical Mediterranean diet. Once you've completed your food journal, look over entries and answer the following questions. For every question you answer yes to, give yourself a point.

1. Do you eat two or more cups of vegetables each day?
2. Do you eat two or more pieces of fruit each day?
3. Do you eat two or more servings of whole grains each day?
4. Do you eat fish or seafood two or more times each week?
5. Do you consume two or more servings of legumes each week?
6. Do you eat a handful of nuts most days of the week?
7. Do you use olive oil instead of other fats?
8. Do you eat two or fewer servings of red meat each week?

Now add up your points based on your yes answers. If you've scored a 7 or above, you can rest assured you are already eating in the Mediterranean style. If you scored a 5 or higher, you're still doing quite well. You can also probably see where you could make some changes, maybe by adding nuts to your snack repertoire or reducing the amount of red meat you consume. If you are within the 3–4 range, you have already adopted some elements of the

Mediterranean diet but there's definite room for improvement. Again, look at the questions where you answered no. Is there an opportunity to make changes there? If you scored a 2 or lower? Well, your score indicates that you aren't following the Mediterranean diet and, as a consequence, are missing out on all those health benefits.

While the Mediterranean diet provides a fantastic foundation for making healthy changes, there's no reason to completely overhaul what you eat. Not only is that kind of sweeping transition unnecessary; without a more moderate approach, you'll probably get frustrated and quickly give up. Instead, make small changes and take it from there. Starting small could include things like switching out vegetable oil for olive oil, adding pumpkin seeds to your favorite trail mix, or throwing a handful of frozen red peppers into your soup. If you're into seafood, you can also add anchovies to a salad or pizza, or order fish tacos the next time you're at a restaurant or food truck. Increasing the nutrient density of your diet won't happen overnight, either. Take your time, and make small moves, so you can support changes that over the long term will allow you to enjoy what you are eating.

Ramsey is a huge proponent of what he calls a "brainbow" salad. Instead of your basic bowl of iceberg lettuce and cucumber, he likes to jazz it up by adding colorful fruits and vegetables. But do it your way with the foods you like to eat. When Ramsey taught me how to make "brainbow" salad, I used what was already in my fridge and based my recipe off a traditional salad called Gỏi that I often make with my wife, who is Vietnamese. My version of a "brainbow" involves tossing chopped green and red cabbage, carrots, red onion, bean sprouts, mint, cilantro, and peanuts in a bowl. We then top it with shrimp, chicken, or tofu, and we use a fish sauce–based dressing to finish it off. My wife and I are getting all those brain-boosting nutrients you find in colorful fruits and vegetables, but we're doing it on our own terms.

When Cory and I talked about his eating habits, he told me that instant ramen was his most convenient go-to food. It's not uncommon for people to gravitate toward carb-heavy meals for a quick mood boost. They are called "comfort" foods for a reason; they tend to increase the amounts of serotonin in the brain. Since Cory wanted to eat ramen, the challenge was to find ways to make it more nutritious. Packing in more nutrient density was an easy fix by adding mushrooms, bok choy, some lean protein, and a soft-boiled egg. "People often feel shame about their dietary preferences—they shouldn't," said Ramsey. "You can find ways to add nutrients that work with your own individual tastes."

Overcoming Food Challenges

While it is easy to say we all have control over what we eat, there are practical challenges for some people when it comes to making necessary changes to their diet. Purchasing whole or organic foods can be expensive, and living in "food deserts," where grocery stores are sparse and fast-food chains are rampant, can make finding so-called super foods even more of a challenge. As I already mentioned, many people may have food sensitivities or allergies to contend with. It's undeniable that these obstacles exist, but there are still ways to improve your diet despite them.

"While, too often, the foods that get the spotlight are organic blueberries, which are very expensive and hard to get out of season, those aren't the only nutrient-dense foods out there," he explained. "The tale we've all been told is that healthy food is expensive, hard to cook, and doesn't taste very good, but that doesn't have to be the case. You can find a way to add some leafy greens to foods you already enjoy. You can grab a can of wild salmon or tuna to get your seafood. You can eat what's available and in season, or what's on sale. There's no one right way to eat your way to better mental health."

This is another reason why it's important to start small and build from there when it comes to making your diet more Mediterranean. You don't have to buy out the health food aisle (or spend your whole paycheck) to add more nutrient density to your meals. You can simply add an egg here, some fresh leafy herbs there, and throw in a handful of nuts where you can. Once you begin to make incremental changes, you'll find new and exciting ways to add more of those little mood-boosting extras to meals you and your loved ones can truly savor.

Nutrients to Consider

We already discussed the Mediterranean Diet Score as a solid foundation for starting basic food switches and swaps, but there are also some foods that are just incredibly nutrient-dense—meaning you can get a lot of brain-boosting nutrition—that we should also address. While Ramsey and LaChance identified twelve major nutrients that can help people prevent and better manage depression, I've found that five nutrients, in particular, are useful to focus on when you are beginning to use food as a self-care strategy for mental health: omega-3 fatty acids, L-theanine, B vitamins, vitamin D, and probiotics.

LONG-CHAIN OMEGA-3 FATTY ACIDS. These polyunsaturated fatty acids (PUFAs) are a type of healthy fat that is found abundantly in oily fish. Eicosatetraenoic acid (EPA) and docosahexaenoic acid (DHA) are among the most important for mental health. You can include these nutrients in your diet by incorporating seafoods like wild salmon, sardines, and bivalves (like mussels and oysters). If you don't like seafood, or you're a vegetarian or a vegan, you can get these nutrients by eating plant-based foods including flaxseed, chia seeds, Brussels sprouts, and walnuts. Plant-based options consist of a fatty acid called alpha-linolenic acid (ALA) that the body naturally converts to EPA and DHA, but generally in small amounts. Another way to increase omega-3s in your diet is to pay attention to food labels when you're at the grocery store. Several brands of milks, juices, and nut butters are fortified with DHA. A diet that's rich in omega-3 fatty acids is great for combating the type of inflammation that's thought to be associated with mental illness. Research has also found reduced DHA levels in the brain's prefrontal cortex from postmortem studies of patients with major depression and bipolar disorder, and victims of suicide. Additional studies have shown that taking an omega-3 supplement consisting mostly of EPA can reduce symptoms of depression and ADHD. That's why psychiatrists are joining cardiologists in recommending adding two to three servings of oily fish to your diet every week (since it's always best to get your nutrients from food). If seafood isn't an option, go for plant-based choices like adding flaxseeds to your smoothies or walnuts to a hearty salad.

L-THEANINE. This amino acid, commonly found in both black and green tea, is one of my favorite recommendations for managing anxiety. L-theanine not only has powerful anti-inflammatory properties, but it also can help instill a sense of calm pretty quickly. Its antianxiety properties are thought to involve its ability to turn down the volume on glutamate (which is responsible for getting us revved up) and turn up the volume on GABA (which helps us calm down). It can also increase serotonin and dopamine production in the brain. It's a great option for a quick and calming mood boost. Since green and black tea also contain caffeine, it can be a great option for inducing a calm state of awareness, without the jitters. For a decent L-theanine fix, I recommend matcha tea, which may contain as much as five times the L-theanine as your common bag of green tea. Unlike common green tea, matcha tea is grown in the shade in the final weeks before harvesting, and then ground into a fine, bright-green powder. I also find the process of making matcha tea to be a calming ritual in and of itself; it involves whisking the powder in a small bowl instead of dropping a tea bag into a cup of warm water. Some studies even show that L-theanine can help reduce blood pressure during a stressful event. It goes to show that tea can satisfy your caffeine fix and add a calming nutrient mood boost for good measure.

B VITAMINS. B vitamins, particularly vitamins B_6, B_{12}, and folate, are nutrients that play a useful role in brain development as well as aid in the production of neurotransmitters (like serotonin and dopamine) that help regulate mood. These vitamins also help build myelin, the fatty "insulation" that allows brain cells and circuits to communicate with each other more efficiently. When your diet doesn't have enough B vitamins, the brain suffers. To protect your mental health, you want to be sure you are incorporating some foods with these nutrients at every meal. You can find B vitamins in leafy greens, whole grains, pork, mussels, and eggs.

VITAMIN D. The United States has a vitamin D problem; many of us are deficient, and that's not ideal. Vitamin D is converted to its active form by sunlight and it's known for its anti-inflammatory properties. Spending just ten minutes per day outside in midday sunlight can help improve vitamin D levels. While there are legitimate concerns about sun exposure and skin cancer, some studies show that you can continue to wear sunscreen without compromising vitamin D production. When it comes to food, egg yolks, mushrooms, salmon, and sardines—as well as vitamin D–fortified foods like milk and cereal—are ways to increase levels of this essential nutrient. Scientists have linked vitamin D deficiency to a host of diseases, ranging from cancer to depression. While researchers are still determining the exact role vitamin D plays in the development and prevention of mental illness, there is some research showing that vitamin D can help reduce symptoms of depression. Since by some accounts, up to 42 percent of the United States population is vitamin D deficient, it makes sense to focus on ways to include vitamin D–rich foods in your diet for improving physical and mental health.

PROBIOTICS. Remember those good bugs that make up your microbiome? You can help keep those populations of bacteria healthy and hearty by eating more fermented foods (yogurt, kefir, kombucha, sauerkraut, and kimchi), fibrous fruits and veggies (bananas, grapefruit, and beans), as well as incorporating more nuts and seeds (almonds or flaxseeds) into your diet. With the brain and gut in such close communication, it pays to have a diverse microbiome. A number of studies suggest that regular probiotic consumption may prevent mental illness, and it can help improve symptoms of depression and anxiety as well.

What About Supplements?

As you read through this, you may be thinking, "I already take a multivitamin. Doesn't that provide enough nutritional insurance?"

The answer isn't a straight yes or no. Many of the studies that have looked at the role of specific nutrients on mental health have used supplements so researchers could more accurately measure the dosage for their analyses. When it comes to a basic multivitamin, however, I haven't come across compelling evidence that it will help treat or prevent mental illness. Some herbs and adaptogens like ashwagandha, maca, and rhodiola do have a growing body of evidence indicating they may be useful for improving mental health and treating illnesses like generalized anxiety or mild forms of depression. Like prescription medications, herbs and adaptogens have potential side effects and, without proper guidance from a health-care professional trained in integrative medicine, they can be dangerous.

Within the medical community, there exists an ongoing debate about the necessity of supplements when it comes to preventing disease and supporting health. Some of my colleagues recommend supplements for all of their patients and others automatically scoff at the idea. It can be equally confusing if you're following the evidence. One day I might come across a study indicating that a specific supplement lowers that risk for cancer and heart disease and the next week I'll read a study suggesting that that same supplement actually increases cancer and heart disease risk. Most health experts agree that the best way to get your nutrients is from food. It's time-tested, doesn't have hidden side effects, and presents nutrition to your body in a way that it can recognize and absorb.

That being said, there are cases where supplementation might make sense. Most ob-gyns, for example, recommend a prenatal vitamin for expectant mothers to reduce the risk of neural tube defects in their unborn child. There's some good evidence for riboflavin supplementation for migraine prevention—and an iron supplement might be recommended for someone with anemia. There are other individualized cases, like supplementing with fish oil or L-theanine if getting these nutrients from food might be challenging for you. It is always best to check with your doctor first before going down the supplement route. If your intention is getting as much of your nutrition from food as possible, that's the best place to start.

The Bottom Line

Nutrition is an essential part of protecting and maintaining your mental health. Ramsey and I agree that eating for mental health goes beyond just the food itself. It's about making the act of eating more mindful and joyful. Prepare dishes you enjoy, cook with your family, and take the time to savor the pleasures that both good food and good company provide.

"My food prescription for patients is seafood, greens, nuts, and beans—and a little bit of dark chocolate," said Ramsey. "For too long, there have been a lot of talking heads arguing about healthy eating—and, frankly, they've been debating the wrong things. In the past, no one has been focused on mental health. But we're learning that when you can add more nutrient-dense foods to your plate in a way that you like, it's a very powerful act that can help you keep your brain healthy."

Your Self-Care Playbook: Tried-and-True Ways to Nourish Your Mental Health

Now that you understand the role food plays in nourishing your mental health, it is even more important to include nutrient-dense meals in your self-care playbook. As previously mentioned, there's no need for a complete overhaul of your diet; that's not what we're going for. Instead, look for small ways that you can add mood-boosting foods to what you already like to eat. That way, you can optimize your mental health and also have a little fun along the way.

Make the Trade

As we talked about before, it's fairly simple to add nutrient-dense foods to your diet just by making some targeted substitutions. Instead of coffee every day, throw in an occasional cup of matcha tea; you'll get a burst of caffeine to help you wake up as well as a calming L-theanine boost. The next time it comes to ordering takeout, consider going for a fish dish, or asking for some roasted veggies instead of french fries on the side. By making these little changes, you're putting yourself in the best position to eventually begin noticing big changes in the way you feel.

Leaf It Up

There's a reason why so many health experts suggest eating a predominately plant-based diet. Fruits and veggies are loaded with phytonutrients that help fight inflammation and provide the building blocks for your brain. To get the most out of these nutrient-dense foods, add more leafy greens to your meals. You can toss some kale or spinach into your favorite chicken soup or stew, and red leaf lettuce tastes great in tacos and wraps. Incorporating more vegetables into your diet, even if you love meat, has evidence-based benefits for your physical and mental health.

Make Comfort Foods More Nutrient-Dense

There's no reason for you to give up your favorite comfort foods, especially if you are dealing with depression or anxiety. Instead, make them the foundation to which you add more nutrient-dense foods. For instance, add sardines to your favorite pasta dish for an omega-3 fix. You can mix kale with your morning smoothie, or even add it to a rich, decadent mac and cheese dish. There's no need to give up the foods you love. Instead, think about ways you can augment them to better nourish your brain.

Think Small

When you start small, you can build up from there, finding your own unique ways to add distinct tastes and flavors to your go-to dishes. Committing yourself to eating your way to happiness by making the right food choices will make you feel better before you even start. Knowing that what you put on your plate can potentially impact your mood is empowering, and that realization gives you more control over your life. When you can be more proactive, taking charge of your food to bolster your mental health, you will get a little extra oomph that will make the food's effects even more pronounced.

CHAPTER 10

MOVING YOUR BODY FOR YOUR MIND

To keep the body in good health is a duty . . . otherwise
we shall not be able to keep our mind strong and clear.
—*Buddha*

Lewis had always been athletic. He had played multiple sports throughout high school and college, and even joined his company softball team once he started working. Now, in his early forties, he didn't have as much time for competitive sports, but he always made sure he had an active gym membership close to home. He had a reliable routine of heading straight there after work, hitting the weights, and then finishing up with a quick run on the treadmill.

During our first visit, Lewis told me he was feeling stuck. He didn't think he had a mental illness, but he was not happy with the way his life was going. He and his long-term girlfriend had recently separated. Although he wanted to regroup and move on with his life, Lewis found himself rehashing the same old disputes and disagreements with his ex. It was clear they were both having a hard time letting go and, instead, remained in a form of relationship purgatory. Not together, not apart—and not doing much more than making each other miserable with their daily quarrels.

Lewis had started seeing a psychologist for talk therapy not long after his breakup, after noticing a post on social media encouraging people to find someone to talk to about their problems before they got out of hand. After a few months of regular visits, however, Lewis felt like he was stuck in the same pattern of going nowhere that he was already in with his ex. Lewis and his therapist were having the same conversations again and again. He couldn't seem to find a way to move forward. By the time Lewis came to see me, he freely admitted he wasn't sure he even knew how to move forward.

At his annual physical, Lewis's primary care physician, after hearing about his change in mood and drop in motivation, as well as noticing a bit of weight gain, prescribed a common antidepressant medication. Lewis took his pills every morning, like clockwork, but he didn't feel like they were doing much of anything. He hoped a different medication, or perhaps a different dosage, might help him come to terms with the breakup, feel less anxious about it, and move on with his life. After months waiting for his life to improve, without much effect, he eventually came to see me.

"I don't like to go out much anymore," he told me. "I'm just so afraid I'll run into my ex. I don't have the bandwidth to deal with it."

Because of that fear, Lewis spent the majority of his free time lying in bed, watching movies, and fielding those contentious phone calls from his old girlfriend. He said he was waiting for something to change, but he wasn't sure what type of change would make the biggest difference. He explained to me that he had even stopped going to the gym over the past few months.

"I haven't felt up to it," he said. "I have a bum hip from football. I hurt it way back in high school. When it acts up, I know I need to stay out of the gym. I don't want to make it worse."

As we talked more, it became clear that Lewis wasn't just taking a break from working out. Rather, he wasn't moving much at all. Each day, Lewis went from his apartment to his car to work to his car and then back to his apartment again. According to his phone, if he cleared three thousand steps in a twenty-four-hour period, it was an active day for him. As a person who had been accustomed to moving his body, this was a precipitous drop in Lewis's regular physical activity. That was one of the things that stood out as a big red flag for me the first time we spoke in my office.

Since Lewis told me his medication wasn't doing anything for him, I initially prescribed a new antidepressant to see if that might help with improving his energy and calming his racing thoughts. A few weeks later, during our appointment, Lewis said that, like the previous prescription, the new one wasn't working, either. He was still living the same kind of *Groundhog Day*–type of life. By this point, he wondered if he even had the capacity to feel better than he already did. After discussing the five pillars of self-care for mental health during one of our visits, Lewis decided that focusing on movement was a good place for him to start.

A few visits later, he came to see me and reported feeling much better. The effect was so dramatic that it initially caught both of us off guard. As we talked, he told me that he had intentionally gone to the gym for some light workouts. After a workout, he noticed dramatic improvements in his mood. He felt more motivated and a sense of calm, even to the extent that he felt in better control of his emotions during tense telephone conversations with his ex. After the next few trips to the gym, he realized he was continuing to feel better, and he allowed himself the space to acknowledge that moving his body was directly improving his mental health. After resuming his gym routine, he was feeling the best he had in a long time.

"I still don't always want to go to the gym," he told me. "But I feel really good when I'm done with my workout—and that feeling lasts. I keep that in mind when I start thinking about skipping."

I could relate to what Lewis was saying. I noticed the same sort of mood-boosting buzz after a yoga class when I was living with depression. Yoga, of course, has the added benefits of intentional breath and a spiritual component to help bolster mental health. But it also is a form of movement—and movement, in any form, is a powerful tool that can help improve your mood as well as your overall sense of well-being.

Moving into Health

Even before I discovered yoga, I recognized that moving my body has the power to make me feel good. When I lived in New York City, I'd spend hours walking from Lincoln Center to Times Square, up to Columbia University, and then back down to Juilliard. I would slip on my headphones, lost in the rhythm of my favorite music, and sometimes walk for hours. I found that those walks did an incredible job of clearing my mind, relaxing my body, and leveling my mood, even on the most stressful days. Since then, I've known, intrinsically, that movement plays an important role in maintaining my mental health. I feel better after going on a quick run, walking my dog, or practicing an hour of yoga. Moving makes me feel good.

You've probably heard a lot of people talk about how "cardiovascular exercise" or "working out" are mental health boosters. Certainly, that's true—and the scientific evidence backs up these claims. What you may not know is that you don't have to run a marathon, engage in high-intensity interval training (HIIT), or dead press 250 pounds to enjoy those mental health effects. All you need is to move your body. It really doesn't take all that much. While Lewis is a fan of quick sprints on the treadmill, and I now gravitate toward my yoga mat, there is also a benefit in taking a short walk around the neighborhood, a quick dance break in the kitchen while making dinner, or working in your garden on a sunny afternoon. What is most important to your mental health is that you find ways to move your body that you actually enjoy, and that you'll stick with, even when you aren't feeling your best. Many people struggle with the idea of adding more movement to their lives but, when you come to understand that movement is actually medicine, like antidepressant medications, it can become an integral part of treatment.

Joseph Firth, PhD, a researcher at the University of Manchester in the United Kingdom, has spent his career looking at the benefits of physical activity on mental health. He is one of an emerging group of scientists who are observing strong evidence that regular movement can not only help prevent and manage physical health problems like cardiovascular disease, type 2 diabetes, and cancer; it can also support strong mental health. In addition to that, it works for everyone. Firth's own research studies have demonstrated that regular movement not only works to prevent mental illness if you're healthy, but it also helps alleviate debilitating symptoms in those diagnosed with more severe mental illnesses, like schizophrenia and bipolar disorder.

"Based on the evidence we're seeing, we're really emphasizing the importance of reducing sedentary behavior," said Firth. "Even the World Health Organization (WHO) has now updated its physical activity guidelines to say that every move counts; acknowledging that doing something is better than nothing. We've got such sedentary lifestyles nowadays that we're not doing what our bodies need to just function normally."

That includes our brains—and when we don't move regularly, our mental health suffers as a result.

An Evolutionary Explanation

In order to understand why movement is critically important for mental health, consider what everyday life was like for our ancestors centuries ago. Long before the advent of supermarkets and kitchen appliances, human beings lived the hunter-gatherer life. To support basic survival, they had to constantly be on the move so they could find ample sources of food and water. They also needed to remain on high alert for any potential predators. That kind of vigilant activity takes a fair amount of brain power. Given the fact that the human brain needs so much energy to work its best—the brain calls dibs on about 20 percent of the body's total energy stores—many evolutionary biologists believe that our brains naturally evolved to work best when our bodies are on the move. Movement enhances the flow of oxygen-rich blood to the brain as well as promotes neural connectivity. When you think about it, it makes a lot of sense.

"As a hunter-gatherer species, you have to move through the environment to survive," said Firth. "When you are active and moving is also when your brain needs to be the most active and switched on. That's because you are hunting, you are looking for berries and other foods. You want to make sure you're not covering the same ground. You are finding new sources of food and you're keeping an eye out for threats."

According to Firth, there's evidence that exercise results in our muscles releasing brain-derived neurotrophic factor (BDNF). Remember that BDNF is that brain molecule that helps keep our brains fit and nimble, so we can better adapt to the world around us, but it also helps to protect our brains from stress. You can imagine that our forebears, as they were traipsing around the savanna looking for food, would benefit from that extra brain "fertilizer." It would keep them sharper, allowing them to be more creative about how they went about finding and acquiring different foods. It would also allow them to watch out for predators without being totally done in by the stress of the endeavor. That extra BDNF could help them keep ahead of any environmental hazards and threats—ensuring their safety and well-being. Not to mention, it would also help motivate them to continue on, even when food, perhaps, had been scarce for some time.

"[The release of BDNF] is an evolved consequence; our bodies were designed so that the brain and body are active together," said Firth. "When we take away that physical activity, you end up taking away that boost for the brain as well."

Today, of course, we don't need to look any further than the local market or convenience store to gather our food. We don't even have to go ourselves—a few taps on a smartphone app means you can have your favorites delivered to your door within the hour. We also, for the most part, don't have to worry as much about predators or environmental hazards. The end result is that the vast majority of us spend our lives seated and sluggish, our bodies doing the bare minimum to stay upright. This can have a profound negative effect on both our physical and our mental health.

"We are doing nowhere near the levels of physical activity that our bodies were designed to do just to function normally," said Firth. "That's why everyone has diabetes, high blood pressure, and other health problems. And, as part of that, we've got no BDNF. We don't have that brain power anymore. That's fundamentally why we need a healthy, moving body to have a healthy mind."

The human body wasn't designed to be sedentary. It needs to move in order to thrive. This doesn't mean you have to emulate the hunter-gatherer lifestyle, said Firth—you probably couldn't if you tried. It doesn't even mean that you have to be a super-athlete of some sort. Leave the marathons and endurance swims for the people who actually enjoy them. Rather, it's all about finding ways to sit less and move more. Doing so not only may prevent physical health problems from emerging but also will help your brain work its best, and that means improved mental health.

Exercise versus Anxiety

Think about the way your body feels when you are nervous or stressed out. You can go back to the grizzly bear approaching the campsite example we discussed in Chapter 6, if you'd like. Or maybe you can conjure how you felt before a public speaking event, a big sports competition, or even those moments just before you asked your partner out for the first time. As you likely recall, in these moments, your sympathetic nervous system kicks in. Your breath quickens, your heart rate accelerates, and your blood pressure starts to rise. Blood rushes to your brain as well as to your arm and leg muscles. Your body, thanks to its sympathetic nervous system response, is ready for you to think fast, move fast, and deal with the situation at hand in the best way possible.

Now, consider how your body responds to physical exertion. Do you notice the similarities? There is quite a bit of overlap between how the body responds to physical exertion and how it responds to anxiety. Shorter, shallower breaths? Check. Elevated heart rate? Indeed. Increased blood pressure? Also, yes. You probably also have sweaty palms and dry mouth. The two states are nearly identical.

I mention the similarities of physiological symptoms here because (a) they help to illustrate how exercise ties together the body and mind through the sympathetic nervous system response, as Firth explained, and (b) exercise offers an opportunity for you to learn how to manage these symptoms in a controlled environment before you go into full sympathetic overdrive.

Let me explain. Another patient of mine, Jess, was a star volleyball player for her college team. Although she played throughout high school without much of an issue, by the time she reached college, NCAA-level competition resulted in her experiencing horrible pre-match anxiety. When she came to see me, she said she'd been spending an hour before each game vomiting in the bathroom.

Antianxiety medications helped calm her down, but they interfered with her performance on the volleyball court. She told me they made her feel tired and decreased her reaction time.

"I'm no longer puking, which is definitely a plus," she told me. "But I'm so much less alert when I get out there. I just feel like I'm in a fog when I need to be at the top of my game."

Her story reminded me of my pre-performance jitters when I was a student at Juilliard. I should tell you that playing live at Avery Fisher Hall in New York City has a way of ratcheting up your nerves. It got to the point where I started doing one hundred jumping jacks or taking a quick run-in-place before I practiced at home, because I wanted to simulate the feeling I'd experience onstage. By using aerobic exercise to engage my sympathetic nervous system, I became more aware of what would likely happen in my body in response to the emotional stress of an audition or a live performance. That helped me to learn, over time, how to acknowledge that physiological response and perform despite my nerves. For example, I learned that if I intentionally activated my sympathetic nervous system by running in place, after I stopped running I could always inactivate my sympathetic response by taking slow, coherent breaths. It took some practice, but eventually I learned that I still had some control over my body's natural response to anxiety. Ultimately, the time I spent practicing how to manage my sympathetic nervous system made a huge difference for those big performances.

When I suggested that Jess try something similar, she was skeptical. She didn't think jumping jacks would do it for her (and let's face it, they might not have; she was in much, much better physical shape than I was as a student). But as we talked more about strategies to help her manage her anxiety, she told me about how, at one volleyball summer camp, the locker room showers had only cold water.

"I hated it so much," she said. "I'd just have worked out for the day, but I'd feel my heart beating out of my chest just anticipating that freezing water. I got out of there as soon as I possibly could."

That physical response to cold water was something she could use to help her simulate her own sympathetic nervous system response. To help better manage her pre-game anxiety, Jess started taking an icy, cold shower before volleyball practice. This mimicked her nervous state and gave her the opportunity to find ways to manage those feelings outside of the high-stakes situation of a college game. Jess also found breath work useful in curbing her stage fright, especially 4-7-8 breathing, and started using the technique before joining her team on the court.

While the shower and breath work combination didn't immediately or completely relieve Jess's anxiety, it had a cumulative effect. Within a few weeks, although she still felt nervous before playing, she managed to perform without losing her lunch before each match. She could use these self-care techniques to help her better manage anxiety so she could concentrate on playing her best game.

The Many Benefits of Movement

As Lewis and I talked more about exercise during our sessions, he told me he enjoyed high-intensity running intervals on the treadmill, where you intersperse bursts of all-out sprints with lower-intensity jogging.

"You do these intervals, and I can sometimes catch a runner's high," he said. "Even if I don't, though, I still end up feeling nice and relaxed for the rest of the day."

Many elite athletes talk about achieving a runner's high during intense physical activity that's accompanied by feelings of euphoria, relaxation, and decreased sensitivity to pain. As we discussed before, the sympathetic nervous system is activated in response to physical movement (including going for a run). The sympathetic nervous system makes the heart pump faster, working hard to get oxygenated blood to where it's most needed. Endorphins (chemicals in the body that may reduce perception of physical pain) are released as well as endocannabinoids (chemicals that regulate emotional stress and mood). Although there's some controversy about the role endorphins play in directly affecting mood in response to physical activity, endocannabinoid levels have been found to be elevated in the blood in response to exercise, and that elevation has direct associations with a boost in mood. In essence, when you move your body, feel-good endocannabinoids are released into the bloodstream. From there, they can move directly into the brain. Endocannabinoids have been found to work almost like an antidepressant as well as to reduce our body's physiological response to stress.

It probably doesn't surprise you to learn, given just how interwoven movement and brain health are, that exercise also promotes the release of BDNF as well as neurotransmitters like dopamine, norepinephrine, and serotonin. We already talked about the benefits of increased BDNF. These particular neurotransmitters are linked to not only mood regulation, but also enhanced learning and memory. After all, your hunter-gatherer ancestors didn't just need to be calm and motivated. They also needed to be sure they were at the top of their mental game so they could find food and water sources as quickly as possible.

"Exercise can lead to overall improved mood," said Firth. "It can improve the workings of the threat detection areas of the brain, and how it processes threats and anxiety. In doing so, it can help you modulate your emotions. But it also helps with cognitive deficits."

Many mental illnesses produce cognitive deficits that make it harder to concentrate or work through complex tasks, and may create short-term and long-term memory problems. Experiencing a cognitive deficit as a result of mental illnesses like depression or dementia can impact almost every aspect of your life.

"This makes it much harder to understand social situations and complex social interactions fully," said Firth. "Obviously, cognitive deficits are an annoyance, but they also impact a person's ability to keep a job, keep a friend, or keep a relationship. It has that knock-on effect that makes it harder for people to just get on in day-to-day life. And when you can't get on in day-to-day life, it becomes a vicious cycle, making it even harder to overcome your mental health condition."

That's another reason why regular exercise is so important for mental health. Firth's own research has shown that patients struggling with schizophrenia demonstrate improved cognition after exercise interventions.

"As an adjunctive treatment, we see that exercise can help reduce psychiatric symptoms and improve cognitive function," said Firth. "These are things that can really help with people's real-world functioning."

Not everyone can achieve the runner's high. In fact, most people don't. It takes some pretty intense exercise to get there. However, even simple physical activity and basic movement have been linked to better mood, increased feelings of calmness, and improved cognition. This is why groups like the World Health Organization are strongly advocating for more movement in general. Even in less intense dosages, movement matters when it comes to promoting mental health and overall well-being.

Additional Benefits of Movement

Movement doesn't just jump-start the release of mood-enhancing molecules and neurochemicals like endocannabinoids, serotonin, and BDNF. It also supports mental health by other means. In fact, physical activity, thanks to the way our brains evolved over time, is linked to a variety of advantages that help bolster brain health and, as a consequence, our mental and emotional well-being.

We already talked about how movement can help improve mood and reduce stress. Regular exercise has also been shown to increase your energy levels. All of our cells have small organelles inside them called mitochondria. You may remember them as the wrinkly-looking cell components from eighth-grade science class. These are the cell's energy factories. They give your cells, including your brain cells, the energy they need to function at the top of their game. When you are physically active, your cells are spurred to make even more mitochondria so they can provide enough energy to meet your metabolic needs. As a result, energy can potentially improve, associated with a reduction in fatigue.

Speaking of fatigue, regular movement also helps promote healthier sleep habits. While scientists aren't exactly sure why or even how exercise has such a powerful influence over the way we sleep, study after study has shown regular physical activity improves how quickly you fall asleep, how long you stay asleep, and how much slow wave, or deep sleep, you get over the course of the night. We've already talked about how important sleep is to mental health in Chapter 7. Regular movement is yet another way to help ensure you are getting sufficient z's to keep your brain in healthy, working order.

That's not all, though. Physical activity can help reduce inflammation across the body. You already know that chronic inflammation is linked to not only physical illnesses like cardiovascular disease and diabetes, but mental illnesses like depression, anxiety, and PTSD as well. When you regularly move your body, regardless of whether you are taking a walk or lifting light weights, anti-inflammatory chemicals are produced. When those chemicals are coursing through your bloodstream, they can help counteract cortisol and other stress hormones in the body and brain—and help prevent chronic inflammation and the corresponding development of mental illness.

A Prescription for Movement

Now that you know how movement makes its mark on the brain, you may be wondering how much is enough to get the mental health benefits. As I've already said, what's good for the heart is good for the brain. So perhaps you've seen the American Heart Association's (AHA) guidelines for exercise. It recommends 150 minutes per week of moderate-intensity exercise, which, loosely defined, is anything that gets your heart beating faster than normal. It should quicken your breathing, but you should still be able to carry on a conversation without too much difficulty. A brisk walk, a bike ride on a flat road, or vacuuming your house during a cleaning spree could count as moderate-intensity movement.

For those of you who already are engaged in some form of regular exercise, the AHA says seventy-five minutes of vigorous aerobic activity each week plus two days of resistance training will do the trick. Vigorous exercise takes things up a notch or two. Remember that comfortable conversation you could have with moderate activity? Once things get to the vigorous level, talking becomes a challenge because you are breathing so hard. Conversation time is over. You need your breath to keep your body going. Activities like running, hiking, and popular sports like basketball and soccer all fall into the vigorous exercise category.

You may be thinking, "Well, that's all well and good for heart health. But I want to improve my mental health." As it so happens, the European Psychiatric Association has published its own physical activity guidelines. Its recommendations are nearly identical to the AHA's—150 to 300 minutes of moderate activity per week. While we are still awaiting official exercise recommendations for mental health in the United States, the evidence is increasingly clear: Movement can be an essential component to managing mental illnesses ranging from depression to bipolar disorder.

Firth's own research into exercise and psychiatric care shows that physical activity is of benefit even in more severe mental illnesses like schizophrenia—helping to alleviate many of their symptoms when prescribed in concert with traditional drug therapies. The evidence is emerging to show that when you regularly move your body, and combine that movement with other conventional treatments, you are positioning yourself to best relieve symptoms that often accompany mental illness, like medication-induced weight gain or brain fog.

When I talk to patients about adding more movement to their routines, invariably, one of the first questions is "How?" Not every patient is as experienced as Lewis or Jess when it comes to regular exercise regimens. With so many exercise options out there, they often don't know what they should be doing or even where to begin. Firth said such concerns are more than understandable. Starting may be a challenge, especially when you may be struggling with your current mood or other symptoms of mental illness.

"It can be hard to try to even justify extra stuff like physical activity interventions when there are real consequences of living with the condition [of severe mental illness]," he said. "There is also a lack of availability on the minimum evidence-based care; people can have difficulty getting access to the right medications or even getting to see a doctor in good time. But I'd add our actual first-line treatments and what we consider evidence-based care for mental health conditions don't always have good outcomes. Physical activity can help."

There's no need to join a high-priced gym or even sign up for the local outdoor boot camp classes. Instead, begin where you feel comfortable. Firth recommends starting with whatever physical activity you'd like to and actually are willing to do. If you enjoy dancing, dance. If a run is more your style, lace up your running shoes. If all you can manage is a short walk around the neighborhood, that works as well. Despite numerous studies trying to identify the "right" kind of exercise to improve mental health, the evidence shows the best physical activity is the one that you'll actually do on a regular basis.

"There's too much emphasis on people trying to figure out what's right," said Firth. "Is it aerobic? Resistance? Outdoor exercise? Group exercise? Sports? Realistically, all of those things are great. You don't have to go for a run if you'd rather lift weights. You don't have to lift weights if you'd rather do a yoga class. The more we delve into the different types of exercise, the more we see that all forms of exercise are created equal in terms of general well-being and benefits for overall health."

That means the first step to adding more movement to your routine is to simply come up with small, concrete intentions for your week. Making room for movement, like incorporating more nutrient-dense foods in your diet, should not require an entire lifestyle overhaul all at once. Firth suggests that you will get the most benefit from physical activity when you start small and build from there. For some people, that may be thirty minutes on the treadmill five times a week. For others, it may be a short walk to the mailbox after lunch. Do what you can.

"Pick a goal that you can achieve for the next week or the next month," Firth said. "Then you can revisit that goal once you've met it. Pick a goal that is easy for you to achieve or something that you feel quite enthusiastic about doing. Obviously, if you are an athlete, there may be specific exercises you need to do. But outside of that, your activity should be whatever game or activity you like to play. You can rest assured that the evidence supports that whatever you are doing is the right thing to be doing—so take your own individualized approach to your exercise regimen."

Moving Off the Couch

Our bodies, including our brains, were made to move. Scientists and clinicians now understand, more than ever before, how important physical activity is to our general health and well-being. That includes our mental health.

"It's never too early to start," said Firth. "And you know, it's never too late to start, either. Just find ways to move more."

When you engage in regular physical activity, you will see a wide variety of benefits with regard to your energy levels, your sleep quality, your mood, and your ability to manage stress. Remember, this isn't about marathons or endurance sports. It's simply about moving your body in ways that feel good to you, which over the long term will help promote your own mental health.

Your Self-Care Playbook: Strategies for Moving Your Body for Your Mind

Now that you understand how movement plays a vital role for your mental health, it's important to find ways to incorporate more physical activity into your daily life. Today, sedentary lifestyles are not uncommon, and that lack of movement has the power to affect both our physical and our mental health in detrimental ways.

As you think about how to add more movement into the mix, remember that Rome was not built in a day. No one is expecting you to start training for a triathlon or to run out and join the town rugby league. Like with your diet, trying to completely overhaul your exercise regimen immediately will probably do nothing more than discourage you. Instead, find small ways to add more movement to your daily schedule. Move in ways you enjoy, and start a physical activity routine that you can build upon over time. Here are a few suggestions to help get you moving into mental health.

Move Mindfully

Like with your breath, exercise is a place where having conscious awareness pays off. You need to pay attention to how you feel after you move in order to truly appreciate its many effects. After you decide how you'd like to get moving, start in whatever fashion you choose, but, most important, take time to evaluate your mood when you finish. Too often, we focus only on the physical sensations after physical activity. We pay attention to the soreness in our legs or how exhausted we feel. But it's also useful to check out what's going on with your mood, too. If you notice that you feel better—whether you're more upbeat or you're experiencing improved mental clarity—acknowledge that feeling. Make the connection that moving makes you feel good. In doing so, it will help motivate you to incorporate more movement, even on days when you don't feel like it.

As you know, I recommend yoga because of the mindfulness elements; however, there are other movement-based practices that also help you move in a more mindful way. Tai Chi, dance, and running all offer an opportunity for you to focus on your breath and pay attention to the way your body responds to your thoughts and feelings.

Meet the Moment

It's important to start where you can when it comes to movement. For example, you can make a point of stretching every morning when you get out of bed, or even taking a walk during your lunch break at work. Perhaps you'll decide to do a quick set of ten jumping jacks before a meeting. You can add a leisurely bike ride to your weekends, or just boogie down in the kitchen while you are making dinner for your family. Whatever way you can and want to move is the right way to do it.

Develop a Routine

Make movement nonnegotiable. The evidence is clear: Movement is medicine. It's important to treat it as such. So put your daily walk on your to-do list. Set some alerts on your phone to remind you to get up and move a little in between conference calls. Schedule your gym time or yoga classes in advance. Make movement, like taking your medications, something you *must* do for your overall health and well-being. When you treat it as a given, like brushing your teeth or taking a shower, you are much more likely to do it.

Add a Social Element

Sometimes it can be hard to hold yourself accountable. If you are having an off day, it's all too easy to say you'll just skip whatever physical activity you might have had planned. When you add a social element to movement, whether you're going to a group class or just meeting some friends for a walk, it's harder to blow it off. People are counting on you to be there! Besides the accountability aspect, however, adding a social element to physical activity often makes it a lot more enjoyable and, as a consequence, gives you another reason to stick with it.

There's an App for That

An app and a fitness tracker and even a free online class! While our smartphones and televisions, in some respects, have led to us moving, as a society, much less than we should, there are plenty of opportunities to use these new technologies for good instead of evil. You don't need to pay for high-priced studio classes, a fitness trainer, or even specialty exercise gear to get the most out of movement. There is a plethora of YouTube videos and free apps that can help you keep up with your movement goals and offer you the opportunity to give new activities a try. Use these different technologies to remind you to get up and move, or just keep your physical activity regimen fresh and fun.

EMBODYING THE FIVE PILLARS OF SELF-CARE

Don't count the days, make the days count.
—Muhammad Ali

Living with mental health is a lifelong journey, one that requires patience, perseverance, and engagement. Finding ways to incorporate the five pillars of self-care into your regular routine can offer a strong foundation to bolster your own mental health, whether you are working through a severe mental illness or feeling discontented with the path your life is currently on. The ultimate intention, however, is to strengthen and maintain a mind that is working for you and not against you. That's what is going to help guide you as you navigate the world in a way that supports living your best life.

The five pillars of self-care for mental health—breath, sleep, spirituality, nutrition, and movement—are intricately intertwined.

When one pillar is neglected, the others suffer. If you don't sleep well, you may find yourself gravitating toward carb-loaded comfort foods the next day. If you aren't consuming more nutrient-dense foods, it can be harder to move your body. If you aren't moving your body, your breath is likely to be affected. And, without spirituality, you may have trouble connecting with the people around you, including connecting with your therapist. Truly, each pillar depends on the others, and living with mental health depends on them all. But start with one small change and see how you feel. Maybe start breathing mindfully a few times a day. That might just inspire you to add a daily walk or a light yoga practice. Bit by bit, these small changes will eventually add up to significant improvement in your physical and mental health—which we know now affect each other.

As you try different ways to pay attention to your breath, sleep, spirituality, nutrition, and movement, know that there will be fits and starts. After all, there's no progress in life that happens in a straight, continuous line; growth is a nonlinear process. I submit that any setbacks you experience are not failures. Instead, consider them as learning opportunities. As Samuel Beckett, the famous Irish novelist and playwright, once wrote, "Try again. Fail again. Fail better."

You may have to try several different practices before you find the right ones for yourself, and you may find that some of them are not as easy as you hoped. Setbacks are an expected part of the process. What's more, they are of benefit, as they can teach you how to make meaningful, personalized changes to your self-care playbook that will keep you moving forward. Even though it may not always seem that way in the moment, it's our setbacks that help us learn how to live with purpose, balance, contentment, and hope.

I understand that it is not easy to let go of outdated notions of mental health, or to accept that modern medicine can't offer a pill or intervention that quickly eradicates life's inevitable challenges. While it is easy to come up with a million reasons that diminish the healing power of self-care, I encourage you to prioritize it as evidence-based medicine. As a psychiatrist, the most rewarding part of my work is watching my patients, many of whom came to me during a time of significant emotional distress, begin to appreciate the complexities and richness of their lives. To smile, to laugh, to feel better. Self-care works; it has been time-tested and has proven itself as much as any aspect of modern medicine to be an intervention we all should take seriously.

My aim, as with any patient I meet, is to provide you with the means to support your own resilience and wellness. Even though it may seem that at times there's nothing you can do, self-care offers a set of skills that you can access anytime and anywhere. It gives you the power, control, and agency to understand how to improve your mental health one step at a time. And, even better, self-care works seamlessly in conjunction with medications, talk therapy, and other mental health interventions to help those treatments work better.

I understand that some of you feel stuck, and you may have felt this way for a very long time—but if you've come to the end of this book, you are already on a path to healing. Asking what you can do is the first step. And while incorporating the practices I have presented here may seem difficult or impractical, or even virtually impossible, keep in mind that every day, you are capable of imagining, dreaming, and considering the possibilities of what could potentially become your reality.

My intention is that you will acquire hope and even joy in the process of implementing self-care. It's a process that is not always simple, nor is it without setbacks and restarts, but if living with mental health remains your guiding light, you increase your chance of attaining what we all seek: a beautiful life filled with purpose, balance, contentment, and hope.

ACKNOWLEDGMENTS

During one of my first conversations with my publisher, I asked if she had any advice before I began writing *The Self-Healing Mind*. At that time, I was comfortable writing academic articles and mental health stories for popular blogs and magazines—I figured writing my first book would be no different. But as I sat on my porch on that midsummer day, she offered some words over the telephone that stuck with me.

"Have fun—and it's harder than you think."

She was right. Writing *The Self-Healing Mind* has been a rewarding yet humbling process. And although I hope it is just the first of many books I will write, I will never forget this experience. So I'd like to begin by extending my sincere thanks to Karen Rinaldi. Thank you for your commitment to this book, for your commitment to mental health, and for giving me a platform to share my ideas about a topic I care about so deeply. And to the entire team at Harper Wave who worked with me, particularly Rebecca Raskin and Kirby Sandmeyer, thank you for your assistance in making the writing process enjoyable and fun.

I also owe a debt of gratitude to my patients, whom I learn from every day. Psychiatry is often a misunderstood area of medicine that has long struggled to break free of the stigma society places on it. And that's just one of many barriers, including the cost of visits and limited health insurance coverage, which make scheduling an appointment with a psychiatrist not only an investment but an act of courage. I admire my patients for seeking treatment and sticking with it. Watching you recover inspires me, and this book would not be possible without you. Thank you for allowing me to take part in your health and wellness journey.

In many ways book writing is like designing a structure that is both beautiful and durable. To Kayt Sukel, thank you for being the architect, and for keeping me on point. You helped me convey my ideas in a way that made sense. I loved working with you and building this project together.

Several stories, expert interviews, and hope narratives were included in the text to help personify self-care. I'd like to thank those who allowed me to include their voices: Dr. Anoop Kumar, Kevin Hines, Dr. Irving Kirsch, Dr. Joseph Firth, Pastor Blake Wilson, Dr. Ronique Wilson, Danae Mercer, Alec Brownridge, Chris Isom, and Marcus Smith. All of you are wellness advocates and stigma fighters. Keep up the good fight.

I'd especially like to acknowledge Dr. Drew Ramsey. Drew not only contributed his expert opinions for the chapter on nutrition but is also my mentor and a good friend. You are paving the way, Drew, for so many psychiatrists and mental health professionals by teaching us that we can extend wellness advocacy beyond the walls of our clinics. Thank you for the constructive criticism, the encouragement, and taking time to share ideas about how we can make mental health accessible to as many people as possible.

I am thankful to the many professional organizations I am a part of—including the Center for Green Psychiatry (particularly my friend and dedicated psychiatric nurse practitioner, Hannah Green), the American Psychiatric Association (APA), and the Dell Medical School at the University of Texas–Austin—that have supported my work. I'd like to especially thank Erin Connors and the APA's media relations team for regularly inviting me to include my expert opinions for stories about mental health in the news. Additionally, to several of my psychiatrist colleagues—Dr. Sue Varma, Dr. Jessi Gold, Dr. Altha Stewart, Dr. Kevin Simon, Dr. Pooja Lakshmin, Dr. Ian Crooks, Dr. Robin May-Davis, Dr. Sonia Krishna, Dr. Cole Weatherby, Dr. Nakia Scott, and Dr. Kristin Yeung Lasseter—my admiration for you motivates me to become the best psychiatrist I can be.

Most of us are thinking about mental health, even if we aren't talking about it. *Men's Health* magazine, where I have written a monthly mental health column and co-hosted a series called *Friday Sessions*, has helped change that by including engaging mental health content in its publications. Ben Court, Rich Dorment, Spencer Dukoff, Nojan Aminosharei, and Marty Munson, thank you for showing guys that taking care of mental health is the coolest thing they can do. I am honored to work with all of you.

To my team at United Talent Agency: Mary Pender, Ana Mijich, Nia Nation, Olivia Fanaro, and Lia Aponte, thank you for supporting my projects and believing in me. And to Dr. Bret Stetka, who has given me a voice on Medscape, thank you for inviting me to discuss evidence-based approaches to mental health for clinicians that include prescriptions for yoga, self-care, and kindness.

I'd also like to thank the men and women I have interviewed about topics related to mental health and self-care, particularly: Common, Ant Anstead, Lisa Ling, Mark Groves, Dr. Travis Stork, Don Lemon, Dr. Kelli Harding, Dr. Jenny Wang, Dr. Paul Song, Dr. David Eagleman, Ruston Kelly, Branden Harvey, and Marcus Smith. I appreciate your commitment to mental health and the kindness you have shown me.

To Joy Tutela and the David Black Literary Agency: I struggle to find words that describe how much I appreciate everything you have done for me. Thank you, Joy, for dreaming with me, telling me what I need to hear, and helping me make ideas happen. So much of my work would not be possible without your guidance, and I am grateful to have you in my corner.

Writing a book takes a team that extends beyond agents, editors, and publishers. I am forever grateful to my wife for her many sacrifices, and for all of those nights and weekends sitting next to me with her head on my shoulder while I typed my next paragraph. And finally, to my parents. You have seen me on both sides of the therapist's couch, and it is your love above all else that has saved me. Thank you.

NOTES

Chapter 1: Redefining Mental Health

19   The American Psychiatric Association (APA) defines mental illness: Ranna Parekh, "What Is Mental Illness?," American Psychiatric Association, August 2018, https://www.psychiatry.org/patients-families /what-is-mental-illness.

24   homosexuality was considered a mental illness: Jack Drescher, "Out of DSM: Depathologizing Homosexuality," *Behavioral Sciences* (Basel, Switzerland) 5, no. 4 (December 2015): 565–75, https://www.ncbi.nlm. nih.gov/pmc/articles/PMC4695779/.

24   mentions of it as a qualifier: Robert P. Cabaj, "Working with LGBTQ Patients," American Psychiatric Association, accessed March 24, 2021, https://www.psychiatry.org/psychiatrists/cultural-competency /education/best-practice-highlights/working-with-lgbtq-patients.

25   depression is one of the leading causes of disability worldwide: "Depression," World Health Organization, accessed March 24, 2021, https://www.who.int/health-topics/depression#tab=tab_1.

25   anxiety disorders: Saloni Dattani, Hannah Ritchie, and Max Roser, "Mental Health," *Our World in Data*, January 20, 2018, https://our worldindata.org/mental-health.

29   mind-body practices like yoga: Catherine Woodyard, "Exploring the Therapeutic Effects of Yoga and Its Ability to Increase Quality of Life," *International Journal of Yoga* 4, no. 2 (July–December 2011): 49–54, https://www.ncbi.nlm.nih.gov/pmc/articles/PMC3193654/.

29   omega-3 fatty acids: Richa Rathod, Anvita Kale, and Sadhana Joshi, "Novel Insights into the Effect of Vitamin B_{12} and Omega-3 Fatty Acids on Brain Function," *Journal of Biomedical Science* 23 (2017): 17, https://www.ncbi.nlm.nih.gov/pmc/articles/PMC4727338/.

29   B vitamins: Lauren M. Young, Andrew Pipingas, David J. White, Sarah

Gauci, and Andrew Scholey, "A Systematic Review and Meta-Analysis of B Vitamin Supplementation on Depressive Symptoms, Anxiety, and Stress: Effects on Healthy and 'At-Risk' Individuals," *Nutrients* 11, no. 9 (September 2019): 2232, https://www.ncbi.nlm.nih.gov/pmc/articles /PMC6770181/.

Chapter 2: Your Beautiful Mind

32 (STAR*D) study: Nhu N. Huynh and Roger S. McIntyre, "What Are the Implications of the STAR*D Trial for Primary Care? A Review and Synthesis," *Primary Care Companion to the Journal of Clinical Psychiatry* 10, no. 2 (2008): 91–96, https://www.ncbi.nlm.nih.gov/pmc/articles /PMC2292446/.

34 prefrontal cortex: A. F. T. Arnsten, "Ameliorating Prefrontal Cortical Dysfunction in Mental Illness: Inhibition of Phosphotidyl Inositol-Protein Kinase C Signaling," *Psychopharmacology* (Berlin) 202, nos. 1–3 (January 2009): 445–55, https://www.ncbi.nlm.nih.gov/pmc/articles /PMC2864782/.

34 amygdala: Cynthia M. Schumann, Melissa D. Bauman, and David G. Amaral, "Abnormal Structure or Function of the Amygdala Is a Common Component of Neurodevelopmental Disorders," *Neuropsychologia* 49, no. 4 (March 2011): 745–59, https://www.ncbi.nlm.nih.gov /pmc/articles/PMC3060967/.

34 limbic system: Ausaf Bari, Tianyi Niu, Jean-Philippe Langevin, and Itzhak Fried, "Limbic Neuromodulation: Implications for Addiction, Posttraumatic Stress Disorder, and Memory," *Neurosurgery Clinics of North America* 25, no. 1 (January 2014): 137–45, https://www.ncbi.nlm .nih.gov/pmc/articles/PMC4445935/#:~:text=The%20limbic%20 system%20is%20involved,memory%20such%20as%20Alzheimer %20disease.

35 through Gage's left eye: Kieran O'Driscoll and John Paul Leach, "'No Longer Gage': An Iron Bar Through the Head: Early Observations of Personality Change After Injury to the Prefrontal Cortex," *BMJ: British Medical Journal* 317, no. 7174 (December 19, 1998): 1673–74, accessed March 24, 2021, https://www.ncbi.nlm.nih.gov/pmc/articles /PMC1114479/.

35 frontal lobe damage could cause dramatic personality shifts: Joseph Barrash, Donald T. Stuss, Nazan Aksan, Steven W. Anderson, Robert D.

Jones, Kenneth Manzel, and Daniel Tranel, "'Frontal Lobe Syndrome'? Subtypes of Acquired Personality Disturbances in Patients with Focal Brain Damage," *Cortex* 106 (September 2018): 65–80, https://www.ncbi.nlm.nih.gov/pmc/articles/PMC6120760/.

35 frontal lobe is in fact associated with distinct behavioral changes: Elisabeth M. Weiss, "Neuroimaging and Neurocognitive Correlates of Aggression and Violence in Schizophrenia," *Scientifica* 2012, article ID 158646, 12 pages (September 24, 2012), https://www.hindawi.com/journals/scientifica/2012/158646/.

35 frontotemporal dementia: Jennifer L. Whitwell, "FTD Spectrum: Neuroimaging Across the FTD Spectrum," *Progress in Molecular Biology and Translational Science* 165 (2019): 187–223, https://www.ncbi.nlm.nih.gov/pmc/articles/PMC7153045/.

35 brain aberration, specifically to the prefrontal cortex: Marcelo Schwarzbold, Alexandre Diaz, Evandro Tostes Martins, Armanda Rufino, Lúcia Nazareth Amante, Maria Emília Thais, João Quevedo, et al., "Psychiatric Disorders and Traumatic Brain Injury," *Neuropsychiatric Disease and Treatment* 4, no. 4 (August 2008): 797–816, https://www.ncbi.nlm.nih.gov/pmc/articles/PMC2536546/.

36 Whitman had visited a campus psychiatrist: M. D. Heatly, "Text of Psychiatrist's Notes on Sniper," *New York Times*, August 3, 1966, https://archive.nytimes.com/www.nytimes.com/library/national/080366tx-shoot.html.

36 compressed a part of the brain called the amygdala: Tuomas K. Pernu and Nadine Elzein, "From Neuroscience to Law: Bridging the Gap," *Frontiers in Psychology* 11 (2020): 1862, https://www.ncbi.nlm.nih.gov/pmc/articles/PMC7642893/.

37 several different brain areas are associated with a depressed mood: Mayur Pandya, Murat Altinay, Donald A. Malone, and Amit Anand, "Where in the Brain Is Depression?" *Current Psychiatry Reports* 14, no. 6 (December 2012): 634–42, https://www.ncbi.nlm.nih.gov/pmc/articles/PMC3619732/#:~:text=The%20main%20subcortical%20limbic%20brain,noted%20in%20subjects%20with%20depression.

38 dopamine led to increased feelings of reward: L. Stein, "Chemistry of Reward and Punishment," in D. H. Efron, ed., *Proceedings of the American College of NeuroPsychopharmacology* (Washington, DC: U.S. Government Printing Office, 1968), 105–23.

38 Alec Coppen's work: Bruno Müller-Oerlinghausen and Mohammed T.

Abou-Saleh, "Alec J. Coppen—A Pioneering Psychiatrist Who Discovered the Pivotal Role of Serotonin in the Pathogenesis of Depression as Well as the Antisuicidal Effect of Lithium," *International Journal of Bipolar Disorders* 7, no. 15 (July 2, 2019), https://journalbipolardisorders.springeropen.com/articles/10.1186/s40345-019-0150-3.

38 pharmacologic treatments for illnesses like schizophrenia and major depression: Chaitra T. Ramachandraiah, Narayana Subramaniam, and Manuel Tancer, "The Story of Antipsychotics: Past and Present," *Indian Journal of Psychiatry* 51, no. 4 (October–December 2009): 324–26, https://www.ncbi.nlm.nih.gov/pmc/articles/PMC2802385/.

38 story of the drug imipramine: Francisco Lopez-Munoz, Cecilio Alamo, and Ramon Cacabelos, "Serendipitous Discovery of First Two Antidepressants," *Taiwanese Journal of Psychiatry* 28, no. 2 (2014): 67–70, http://www.sop.org.tw/sop_journal/Upload_files/28_2/003.pdf.

39 Prozac, a new SSRI: Todd M. Hillhouse and Joseph H. Porter, "A Brief History of the Development of Antidepressant Drugs: From Monoamines to Glutamate," *Experimental and Clinical Psychopharmacology* 23, no. 1 (February 2015): 1–21, https://www.ncbi.nlm.nih.gov/pmc/articles/PMC4428540/.

39 400 percent increase in antidepressant prescriptions: "Products—Data Briefs—Number 76—October 2011," Centers for Disease Control and Prevention, November 6, 2015, https://www.cdc.gov/nchs/products/databriefs/db76.htm.

39 one of the first Zoloft commercials: SuperBowlSammy, "Original Zoloft Commercial," YouTube, March 12, 2009, https://www.youtube.com/watch?v=twhvtzd6gXA.

40 tens of millions of Americans are prescribed antidepressants each year: "Products—Data Briefs, Number 76—October 2011."

41 Ketamine promises a rapid reversal: David Dadiomov and Kelly Lee, "The Effects of Ketamine on Suicidality Across Various Formulations and Study Settings," *The Mental Health Clinician* 9, no. 1 (January 2019): 48–60, https://www.ncbi.nlm.nih.gov/pmc/articles/PMC6322816/.

44 up to a third of patients won't respond to antidepressant drugs: Khalid Saad Al-Harbi, "Treatment-Resistant Depression: Therapeutic Trends, Challenges, and Future Directions," *Patient Preference and Adherence* 6 (2012): 369–88, https://www.ncbi.nlm.nih.gov/pmc/articles/PMC3363299/.

45   ketamine can reduce suicidal ideation: Dadiomov and Lee, "The Effects of Ketamine on Suicidality Across Various Formulations and Study Settings."

46   "thinking thing": Kurt Smith, "Descartes' Theory of Ideas," *Stanford Encyclopedia of Philosophy*, Stanford University, June 14, 2017, rev. August 3, 2021, https://plato.stanford.edu/entries/descartes-ideas/.

Chapter 3: Healing beyond Medicine

58   Numerous research studies: Allison L. Baier, Alexander C. Kline, and Norah C. Feeny, "Therapeutic Alliance as a Mediator of Change: A Systematic Review and Evaluation of Research," *Clinical Psychology Review* 82 (December 2020): 101921, https://www.sciencedirect.com/science/article/abs/pii/S0272735820301094?dgcid=rss_sd_all.

58   therapeutic alliance: Dorothy E. Stubbe, "The Therapeutic Alliance: The Fundamental Element of Psychotherapy," *Focus* 16, no. 4 (Fall 2018): 402–3, https://focus.psychiatryonline.org/doi/10.1176/appi.focus.20180022.

58   better connect with patients: Tori DeAngelis, "Better Relationships with Patients Lead to Better Outcomes," *Monitor on Psychology* 50, no. 10 (November 1, 2019): 38, accessed March 26, 2021, https://www.apa.org/monitor/2019/11/ce-corner-relationships.

59   about ten days: Sungkyu Lee, Aileen B. Rothbard, and Elizabeth L. Noll, "Length of Inpatient Stay of Persons with Serious Mental Illness: Effects of Hospital and Regional Characteristics," *Psychiatric Services* 63, no. 9 (September 2012): 889–95, https://ps.psychiatryonline.org/doi/10.1176/appi.ps.201100412.

61   mind believes that placebo works: Sarah Ballou, Alissa Beath, Ted J. Kaptchuk, William Hirsch, Thomas Sommers, Judy Nee, Johanna Iturrino, et al., "Factors Associated with Response to Placebo in Patients with Irritable Bowel Syndrome and Constipation," *Clinical Gastroenterology and Hepatology* 16, no. 11 (November 2018): 1738–44.e1, https://www.ncbi.nlm.nih.gov/pmc/articles/PMC6414074/.

61   chronic pain disorder: Regine Klinger, Julia Stuhlreyer, Marie Schwartz, Julia Schmitz, and Luana Colloca, "Clinical Use of Placebo Effects in Patients with Pain Disorders," *International Review of Neurobiology* 139 (2018): 107–28, https://www.ncbi.nlm.nih.gov/pmc/articles/PMC6175283/.

61   Kirsch claimed that the placebo response: Irving Kirsch, "Anti-

depressants and the Placebo Effect," *Zeitschrift fur Psychologie* 222, no. 3 (2014): 128–34, https://www.ncbi.nlm.nih.gov/pmc/articles/PM C4172306/.

65 research reviewed in the *Lancet*: Paul Enck, "Placebo Response in Depression: Is It Rising?" *Lancet* 3, no. 11 (October 7, 2016): 1005–6, https://www.thelancet.com/journals/lanpsy/article/PIIS2215-036 6(16)30308-X/fulltext.

68 lifestyle interventions can improve your mental health: Darren P. Morton, "Combining Lifestyle Medicine and Positive Psychology to Improve Mental Health and Emotional Well-Being," *American Journal of Lifestyle Medicine* 12, no. 5 (September–October 2018): 370–74, https://www.ncbi.nlm.nih.gov/pmc/articles/PMC6146362/.

Chapter 4: Survival of the Fittest

74 defined by the American Psychological Association: "Building Your Resilience," American Psychological Association, accessed March 27, 2021, https://www.apa.org/topics/resilience.

76 some genes: S. Maul, I. Giegling, C. Fabbri, F. Corponi, A. Serretti, and D. Rujescu, "Genetics of Resilience: Implications from Genome-Wide Association Studies and Candidate Genes of the Stress Response System in Posttraumatic Stress Disorder and Depression," *American Journal of Medical Genetics. Part B, Neuropsychiatric Genetics* 183, no. 2 (March 2020): 77–94, accessed March 27, 2021, https://pubmed.ncbi .nlm.nih.gov/31583809/.

76 identified a number of genes: Maul, Giegling, Fabbri, et al., "Genetics of Resilience: Implications from Genome-Wide Association Studies and Candidate Genes of the Stress Response System in Posttraumatic Stress Disorder and Depression."

76 Several of these genes: Deborah J. Walder, Hanan D. Trotman, Joseph F. Cubells, Joy Brasfield, Yilang Tang, and Elaine F. Walker, "Catechol-O-Methyltransferase (COMT) Modulation of Cortisol Secretion in Psychiatrically At-risk and Healthy Adolescents," *Psychiatric Genetics* 20, no. 4 (August 2010): 166–70, https://www.ncbi.nlm.nih.gov/pmc /articles/PMC3522124/.

76 Stress, simply defined: Paul J. Lucassen, Jens Pruessner, Nuno Sousa, Osborne F. X. Almeida, Anne Marie Van Dam, Grazyna Rajkowska, Dick F. Swaab, et al., "Neuropathology of Stress," *Acta Neuropatho-*

logica 127 (2014): 109–35, https://link.springer.com/article/10.1007/s00401-013-1223-5.

77   allostatic overload: Bruce S. McEwen, "Central Effects of Stress Hormones in Health and Disease: Understanding the Protective and Damaging Effects of Stress and Stress Mediators," *European Journal of Pharmacology* 583, no. 2–3 (April 7, 2008): 174–85, https://www.ncbi.nlm.nih.gov/pmc/articles/PMC2474765/.

78   changes in areas of the brain: McEwen, "Central Effects of Stress Hormones in Health and Disease."

78   cause you to feel: "Stress Effects on the Body," American Psychological Association, accessed March 27, 2021, https://www.apa.org/topics/stress/body.

78   Inflammation: Vasiliki Michopoulos, Abigail Powers, Charles F. Gillespie, Kerry J. Ressler, and Tanja Jovanovic, "Inflammation in Fear- and Anxiety-Based Disorders: PTSD, GAD, and Beyond," *Neuropsychopharmacology* 42, no. 1 (January 2017): 254–70, https://www.ncbi.nlm.nih.gov/pmc/articles/PMC5143487/.

78   depression: Charles L. Raison and Andrew H. Miller, "Is Depression an Inflammatory Disorder?" *Current Psychiatry Reports* 13, no. 6 (December 2011): 467–75, https://www.ncbi.nlm.nih.gov/pmc/articles/PMC3285451/.

78   gene variants: Isabelle Ouellet-Morin, Michel Boivin, Ginette Dionne, Sonia J. Lupien, Louise Arseneault, Ronald G. Barr, Daniel Pérusse, et al., "Variations in Heritability of Cortisol Reactivity to Stress as a Function of Early Familial Adversity Among 19-Month-Old Twins," *Archives of General Psychiatry* 65, no. 2 (2008): 211–18, https://jamanetwork.com/journals/jamapsychiatry/fullarticle/482596.

80   reshape themselves: Richard G., Hunter, Jason D. Gray, and Bruce S. McEwen, "The Neuroscience of Resilience," *Journal of the Society for Social Work and Research* 9, no. 2 (2018): 305–39, accessed March 27, 2021, https://www.journals.uchicago.edu/doi/10.1086/697956.

80   ten thousand hours of practice to master a task: Malcolm Gladwell, *Outliers: The Story of Success* (New York: Back Bay Books/Little, Brown, 2009).

81   evolved into their robustness: Michael Marshall, "Tardigrades: Nature's Great Survivors," *Guardian*, March 20, 2021, https://www.theguardian.com/science/2021/mar/20/tardigrades-natures-great-survivors.

82   first opportunity: Adrianna Freedman, "Marcus Smith's Key to Staying

Healthy? Starting Therapy," *Men's Health*, August 10, 2020, https://www.menshealth.com/entertainment/a33563142/marcus-smith-nfl-therapy/.

84 "They're often times quiet about some of the things they deal with because they don't want the coaches to know . . . coaches will look at it as if he's not mentally tough, and they want people already mentally tough in the NFL": *Men's Health* magazine (@menshealthmag), "Friday Sessions w/ @moneymarc91 and @gregorysbrownmd," Instagram video, August 7, 2020, https://www.instagram.com/tv/CDmVjw_BYjf/.

Chapter 5: Giving Up on Death

93 "'Hey, kid. Are you okay? Do you need help?'": Goalcast, "This Suicide Survivor Story Will Change Your PERSPECTIVE ON EVERYTHING | Goalcast," YouTube, November 12, 2020, https://www.youtube.com/watch?v=vGPktsXlhTA.

94 "What the hell is wrong with that guy?": Ibid.

94 "That's it. Nobody cares": Kevin Hines, Alys Cole-King, and Mel Blaustein, "Hey Kid, Are You OK? A Story of Suicide Survived," *Advances in Psychiatric Treatment* 19 (2013): 292–94.

94 more than fifteen hundred people: "Golden Gate Bridge Suicides—History," Bridge Rail Foundation, accessed April 6, 2021, http://www.bridgerail.net/golden-gate-bridge-suicides/history.

94 Fewer than thirty-five have survived: Ibid.

94 many reported that they regretted their decision: "Golden Gate Bridge Suicides—Demographics."

95 "No one would ever know that I regretted what I had done": Goalcast, "This Suicide Survivor Story Will Change Your PERSPECTIVE ON EVERYTHING."

95 nine out of ten people: David Owens, Judith Horrocks, and Allan House, "Fatal and Non-fatal Repetition of Self-Harm. Systematic Review," *British Journal of Psychiatry* 181 (September 2002): 193–99, accessed March 16, 2021, https://pubmed.ncbi.nlm.nih.gov/12204922/.

96 one suicide every forty seconds: "Suicide Data," World Health Organization, accessed March 16, 2021, https://www.who.int/teams/mental-health-and-substance-use/suicide-data.

96   intentional self-harm: "FastStats—Deaths and Mortality," Centers for Disease Control and Prevention, accessed March 1, 2021, https://www .cdc.gov/nchs/fastats/deaths.htm.

97   130 suicides: "Suicide Statistics," American Foundation for Suicide Prevention, accessed March 9, 2021, https://afsp.org/suicide-statistics/.

99   once may at some point try again: Isabel Parra-Uribe, Hilario Blasco-Fontecilla, Gemma Garcia-Parés, Luis Martínez-Naval, Oliver Valero-Coppin, Annabel Cebrià-Meca, Maria A. Oquendo, et al., "Risk of Re-attempts and Suicide Death After a Suicide Attempt: A Survival Analysis," *BMC Psychiatry* 17, no. 163 (2017), https://bmcpsychiatry .biomedcentral.com/articles/10.1186/s12888-017-1317-z.

101   millions of dollars: "FY 2019 Budget—Congressional Justification," National Institute of Mental Health, U.S. Department of Health and Human Services, accessed April 6, 2021, https://www.nimh .nih.gov/about/budget/fy-2019-budget-congressional-justification.s html.

102   85 percent of the time: G. E. Simon, E. Johnson, J. M. Lawrence, R. C. Rossom, B. Ahmedani, F. L. Lynch, A. Beck, et al., "Predicting Suicide Attempts and Suicide Deaths Following Outpatient Visits Using Electronic Health Records," *American Journal of Psychiatry* 175, no. 10 (October 1, 2018): 951–60, accessed March 17, 2021, https://pubmed.ncbi .nlm.nih.gov/29792051/.

108   mantra meditation: Julie Lynch, Lucia Prihodova, Pádraic J. Dunne, Áine Carroll, Cathal Walsh, Geraldine McMahon, and Barry White, "Mantra Meditation for Mental Health in the General Population: A Systematic Review," *European Journal of Integrative Medicine* 23 (October 2018): 101–8, https://www.sciencedirect.com/science/article/pii /S1876382018304591.

111   reasons they supported it: D. H. Rosen, "Suicide Survivors: A Follow-up Study of Persons Who Survived Jumping from the Golden Gate and San Francisco–Oakland Bay Bridges," *Western Journal of Medicine* 122, no. 4 (April 1975): 289–94, https://www.ncbi.nlm.nih.gov/pmc /articles/PMC1129714/?page=1.

112   anticipating positive events: Yangmei Luo, Xuhai Chen, Senqing Qi, Xuqun You, and Xiting Huang, "Well-Being and Anticipation for Future Positive Events: Evidences from an FMRI Study," *Frontiers in Psychology* 8 (2017): 2199, https://www.ncbi.nlm.nih.gov/pmc/articles /PMC5767250/.

Chapter 6: Bringing Attention to Breath

125 A study by *Yoga Journal* and Yoga Alliance: "2016 Yoga in America Study Conducted by Yoga Journal and Yoga Alliance Reveals Growth and Benefits of the Practice," Yoga Alliance, accessed April 11, 2021, https://www.yogaalliance.org/Get_Involved/Media_Inquiries/2016 _Yoga_in_America_Study_Conducted_by_Yoga_Journal_and_Yoga _Alliance_Reveals_Growth_and_Benefits_of_the_Practice.

127 as the human brain evolved: Bret Stetka, *A History of the Human Brain: From the Sea Sponge to CRISPR, How Our Brain Evolved* (Portland, Ore.: Timber Press, 2021).

133 approximately 280 million people worldwide: Saloni Dattani, Hannah Ritchie, and Max Roser, "Mental Health," *Our World in Data*, January 20, 2018, https://ourworldindata.org/mental-health.

133 people report becoming more and more anxious: "Americans Say They Are More Anxious than a Year Ago; Baby Boomers Report Greatest Increase in Anxiety," American Psychiatric Association, news release, accessed April 26, 2021, https://www.psychiatry.org/newsroom /news-releases/americans-say-they-are-more-anxious-than-a-year -ago-baby-boomers-report-greatest-increase-in-anxiety.

135 increase in GABA: Chris Streeter, Patricia L. Gerbarg, Greylin H. Niel- sen, Richard P. Brown, J. Eric Jensen, and Marisa Silveri, "Effects of Yoga on Thalamic Gamma-Aminobutyric Acid, Mood and Depres- sion: Analysis of Two Randomized Controlled Trials," *Neuropsychiatry* 8, no. 6 (2018), https://www.jneuropsychiatry.org/peer-review/effects-of -yoga-on-thalamic-gammaaminobutyric-acid-mood-and-depression -analysis-of-two-randomized-controlled-trials-12856.html.

144 Studies: Anant Narayan Sinha, Desh Deepak, and Vimal Singh Gusain, "Assessment of the Effects of Pranayama/Alternate Nostril Breathing on the Parasympathetic Nervous System in Young Adults," *Journal of Clinical and Diagnostic Research* 7, no. 5 (May 2013): 821–23, https:// www.ncbi.nlm.nih.gov/pmc/articles/PMC3681046/.

145 Navy SEALs: Noma Nazish, "How to De-Stress in 5 Minutes or Less, According to a Navy SEAL," *Forbes*, May 31, 2019, https://www.forbes .com/sites/nomanazish/2019/05/30/how-to-de-stress-in-5-minutes -or-less-according-to-a-navy-seal/?sh=37ef574c3046.

145 largely popularized by Dr. Andrew Weil: "Video: Dr. Weil's Breathing Exercises: 4-7-8 Breath," DrWeil.com, March 22, 2019, https://www .drweil.com/videos-features/videos/breathing-exercises-4-7-8-breath/.

Chapter 7: The Sleep Solution

149   interfere with serotonin production: Viktor Roman, Irene Walstra, Paul
       G. M. Luiten, and Peter Meerlo, "Too Little Sleep Gradually Desensi-
       tizes the Serotonin 1A Receptor System," *Sleep* 28, no. 12 (December
       2005): 1505–10, accessed May 3, 2021, https://pubmed.ncbi.nlm.nih
       .gov/16408408/.

149   over 80 percent of patients: David Nutt, Sue Wilson, and Louise Pat-
       erson, "Sleep Disorders as Core Symptoms of Depression," *Dialogues
       in Clinical Neuroscience* 10, no. 3 (September 2008): 329–36, https://
       www.ncbi.nlm.nih.gov/pmc/articles/PMC3181883/.

149   affecting cognition, mood, concentration: Adam J. Krause, Eti Ben Si-
       mon, Bryce A. Mander, Stephanie M. Greer, Jared M. Saletin, Andrea
       N. Goldstein-Piekarski, and Matthew P. Walker, "The Sleep-Deprived
       Human Brain," *Nature Reviews Neuroscience* 18, no. 7 (July 2017): 404–
       18, https://www.ncbi.nlm.nih.gov/pmc/articles/PMC6143346/.

149   hampered immune response: Luciana Besedovsky, Tanja Lange, and
       Monika Haack, "The Sleep-Immune Crosstalk in Health and Disease,"
       Physiological Reviews 99 (2019): 1325–80, https://journals.physiology
       .org/doi/full/10.1152/physrev.00010.2018.

151   consolidating new memories: Björn Rasch and Jan Born, "About
       Sleep's Role in Memory," *Physiological Reviews* 93, no. 2 (April 2013):
       681–766, https://www.ncbi.nlm.nih.gov/pmc/articles/PMC3768102/.

151   serotonin, histamine, and norepinephrine: Andy R. Eugene and Jolanta
       Masiak, "The Neuroprotective Aspects of Sleep," *MEDtube Science* 3,
       no. 1 (March 2015): 35–40, https://www.ncbi.nlm.nih.gov/pmc/articles
       /PMC4651462/.

152   purpose of REM sleep: Dale Purves, "The Possible Functions of REM
       Sleep and Dreaming," in D. Purves, G. J. Augustine, D. Fitzpatrick, et
       al., eds., *Neuroscience*, 2nd ed. (Sunderland, Mass.: Sinauer Associates,
       2001), https://www.ncbi.nlm.nih.gov/books/NBK11121/.

153   sleep problems: "Sleep and Sleep Disorder Statistics," American Sleep
       Association, accessed May 5, 2021, https://www.sleepassociation.org
       /about-sleep/sleep-statistics/.

154   around age sixty: Junxin Li, Michael V. Vitiello, and Nalaka S. Goon-
       eratne, "Sleep in Normal Aging," *Sleep Medicine Clinics* 13, no. 1
       (March 2018): 1–11, https://www.ncbi.nlm.nih.gov/pmc/articles/PMC
       5841578/.

156   include the amygdala: Zahid Saghir, Javeria N. Syeda, Adnan S.

Muhammad, and Tareg H. Balla Abdalla, "The Amygdala, Sleep Debt, Sleep Deprivation, and the Emotion of Anger: A Possible Connection?" *Cureus* 10, no. 7 (July 2, 2018): e2912, https://www.ncbi.nlm.nih .gov/pmc/articles/PMC6122651/.

156   compared to people who aren't depressed: Andrés Barrera Medina, DeboraYoaly Arana Lechuga, Oscar Sánchez Escandón, and Javier Velázquez Moctezuma, "Update of Sleep Alterations in Depression," *Sleep Science* 7, no. 3 (September 2014): 165–69, https://www.science direct.com/science/article/pii/S1984006314000534.

157   associated with conditions like major depression and fatigue: Chieh-Hsin Lee and Fabrizio Giuliani, "The Role of Inflammation in Depression and Fatigue," *Frontiers in Immunology* 10 (2019): 1696, https:// www.ncbi.nlm.nih.gov/pmc/articles/PMC6658985/.

157   times of heightened emotional stress: Maria Basta, George P. Chrousos, Antonio Vela-Bueno, and Alexandros N. Vgontzas, "Chronic Insomnia and Stress System," *Sleep Medicine Clinics* 2, no. 2 (June 2007): 279–91, https://www.ncbi.nlm.nih.gov/pmc/articles/PMC2128619/.

158   imaged the brains of mice as they slept: Benjamin A. Plog and Maiken Nedergaard, "The Glymphatic System in Central Nervous System Health and Disease: Past, Present, and Future," *Annual Review of Pathology* 13 (January 24, 2018): 379–94, accessed May 5, 2021, https:// pubmed.ncbi.nlm.nih.gov/29195051/.

161   medications like benzos:, Jaime M. Monti, Pablo Torterolo, and Seithikurippu R. Pandi-Perumal, "The Effects of Benzodiazepine and Nonbenzodiazepine Agents, Ramelteon, Low-Dose Doxepin, Suvorexant, and Selective Serotonin 5-HT2A Receptor Antagonists and Inverse Agonists on Sleep and Wakefulness," *Clinical Medicine Insights: Therapeutics* 8 (2016), https://doi.org/10.4137/cmt.s38232.

161   melatonin can be useful: Nava Zisapel, "The Role of Melatonin in Sleep Regulation," in D. P. Cardinali and S. R. Pandi-Perumal, eds., *Neuroendocrine Correlates of Sleep/Wakefulness* (Boston: Springer, 2006), 295–309, https://doi.org/10.1007/0-387-23692-9_15.

162   Long-term alcohol abuse: Ian M. Colrain, Sharon Turlington, and Fiona C. Baker, "Impact of Alcoholism on Sleep Architecture and EEG Power Spectra in Men and Women," *Sleep* 32, no. 10 (October 2009): 1341–52, https://academic.oup.com/sleep/article/32/10/1341/2454479.

167   eleven-minute Nidra meditation: Esther N. Moszeik, Timo von Oertzen, and Karl-Heinz Renner, "Effectiveness of a Short Yoga Nidra Meditation on Stress, Sleep, and Well-Being in a Large and Diverse Sample,"

Current Psychology (2020), https://link.springer.com/article/10.1007 /s12144-020-01042-2.

Chapter 8: Tapping into Your Spiritual Self

170   a survey of physicians: K. A. Robinson, M.-R. Cheng, P. D. Hansen, and R. J. Gray, "Religious and Spiritual Beliefs of Physicians," *Journal of Religion and Health* 56, no. 1 (February 2017): 205–225, accessed May 7, 2021, https://pubmed.ncbi.nlm.nih.gov/27071796/.

171   "relating to, consisting of, or affecting the spirit; incorporeal": "Spiritual," *Merriam-Webster*, accessed May 7, 2021, https://www.merriam -webster.com/dictionary/spiritual.

172   "Spirituality," she writes: Maya Spencer, "What Is Spirituality? A Personal Exploration," Royal College of Psychiatrists, 2012, https://www .rcpsych.ac.uk/Docs/Default-Source/Members/Sigs/Spirituality -Spsig/What-Is-Spirituality-Maya-Spencer-X.pdf?Sfvrsn=f28df0 52_2.

175   a Bible verse: "Bible Gateway Passage: Jeremiah 29:11—New International Version," Bible Gateway, accessed May 7, 2021, https://www.bible gateway.com/passage/?search=Jeremiah+29%3A11&version=NIV.

179   20 to 30 percent: Walter Alexander, "Pharmacotherapy for Post-Traumatic Stress Disorder in Combat Veterans: Focus on Antidepressants and Atypical Antipsychotic Agents," *P & T* 37, no. 1 (January 2012): 32–38, https://www.ncbi.nlm.nih.gov/pmc/articles/PMC32781 88/.

179   not all studies have reached the same conclusion: Laurel L. Hourani, Jason Williams, Valerie Forman-Hoffman, Marian E. Lane, Belinda Weimer, and Robert M. Bray, "Influence of Spirituality on Depression, Posttraumatic Stress Disorder, and Suicidality in Active Duty Military Personnel," *Depression Research and Treatment* 2012, article ID 425463, 9 pages, https://www.hindawi.com/journals/drt/2012/4254 63/.

181   goes on to state: "Bhagavad Gita Chapter 6 Verse 10," Bhajan Katha and satsang, accessed May 9, 2021, https://www.yugalsarkar.com/bhagwad -gita-chapter-6-shlok-10-english.

182   Researchers from Aarhus University in Denmark: Else-Marie Elmholdt Jegindø, Lene Vase, Joshua Charles Skewes, Astrid Juhl Terkelsen, John Hansen, Armin W. Geertz, Andreas Roepstorff, et al., "Expectations Contribute to Reduced Pain Levels During Prayer in Highly Religious

Participants," *Journal of Behavioral Medicine* 36 (2013): 413–26, https://link.springer.com/article/10.1007%2Fs10865-012-9438-9.

184 prayer has positive benefits: James W. Anderson and Paige A. Nunnelley, "Private Prayer Associations with Depression, Anxiety and Other Health Conditions: An Analytical Review of Clinical Studies," *Postgraduate Medicine* 128, no. 7 (September 2016): 635–41, accessed May 9, 2021, https://pubmed.ncbi.nlm.nih.gov/27452045/.

184 engaging in prayer: Arjan W. Braam and Harold G. Koenig, "Religion, Spirituality and Depression in Prospective Studies: A Systematic Review," *Journal of Affective Disorders* 257 (October 1, 2019): 428–38, accessed May 9, 2021, https://pubmed.ncbi.nlm.nih.gov/31326688/.

184 changes in the brain: I-Wen Su, Fang-Wei Wu, Keng-Chen Liang, Kai-Yuan Cheng, Sung-Tsang Hsieh, Wei-Zen Sun, and Tai-Li Chou, "Pain Perception Can Be Modulated by Mindfulness Training: A Resting-State fMRI Study," *Frontiers in Human Neuroscience* 10, November 10, 2016, https://www.frontiersin.org/articles/10.3389/fnhum.2016.00570/full.

184 Practicing mindful meditation: Wiveka Ramel, Philippe R. Goldin, Paula E. Carmona, and John R. McQuaid, "The Effects of Mindfulness Meditation on Cognitive Processes and Affect in Patients with Past Depression," *Cognitive Therapy and Research* 28 (2004): 433–55, accessed May 9, 2021, https://link.springer.com/article/10.1023/B:COTR.0000045557.15923.96.

185 brain activity of Tibetan monks: Haiteng Jiang, Bin He, Xiaoli Guo, Xu Wang, Menglin Guo, Zhou Wang, Ting Xue, et al., "Brain-Heart Interactions Underlying Traditional Tibetan Buddhist Meditation," *Cerebral Cortex* 30, no. 2 (March 21, 2020): 439–50, accessed May 9, 2021, https://pubmed.ncbi.nlm.nih.gov/31163086/.

187 physicians actually do believe in God: Robinson, Cheng, Hansen, and Gray, "Religious and Spiritual Beliefs of Physicians."

187 consider themselves religious: "Doctors Differ from Patients on Religion," *WebMD*, June 22, 2005, https://www.webmd.com/women/news/20050622/doctors-differ-from-patients-on-religion.

187 demonic possession: Simon Kemp and Kevin Williams, "Demonic Possession and Mental Disorder in Medieval and Early Modern Europe: Psychological Medicine," *Psychological Medicine* 17, no. 1 (1987): 21–29, https://www.cambridge.org/core/journals/psychological-medicine/article/abs/demonic-possession-and-mental-disorder-in-medieval-and-early-modern-europe/2D5330B11623135975112F57C4E8B311.

187   exorcisms: Carlos Espí Forcén and Fernando Espí Forcén, "Demonic Possessions and Mental Illness: Discussion of Selected Cases in Late Medieval Hagiographical Literature," *Early Science and Medicine* 19, no. 3 (2014): 258–79, accessed May 9, 2021, https://pubmed.ncbi.nlm.nih.gov/25208453/.

187   Muslims and Mental Health Lab at Stanford University: "Muslims and Mental Health Lab," Department of Psychiatry and Behavioral Sciences, accessed May 9, 2021, https://med.stanford.edu/psychiatry/research/MuslimMHLab.html.

187   Mental Health and Faith Community Partnership: "Mental Health and Faith Community Partnership," American Psychiatric Association, accessed May 9, 2021, https://www.psychiatry.org/psychiatrists/cultural-competency/engagement-opportunities/mental-health-and-faith-community-partnership.

Chapter 9: The Medicine on Your Plate

199   a fiber-rich diet: Seth Ramin, Margaret A. Mysz, Katie Meyer, Benjamin Capistrant, DeAnn Lazovich, and Anna Prizment, "A Prospective Analysis of Dietary Fiber Intake and Mental Health Quality of Life in the Iowa Women's Health Study," *Maturitas* 131 (January 2020): 1–7, accessed May 19, 2021, https://pubmed.ncbi.nlm.nih.gov/31787141/.

201   a number of mental illnesses: Joseph Firth, Nicola Veronese, Jack Cotter, Nitin Shivappa, James R. Hebert, Carolyn Ee, Lee Smith, et al., "What Is the Role of Dietary Inflammation in Severe Mental Illness? A Review of Observational and Experimental Findings," *Frontiers in Psychiatry* 10 (2019): 350, https://www.ncbi.nlm.nih.gov/pmc/articles/PMC6529779/.

201   anxiety: Tim Newman, "Anxiety and Inflammation: What Is the Link?" *Medical News Today*, March 16, 2021, accessed May 12, 2021, https://www.medicalnewstoday.com/articles/anxiety-and-inflammation-is-there-a-link#The-evidence.

201   ADHD: Douglas Teixeira Leffa, Iraci L. S. Torres, and Luis Augusto Rohde, "A Review on the Role of Inflammation in Attention-Deficit/Hyperactivity Disorder," *Neuroimmunomodulation* 25 (2018): 328–33, https://www.karger.com/Article/FullText/489635.

201   "Seven Countries Study": A. Keys, A. Menotti, M. J. Karvonen, C. Aravanis, H. Blackburn, R. Buzina, B. S. Djordjevic, et al., "The Diet and 15-Year Death Rate in the Seven Countries Study," *American Journal*

of Epidemiology 124, no. 6 (December 1986): 903–15, accessed May 12, 2021, https://pubmed.ncbi.nlm.nih.gov/3776973/.

201 in the development of cardiovascular disease: Jane E. Brody, "Dr. Ancel Keys, 100, Promoter of Mediterranean Diet, Dies," *New York Times*, November 23, 2004, https://www.nytimes.com/2004/11/23/obituaries /dr-ancel-keys-100-promoter-of-mediterranean-diet-dies.html.

202 Mediterranean diet: C. T. McEvoy, H. Guyer, K. M. Langa, and K. Yaffe, "Neuroprotective Diets Are Associated with Better Cognitive Function: The Health and Retirement Study," *Journal of the American Geriatrics Society* 65, no. 8 (August 2017): 1857–62, accessed May 19, 2021, https://pubmed.ncbi.nlm.nih.gov/28440854/.

202 specific types of cancers: Maria Chiara Mentella, Franco Scaldaferri, Caterina Ricci, Antonio Gasbarrini, and Giacinto Abele Donato Miggiano, "Cancer and Mediterranean Diet: A Review," *Nutrients* 11, no. 9 (September 2019): 2059, https://www.ncbi.nlm.nih.gov/pmc/articles /PMC6770822/.

202 stay sharper as we age: McEvoy, Guyer, Langa, and Yaffe, "Neuroprotective Diets Are Associated with Better Cognitive Function."

202 Researchers at the University of Navarra in Spain: Silvia Carlos, Carmen De La Fuente-Arrillaga, Maira Bes-Rastrollo, Cristina Razquin, Anaïs Rico-Campà, Miguel Angel Martínez-González, et al., "Mediterranean Diet and Health Outcomes in the SUN Cohort," *Nutrients* 10, no. 4 (March 31, 2018): 439, accessed May 12, 2021, https://pubmed .ncbi.nlm.nih.gov/29614726/.

203 buffer against depression: Almudena Sánchez-Villegas, Miguel Delgado-Rodríguez, Alvaro Alonso, Javier Schlatter, Francisca Lahortiga, Lluis Serra Majem, and Miguel Angel Martínez-González, "Association of the Mediterranean Dietary Pattern with the Incidence of Depression: The Seguimiento Universidad De Navarra/University of Navarra Follow-up (SUN) Cohort," *Archives of General Psychiatry* 66, no. 10 (October 2009): 1090–98, https://jamanetwork.com/journals/jama psychiatry/fullarticle/210386.

203 developing depression and anxiety: Camille Lassale, G. David Batty, Amaria Baghdadli, Felice Jacka, Almudena Sánchez-Villegas, Mika Kivimäki, and Tasnime Akbaraly, "Healthy Dietary Indices and Risk of Depressive Outcomes: A Systematic Review and Meta-Analysis of Observational Studies," *Molecular Psychiatry* 24 (2019): 965–86, https:// www.nature.com/articles/s41380-018-0237-8.

203 may increase the risk: Ye Li, Mei-Rong Lv, Yan-Jin Wei, Ling Sun, Ji-Xiang Zhang, Huai-Guo Zhang, and Bin Li, "Dietary Patterns and Depression Risk: A Meta-Analysis," *Psychiatry Research* 253 (July 2017): 373–82, https://www.sciencedirect.com/science/article/abs/pii/S0165178117301981.

203 seminal 2013 study: Felice N. Jacka, Adrienne O'Neil, Rachelle Opie, Catherine Itsiopoulos, Sue Cotton, Mohammedreza Mohebbi, David Castle, et al., "A Randomised Controlled Trial of Dietary Improvement for Adults with Major Depression (the 'SMILES' Trial)," *BMC Medicine* 15, no. 23 (2017), https://bmcmedicine.biomedcentral.com/articles/10.1186/s12916-017-0791-y.

205 Antidepressant Food Scale: Laura R. LaChance and Drew Ramsey, "Antidepressant Foods: An Evidence-Based Nutrient Profiling System for Depression," *World Journal of Psychiatry* 8, no. 3 (September 20, 2018): 97–104, https://www.wjgnet.com/2220-3206/full/v8/i3/97.htm.

206 irritable bowel syndrome (IBS): Stephanie A. Flowers, Kristen M. Ward, and Crystal T. Clark, "The Gut Microbiome in Bipolar Disorder and Pharmacotherapy Management," *Neuropsychobiology* 79 (2020): 43–49, https://www.karger.com/Article/FullText/504496.

206 bacteria help the gut and the brain: Majella O'Neill, "Psychobiotic Revolution: Mood, Food and the New Science of the Gut-Brain Connection" (website), accessed May 12, 2021, http://psychobiotic-revolution.com/.

206 abnormal changes to the microbiome: Megan Clapp, Nadia Aurora, Lindsey Herrera, Manisha Bhatia, Emily Wilen, and Sarah Wakefield, "Gut Microbiota's Effect on Mental Health: The Gut-Brain Axis" *Clinics and Practice* 7, no. 4 (September 15, 2017): 987, https://www.ncbi.nlm.nih.gov/pmc/articles/PMC5641835/.

206 the answer is yes: H. Aslam, J. Green, F. N. Jacka, F. Collier, M. Berk, J. Pasco, and S. L. Dawson, "Fermented Foods, the Gut and Mental Health: A Mechanistic Overview with Implications for Depression and Anxiety," *Nutritional Neuroscience* 23, no. 9 (September 2020): 659–71, accessed May 14, 2021, https://pubmed.ncbi.nlm.nih.gov/30415609/.

207 BDNF levels: Tao Yang, Zheng Nie, Haifeng Shu, Yongqin Kuang, Xin Chen, Jingmin Cheng, Sixun Yu, et al., "The Role of BDNF on Neural Plasticity in Depression," *Frontiers in Cellular Neuroscience*

14, no. 82 (April 2020), https://www.frontiersin.org/articles/10.3389/fncel.2020.00082/full.

207 increase BDNF levels: A. Sánchez-Villegas, C. Galbete, M. A. Martinez-González, J. A. Martinez, C. Razquin, J. Salas-Salvadó, R. Estruch, et al., "The Effect of the Mediterranean Diet on Plasma Brain-Derived Neurotrophic Factor (BDNF) Levels: the PREDIMED-NAVARRA Randomized Trial," *Nutritional Neuroscience* 14, no. 5 (September 2011): 195–201, accessed May 14, 2021, https://pubmed.ncbi.nlm.nih.gov/22005283/.

209 The Mediterranean Diet Food Score: Denes Stefler, Sofia Malyutina, Ruzena Kubinova, Andrzej Pajak, Anne Peasey, Hynek Pikhart, Eric J. Brunner, and Martin Bobak, "Mediterranean Diet Score and Total and Cardiovascular Mortality in Eastern Europe: The HAPIEE Study," *European Journal of Nutrition* 56, no. 1 (2017): 421–49, https://www.ncbi.nlm.nih.gov/pmc/articles/PMC5290049/.

213 reduced DHA: H. M. Chandola and Ila Tanna, "Role of Omega-3 Fatty Acids in Brain and Neurological Health with Special Reference to Clinical Depression," in *Omega-3 Fatty Acids in Brain and Neurological Health* (London: Elsevier/Academic Press, 2014), 163–79, https://www.sciencedirect.com/science/article/pii/B9780124105270000144.

213 consisting mostly of EPA: E. M. Sublette, S. P. Ellis, A. L. Geant, and J. J. Mann, "Meta-Analysis of the Effects of Eicosapentaenoic Acid (EPA) in Clinical Trials in Depression," *Journal of Clinical Psychiatry* 72, no. 12 (December 2011): 1577–84, accessed May 18, 2021, https://pubmed.ncbi.nlm.nih.gov/21939614/.

213 ADHD: Jane Pei-Chen Chang, Kuan-Pin Su, Valeria Mondelli, and Carmine M. Pariante, "Omega-3 Polyunsaturated Fatty Acids in Youths with Attention Deficit Hyperactivity Disorder: A Systematic Review and Meta-Analysis of Clinical Trials and Biological Studies," *Neuropsychopharmacology* 43, no. 3 (February 2018): 534–45, accessed May 18, 2021, https://www.ncbi.nlm.nih.gov/pmc/articles/PMC5669464/.

214 serotonin and dopamine: Rajsekhar Adhikary and Vivekananda Mandal, "L-Theanine: A Potential Multifaceted Natural Bioactive Amide as Health Supplement," *Asian Pacific Journal of Tropical Biomedicine* 7, no. 9 (September 2017): 842–48, https://www.sciencedirect.com/science/article/pii/S2221169117308420.

214 can help reduce blood pressure: Ai Yoto, Mao Motoki, Sato Murao, and Hidehiko Yokogoshi, "Effects of L-Theanine or Caffeine Intake on

Changes in Blood Pressure Under Physical and Psychological Stresses," *Journal of Physiological Anthropology* 31, no. 28 (2012), https://jphysio lanthropol.biomedcentral.com/articles/10.1186/1880-6805-31-28.

215 continue to wear sunscreen: T. Passeron, R. Bouillon, V. Callender, T. Cestari, T. L. Diepgen, A. C. Green, J. C. van der Pols, et al., "Sunscreen Photoprotection and Vitamin D Status," *British Journal of Dermatology* 181, no. 5 (November 2019): 916–31, https://www.ncbi.nlm.nih .gov/pmc/articles/PMC6899926/#:~:text=Conclusions,when%20 applied%20under%20optimal%20conditions.

215 vitamin D deficiency: G. B. Parker, H. Brotchie, and R. K. Graham, "Vitamin D and Depression," *Journal of Affective Disorders* 208 (January 15, 2017): 56–61, accessed May 18, 2021, https://pubmed.ncbi.nlm.nih .gov/27750060/.

215 reduce symptoms of depression: F. Vellekkatt and V. Menon, "Efficacy of Vitamin D Supplementation in Major Depression: A Meta-Analysis of Randomized Controlled Trials," *Journal of Postgraduate Medicine* 65, no. 2 (April–June 2019): 74–80, https://www.ncbi.nlm.nih.gov/pmc /articles/PMC6515787/.

215 42 percent of the United States population: S. Wheeler, "42% of Americans Are Vitamin D Deficient. Are You Among Them?" Mercy Medical Center, July 1, 2018, https://www.cantonmercy.org/healthchat /42-percent-of-americans-are-vitamin-d-deficient/.

215 depression and anxiety: R. T. Liu, R. F. L. Walsh, and A. E. Sheehan, "Prebiotics and Probiotics for Depression and Anxiety: A Systematic Review and Meta-Analysis of Controlled Clinical Trials," *Neuroscience and Biobehavioral Reviews* 102 (July 2019): 13–23, accessed May 18, 2021, https://pubmed.ncbi.nlm.nih.gov/31004628/.

Chapter 10: Moving Your Body for Your Mind

232 boost in mood: J. D. Meyer, K. M. Crombie, D. B. Cook, C. J. Hillard, and K. F. Koltyn, "Serum Endocannabinoid and Mood Changes After Exercise in Major Depressive Disorder," *Medicine and Science in Sports and Exercise* 51, no. 9 (September 2019): 1909–17, accessed May 19, 2021, https://pubmed.ncbi.nlm.nih.gov/30973483/.

232 Endocannabinoids: Mario Stampanoni Bassi, Luana Gilio, Pierpaolo Maffei, Ettore Dolcetti, Antonio Bruno, Fabio Buttari, Diego Centonze, et al., "Exploiting the Multifaceted Effects of Cannabinoids on Mood to Boost Their Therapeutic Use Against Anxiety and Depression,"

Frontiers in Molecular Neuroscience 11, November 20, 2018, https://www.frontiersin.org/articles/10.3389/fnmol.2018.00424/full.

232   exercise also promotes: F. Chaouloff, "Physical Exercise and Brain Monoamines: A Review," *Acta Physiologica Scandinavica* 137, no. 1 (September 1989): 1–13, accessed May 20, 2021, https://pubmed.ncbi.nlm.nih.gov/2678895/.

233   Firth's own research: J. Firth, B. Stubbs, S. Rosenbaum, D. Vancampfort, B. Malchow, F. Schuch, R. Elliott, et al., "Aerobic Exercise Improves Cognitive Functioning in People with Schizophrenia: A Systematic Review and Meta-Analysis," *Schizophrenia Bulletin* 43, no. 3 (May 2017): 546–56, accessed May 20, 2021, https://pubmed.ncbi.nlm.nih.gov/27521348/.

234   mitochondria: J. R. Huertas, R. A. Casuso, P. H. Agustín, and S. Cogliati, "Stay Fit, Stay Young: Mitochondria in Movement: The Role of Exercise in the New Mitochondrial Paradigm," *Oxidative Medicine and Cellular Longevity* 2019 (June 19, 2019): 7058350, accessed May 20, 2021, https://pubmed.ncbi.nlm.nih.gov/31320983/.

234   regular physical activity: M. A. Kredlow, M. C. Capozzoli, B. A. Hearon, A. W. Calkins, and M. W. Otto, "The Effects of Physical Activity on Sleep: A Meta-Analytic Review," *Journal of Behavioral Medicine* 38, no. 3 (June 2015): 427–49, accessed May 20, 2021, https://pubmed.ncbi.nlm.nih.gov/25596964/.

234   anti-inflammatory chemicals: T. You, N. C. Arsenis, B. L. Disanzo, and M. J. Lamonte, "Effects of Exercise Training on Chronic Inflammation in Obesity: Current Evidence and Potential Mechanisms," *Sports Medicine* (Auckland, New Zealand) 43, no. 4 (April 2013): 243–56, accessed May 20, 2021, https://pubmed.ncbi.nlm.nih.gov/23494259/.

235   American Heart Association's (AHA) guidelines for exercise: "American Heart Association Recommendations for Physical Activity in Adults and Kids," www.heart.org, accessed May 20, 2021, https://www.heart.org/en/healthy-living/fitness/fitness-basics/aha-recs-for-physical-activity-in-adults.

235   physical activity guidelines: "New Guidelines: Exercise Key Part of Mental Health Treatment," Psychiatry & Behavioral Health Learning Network, October 15, 2018, https://www.psychcongress.com/article/new-guidelines-exercise-key-part-mental-health-treatment.

236   bipolar disorder: Daniel Thomson, Alyna Turner, Sue Lauder, Margaret E. Gigler, Lesley Berk, Ajeet B. Singh, Julie A. Pasco, et al., "A Brief

Review of Exercise, Bipolar Disorder, and Mechanistic Pathways," *Frontiers in Psychology* 6 (2015): 147, https://www.ncbi.nlm.nih.gov/pmc/articles/PMC4349127/.

236   Firth's own research: Joseph Firth, Marco Solmi, Robyn E. Wootton, Davy Vancampfort, Felipe B. Schuch, Erin Hoare, Simon Gilbody, et al., "A Meta-Review of 'Lifestyle Psychiatry': The Role of Exercise, Smoking, Diet and Sleep in the Prevention and Treatment of Mental Disorders," *World Psychiatry* 19, no. 3 (September 15, 2020): 360–80, https://onlinelibrary.wiley.com/doi/full/10.1002/wps.20773.

INDEX

ABOUT THE AUTHOR

GREGORY SCOTT BROWN, MD, is a board-certified psychiatrist, writer, and wellness advocate. His commentary has appeared in the *New York Times*, in the *Huffington Post*, in *Psychology Today*, on the *Today Show*, and on NPR. He is an advisory board member for *Men's Health* magazine, where he regularly contributes content for mental health stories.

Dr. Brown trained at the Academy of Integrative Health and Medicine, at the McGovern Medical School in Houston, and at the University of Texas Dell Medical School, where he is currently an affiliate faculty member in the department of psychiatry. He is an alumnus of Rice University, where he received a bachelor's degree in anthropology, and Johns Hopkins University, where he completed a post-baccalaureate premedical program.

In addition to his clinical work, Dr. Brown works diligently to fight stigma, in part by hosting candid conversations about mental health with well-known actors, journalists, musicians, and professional athletes. Dr. Brown loves staying active, and most days he devotes time to practicing yoga with his wife or going for a run with his rescue dog, Kai.

Learn more at gregoryscottbrown.com.